*Reston Land Corporation
and the Reston Board of Commerce
join in publishing this historical record
of the New Town of Reston.
We dedicate it to Robert E. Simon, Jr.,
the community's founder,
and to the individuals, businesses,
and organizations, past and present,
who have made Reston a beautiful,
stimulating and special place
in which to live, work, and play.*

THE
DONNING COMPANY
PUBLISHERS
NORFOLK/VIRGINIA BEACH

Reston

A NEW TOWN IN THE OLD DOMINION

A PICTORIAL HISTORY

Nan Netherton

The Donning Company/Publishers,
5659 Virginia Beach Boulevard,
Norfolk, Virginia 23502

Edited by Richard A. Horwege

Library of Congress Cataloging-in-Publication Data:

Netherton, Nan.
    Reston : new town in the Old Dominion : a pictorial
history / by Nan Netherton.
        p.   cm.
        Bibliography: p.
        Includes index.
        ISBN 0-89865-782-2 (lim. ed.)
        1. Reston (Va.)—History—Pictorial works.   2. Reston
(Va.)—Description—Views.   I. Title.
F234.R47N48   1989   89-11946
975.5'291—dc20   CIP

Printed in the United States of America

RESTON

Reston's Master Plan is shown here in full color, keyed to land uses in the eleven-square-mile area which is enclosed by the boundaries shown.
Courtesy of Reston Land Corporation

Contents

Opposite page: Heron House and Washington Plaza on Lake Anne have served as the symbol of the new town of Reston since they were completed in 1964. The Lake Anne Village Center, of which these features are a part, was placed in a historic district by the Fairfax County Board of Supervisors in 1984.
Courtesy of Reston Land Corporation

The street furniture and sculpture on Washington Plaza were all planned by well-known artists and designers. This light fixture design was used through-out Lake Anne Village Center and was conceived by Seymour Evans Associates.
Courtesy of Reston Land Corporation

Meenehan's Hardware was important in more ways than the name suggests. They also had a garden shop useful to new homeowners in a brand new community where yards and gardens needed attention. "Meenehan's fleet" was an amusing name given to the entrepreneur's boat rental business at the quay on Lake Anne.
Courtesy of Reston Land Corporation

The large fountain nestled among the shops on Washington Plaza was designed by James Rossant. The sprays of water are forced out of different openings to create a fascinating design of their own in the sunlight.
Courtesy of Reston Land Corporation

Foreword

Reston is the direct result of a man who had a dream and the dogged determination to implement it. Robert Simon, and the two developers who followed him, Gulf Reston and Reston Land Corporation, have for twenty-five years demonstrated a sensitivity to the natural beauty of the 11.5 square miles of land on which our new town is being built. These considerations have created an unusually attractive community which over fifty-three thousand people now call home.

Following World War II, veterans and others who had been involved in the war effort were eager to return to a normal life, working at peacetime occupations. Most of them wanted to find homes, marry, and raise families. There was great pressure on local governments and on the building industries to provide land and housing. Numerous developers built houses on subdivided land, usually close to large cities, sold them and moved on. City, town, and county officials across the country found that very soon they had not only to provide services and schools, but that taxes had to be raised and new ordinances had to be passed in order to ensure that builders and householders would share in the financial burdens caused by subdivision development.

In 1961, Robert Simon wanted to reinvest the proceeds from his recent sale of the family's property, Carnegie Hall, in New York City. He found

the largest piece of land for sale in one ownership close to a major city in the United States. He literally fell in love with this tract nestled in the midst of Northern Virginia's famed hunt country near Washington, D.C. It was a special place of rolling forested hills and meadows and clear rippling streams. Here he would build an urban landscape in a rural setting, designed at a human scale, a place which would emphasize the quality of life and the importance and dignity of each individual, with opportunities, in a self-contained design, to live, work, and play. The whole plan would be in contrast to the typical postwar suburban housing developments which had sprung up everywhere, dotting the landscape with residences with little or no thought given to needs for schools, services, employment and shopping centers, recreational and cultural opportunities, and provision of open space.

Bob Simon engaged noted planners and architects to prepare a grand design for the development of his land and a talented environmentalist to plan for the management of the open space. He persuaded the Fairfax County Board of Supervisors to pass an ordinance making possible the clustering of housing closely together so that open space with fields and trees could serve as large areas of commonly held land to improve the physical appearance and the environmental quality of the community. Natural streams were

Linda Carruthers moved to Reston in 1964 because she found the sense of community a welcome change from the usual anonymous suburban sprawl. From a modest beginning selling cut flowers in 1974 from this van at Lake Anne Center, the Lake Anne Florist business has grown rapidly and now employs a staff of twenty at peak holiday periods. Linda is also a partner in a commercial interior landscaping firm, The Plant People. She serves on the Horticultural Advisory Committee of the Northern Virginia Community College.
Courtesy of Linda Carruthers

Washington Plaza is a people-place, human scale, and a destination for grocery shopping, finding a book, meeting a friend, or just taking a walk, as is illustrated by this photograph taken in 1967.
Courtesy of the Reston Land Corporation

The art gallery in Heron House became headquarters for GRACE—the Greater Reston Art Center—when it was organized in 1973. When GRACE moved to temporary quarters at Town Center in February 1988, the Reston Art Gallery leased the space. Photograph by Anthony Hathaway
Courtesy of Reston Land Corporation

dammed to form lakes, and village centers were designed to provide shopping facilities and other services. Lake Anne Village Center with its tall apartment building, Heron House, and innovative townhouses surrounding the lake like a European coastal village, became an internationally recognized symbol of this growing American New Town.

Providing the services of roads, streets, sewer, water, shopping centers, parklands, and recreational facilities, and working with county officials to provide schools, libraries, and other necessities became too great a burden for one man's bank account. One of his principal investors, Gulf Oil, stepped in to save the project from bankruptcy in 1967. It is to their lasting credit that Gulf Reston officials continued development of the New Town and for more that ten years encouraged a diversity in housing sizes, styles, and prices. The company actively sought businesses and organizations that would establish themselves in Reston and thus provide opportunities for residents to work near the places where they lived. The residents organized the Reston Community Association at the time of the change in developer to ensure that the new administrators were kept informed of Restonians' desire for continuation of the original master plan. This proved to be a beneficial dialogue between the residents and the developer.

Restonians were resourceful and energetic in other ways as well. Civic, cultural, sports, and religious organizations were formed and flourished. A citizens' effort of major significance was the building of the Reston Community Center at Hunters Woods Village. It required seven years of planning and design to provide space for programming which would appeal to a wide range of community interests. Close cooperation with Fairfax County officials was needed to establish an administrative board and a special taxing district to fund the ambitious plan.

When the Mobil Corporation bought the remaining undeveloped land from Gulf Reston in 1978, Reston Land Corporation was formed as a subsidiary. The new developer also followed Simon's master plan for the development of the New Town. Long-planned projects came into being; additional schools and parks, a regional county branch library building, the Reston Hospital Center, a shelter for the homeless, a county mag-

isterial district office building, and the Cameron Glen nursing center for the elderly. High technology firms found campus-like office or R&D park designs desirable and the location close to Washington a strong factor in the decision to build or lease facilities in Reston. The business community banded together in 1984 and established the Reston Board of Commerce, now consisting of some five hundred members working to strengthen effectiveness and ties between businesses and the community.

By the end of 1988, over fourteen hundred companies had established themselves in Reston, employing thirty-one thousand people, more than an average of one and one-half jobs per household. High technology firms like Sperry were followed by others, especially after the Dulles Toll Road opened in 1984, shortening the driving time to Tysons Corner and Washington. Time and again, company officials spoke of the community design, housing, amenities, and the talented work force as being major factors in their decisions to settle their businesses in Reston. The overwhelming commitment of numerous businesses to Reston, starting in the early years with USGS, has provided the broad employment base so vital to the new town concept.

Another key component in Bob Simon's original master plan for Reston was the Town Center, the heart of this urban landscape in a rural setting. It is now under development, invested with ideas from some of the best designers in the country who have thought about how people can be served in an interesting and exciting way, and how their lives can be enriched. Town Center will not only have attractive places in which to live, work, shop, and be entertained, but it will become a destination, a place to visit, for people from both near and far. It is the coming of age of our community.

Our New Town concept has permitted an outpouring of creative energy that has resulted in a major success. Reston will continue to attract national and worldwide attention as it has from the beginning. Bob Simon's gigantic gamble has paid off.

James Cleveland
President
Reston Land Corporation

Acknowledgments

A book which encompasses several centuries, hundreds of people, and thousands of acres of land necessarily involves a great deal of research. The officials and staff at Reston Land Corporation were most cooperative in providing information, photographs, and assistance of all kinds. James Cleveland, president of Reston Land; Gregory Friess, executive vice president; William Steiner, director of residential marketing; and Linda Miller, marketing services supervisor, all took a deep interest in the project. Jean Balderson, executive secretary to the president and executive president of Reston Land, provided insights from her experience and staff support in numerous ways, not the least of which was conversion of the manuscript to a word processor. She made a difficult job seem easy. Helping her were Arlene Ashton, Joy Caveney, Marta Echard, Polly Erksa, Nancy Fiske, Donna Hodgkins, Janet Humston, Julie Peet, Connie Rudacille, Joan Shields, and Karen Williams.

Dr. Mel Bolster spent many hours assisting with research at the National Archives, Library of Congress, Fairfax County's Public Library Virginia Room, and the Reston Regional Library. Cathy Tunis, at the latter institution, read the manuscript, asked questions, and made constructive suggestions based on her experience with reference questions. She also helped with the indexing.

Connie Ring, Edith Sprouse, and Beth Mitchell assisted me at the Fairfax County Judicial Center Archives. The Virginia Room staff were their usual efficient, helpful selves. Special thanks go to Suzanne Levy, Eric Grundset, Paula Grundset, Anita Ramos, and Brian Conley at the library.

The following people helped with interviews, pictures, information, or assisted in other ways: Liz Anderson, Arthur Arundel, Jean Balderson, S. Curry Belfield, Lois Biddison, Richard Bonar, Larry Butler, Carlos Campbell, Linda Carruthers, Jack Carver, Ken Chamberlain, Robert Clay, James Cleveland, Karen Connell, Mary Cremonese, Cuba Curtice, Arvil Daniels, Margo Daniels, Gladys Dalby, Greg Davidson, Nancy and Hart Davis, Robert Dawson, Carol Dunlap, Abbie Edwards, Don Edwing, Meg Elliott, George Felton, Merni Fitzgerald, Fred Flaxman, Madeline Flynn, Ken Frager, Beverly Frederick, Monroe Freeman, Robert Frye, Daphne Gentry, T. Keith Glennan, Al and Judy Goldsmith, Judy Green, Tom Grubisich, John Guilfoyle, John Guinee, Noel Harrison, Michael Healy, Peter Henriques, Nancy Herwig, Janet Howell, Karl Ingebritsen, Susan Jones, Edith Keenan, W. Herman Kephart, James Kirby, Melissa Kirkpatrick, Jack Kutner, Nancy Larson, Robert E. Lee IV, Carolyn Lindberg, Josie Macias, Stewart Macdonald, William Magness, Warren Mattox, Peter McCandless, Karen Moore, Deborah Odell Moss, William Moyles, Harry Mustakos, Barbara Naef, Nancy Netherton, Ross Netherton, Bernard Norwitch, Gail Osberg, Bryn Pavek, Martha Pennino, Lindsay Petersen, Constance Pettinger, Kenneth Plum, Shirley Price, E. A. Prichard, Doug Reans, Hunter Richardson, Fran Robinson, Allan Rosenbaum, Linda Rutledge, Robert Ryan, Glenn Saunders, John Scherzer, Brad Shipp, Robert E. Simon, Jr., Claudia Smith, Francis Steinbauer, Robert Stelling, John Stokely, Geoffrey Styles, Anne Thomas, David Toatley, James Todd, Judi Ushio, Ronald Varner, Elfriede Walker, Vernon Walker, Michael Was, Daniel Weimer, Kohann Whitney, Russell Wright, and Cheri S. Wubbels.

Introduction

One man had a dream of building a special kind of community—an urban landscape in a rural setting. It would provide an environment that fosters the feeling that people's lives exist within a framework which helps to give meaning to what they do and plan. Robert E. Simon, Jr., decided to develop a New Town in Northern Virginia at a time in the early 1960s when the American landscape was being plowed under at a rate of a million acres a year for the building of monotonous suburbs. His community would be a place where people could make a living and make a life in close proximity to one another. This would be accomplished through seven goals which he set for the realization of his dream. The New Town of Reston would provide: a wide range of recreational and cultural facilities as well as an environment for privacy; the fullest range of housing styles, sizes, and prices; recognition of the importance and dignity of each individual; means by which people could both live and work in the community; commercial, cultural, and recreational facilities at the outset of development and not years later; structural and natural beauty as a necessity of the good life; that Reston would be a financial success.

The dream was eventually realized with a combination of tenacious personal vision, an obstacle course to excellence, and the understanding and endorsement of his goals as the work was carried toward completion by two other developers, Gulf Reston and Mobil's Reston Land Corporation.

Reston is located in the northwest corner of Fairfax County, close to thirty-nine degrees latitude north of the equator, in the northeastern corner of Virginia. Its elevation above sea level varies from two hundred to four hundred feet, and it is in the Piedmont transition zone above the coastal plain with the Bull Run and Blue Ridge Mountains observable on the distant skyline to the west and north, respectively.

The temperate and usually pleasant climate is humid, with approximately forty-one inches of precipitation annually. Winters are mild because of the sheltering influence of the Appalachian Mountains to the west and the proximity to Chesapeake Bay and the Atlantic Ocean on the east. The frost-free season lasts about two hundred days, long enough for the maturing of a wide variety of field crops, vegetables, and fruits. The ground is generally frozen only to shallow depths in the winter.

The land upon which the New Town of Reston is being built has for more than three centuries been an exceptionally large parcel relative to surrounding lands. For almost a century it was part of the 5,200,000-acre Northern Neck Proprietary, a 1649 royal grant from Charles II of England to seven loyal followers. Then for more than a century, it was a Fairfax family property of over

12,000 acres, called Great Falls Manor.

An Englishman, Benjamin Thornton, purchased over 8,000 acres from Reginald Fairfax in 1848. Forest timber was cut during most of Thornton's ownership period and continued when Dr. C. A. Max Wiehle and Gen. William McKee Dunn purchased the property in 1886. Wiehle dreamed of building a health and vacation resort which would be patronized by Washington vacationers commuting on the Bluemont Branch of the Southern Railway which ran right through the property. A town plat was laid out in 1892 showing a plan with streets, parks, and an area set aside for industrial use. Only a few buildings were constructed; Dr. Wiehle went bankrupt and died, and the town idea died with him.

Dr. Hugh Barbour Hutchison of Herndon purchased the property in 1908; he cut timber, cleared meadows, and raised dairy cows and poultry. A. Smith Bowman purchased the land from Hutchison's estate in 1927, raised beef cattle and, when Prohibition was repealed, he set up a bourbon distillery as well, feeding the leftover sour mash to the cattle.

As Fairfax County land became more valuable for residential subdivisions than for farm use, the Bowmans tried to develop a planned subdivision. Several problems, including lack of central sewer service and the Federal Aviation Administration's plans for building a new access road through the property to the Chantilly Airport (now Dulles) made a sale of the property desirable. A Florida subdivision developer, Lefcourt Realty, purchased Sunset Hills first, but financial problems developed, so the 7,000-plus acres were put on the market again. In 1961 Robert E. Simon, Jr., a New York City real estate developer, purchased the acreage. At the time it was one of the largest pieces of land in one ownership in any close-in metropolitan area of the United States. The funds for the purchase had come from the sale of his family-owned Carnegie Hall in New York.

Simon decided to build a New Town patterned after those in Great Britain and other European countries, with planned physical and visual de-

sign, a place where men and women would have varied opportunities for housing, employment, and personal growth through recreation, the arts, civic activity, and close contact with the natural environment. The name "Reston" was formed from Simon's initials and the English suffix for "town."

Building a new town was costly; Simon had to borrow money to keep it going. One of the lenders was Gulf Oil Corporation. Through a combination of external circumstances and business management decisions, Simon had to step aside and let Gulf take over the project. It was done primarily to protect their investment because Gulf was not in the real estate development business. Gulf Reston, Inc., a separate company which took over the land development, stayed with the project, building houses, apartments, commercial rental space, and the national headquarters of the United States Geological Survey, a big employment center in and for the New Town. Then, in 1977, Gulf decided to get out of the real estate development business and concentrate on the energy business.

The Mobil Corporation, which had entered the real estate development business by choice in 1966, purchased the project's undeveloped land totalling thirty-seven hundred acres in 1978. The Mobil Land Development Corporation's objective was, through creative planning, "to provide attractive living and recreation areas consistent with protection of the environment."

This book tells the history of the land and its owners, how Mobil's subsidiary, the Reston Land Corporation, has developed a rapport with the citizens of Reston, and the local government structure, and followed the master plan first developed by Robert Simon. The variety of options available for housing, "high tech" and other industry, and numerous amenities contribute to a successful and pleasant live-work-play environment with open space, trees, and recreational facilities. There is a true sense of community in Reston which appears repeatedly in the experiences and comments of its residents.

The Reston Festival has been by the
Reston Community Association since its
establishment in 1967. This scene on
Washington Plaza at Lake Anne was
taken at the May 1988 festival by Hart
Davis.
        Courtesy of the photographer

The Northern Neck Proprietary Survey of over 5,200,000 acres of Virginia land. The British Crown Commissioners appointed William Mayo and Robert Brooke as chief engineers. Thomas, Sixth Lord Fairfax, engaged surveyor John Warner. His map, which was redrawn as the result of the efforts of several others as well, determined the boundaries and settled the suit of Virginia v. Fairfax in 1745. Library of Congress.

Courtesy of the Virginia Room, Fairfax County Public Library

1

The Lords of the Great Falls Manor

When Fairfax County was formed in 1742 from the upper part of Prince William County, it was part of the Northern Neck Proprietary. There were no towns within its boundaries and very few settlers on the land. The Potomac River bounded it on the northeast and south, Bull Run and the Occoquan River on the southwest, and the Blue Ridge Mountains on the northwest. The area consisted of over eight hundred square miles and included the land which later was cut off to form Loudoun County. The county seat was moved to Alexandria in 1752, after it was founded in 1749.

The county was named for Thomas, Sixth Lord Fairfax, for whom his cousin William acted as agent for the Proprietary as well as collector of customs on South Potomac.

The Northern Neck Proprietary grant had been given by Charles II in 1649 to seven loyal Englishmen in exile with him in France. He had fled from England following the beheading of his father, Charles I, by the parliamentary forces in the English Civil War. The grantees of the Proprietary had the rights of an English court baron of the feudal system of the Middle Ages. "They could build towns, castles and forts, could create and endow colleges and schools, and were to enjoy the patronage of churches." They could give, grant, or lease lands within the grant for rents or other considerations. Charles II was restored to

the English throne in 1660, thereby making the gift valid as a royal grant.

After some years had passed, the rights to the Proprietary devolved on cousins, sons of two of the original seven: Thomas, Second Lord Culpeper, and his cousin Alexander Culpeper. Lord Culpeper died in 1689, leaving his shares of the Proprietary to his only legitimate heir, Catherine. A year later she married Thomas, Fifth Lord Fairfax. Their son, Thomas, became the Sixth Lord Fairfax upon the death of his father in 1710. The young lord came into a family estate which had been drastically depleted by his father's profligate spending on a number of unsuccessful investment ventures.

Thomas, Sixth Lord Fairfax, the first son, was born in 1693 at Leeds Castle, Kent, an edifice and site with a proud heritage dating back to 857 as a fortress, palace, and residence. Much of its history had been linked with English royalty. It had been purchased by Sir John Culpeper for his family's use in 1632.

Thomas Fairfax attended Oriel College, Oxford, and enjoyed several years of study there, generously interspersed with a pleasing variety of extracurricular activities. When his mother, Catherine Culpeper Fairfax, died in 1719, he became head of the family with responsibilities which included guardianship of a minor brother and three unmarried sisters who needed dowries

The Right Honorable Thomas, Sixth Lord Fairfax, Baron of Cameron, and Proprietor of the Northern Neck. He once owned the Great Falls Manor on which the modern "new town" of Reston has been developed. This portrait of him is attributed to Sir Joshua Reynolds.
Courtesy of Alexandria-Washington Lodge No. 22, A.F.&A.M., Alexandria, Virginia

in order to marry well. It soon became abundantly clear that the income required to provide a comfortable living for all of the family members made the economic development of the Virginia Proprietary imperative.

When the agent for the Northern Neck Proprietary, Robert "King" Carter, died in 1732, Thomas moved quickly to have his boyhood friend and first cousin, William Fairfax, transferred from collector of customs at Salem, Massachusetts, to collector of customs on South Potomac and his agent for the Proprietary. William and his third wife, Deborah Clarke, moved from Salem to Virginia in 1734 and first settled in Westmoreland County, where in 1736 their son Bryan was born.

During this time, Thomas, Sixth Lord Fairfax, paid his first visit to the Virginia lands his father and mother had never seen. He explored them quite thoroughly and arranged to have his own team of surveyors mark out for the first time the boundaries of his Proprietary. When all the technical requirements with chain, pole, and transit had been satisfied, the Proprietary area was found to include 5,280,000 acres. Pleased with what he had learned and seen, he returned to England to confirm the grant with the Privy Council.

He left orders to have several manors surveyed within the Proprietary when he returned to England to confirm the Proprietary grant in 1737. One of them was Great Falls Manor, surveyed by John Warner in 1739. It contained 12,588 acres and abutted on the southeast side of Col. Robert "King" Carter's copper mine tract near present-day Herndon.

In 1741, William Fairfax and his family moved up the Potomac to what was then Prince William County to their new home, Belvoir. William succeeded with his efforts to form a new county, which was given the family name. Two years later, a neighbor up the river on the next peninsula, Maj. Lawrence Washington of Mount Vernon, married William's daughter Anne.

Meanwhile, Thomas put his affairs in order in England and gave his life interest in Leeds Castle as well as other English lands to his brother

Robert in return for full control over the Proprietary for his lifetime. Lord Fairfax emigrated to Virginia and set about having his lands surveyed in the Shenandoah Valley with the idea of establishing his permanent residence there. One of William's sons, George William, and a new lad in the neighborhood, George Washington, went along to improve their knowledge of both the country and the gentlemanly art of surveying. Washington had just moved up the Potomac from his widowed mother's plantation near Fredericksburg to live with his brother Lawrence and was immediately drawn to the Fairfax family at Belvoir as they were to him. On the trip with George William Fairfax, he struck up a friendship which was to last a lifetime.

George William's younger half-brother, Bryan Fairfax, also became a good friend of George Washington's. Their forty-five-year correspondence reveals the interesting personal and political development of the frontiersman who became the Revolutionary War general and later president of the new country, and the steadfast aristocrat who later became the eighth baron of Cameron.

It was to Bryan Fairfax that Thomas, Sixth Lord Fairfax, gave the Great Falls Manor, in 1765, when it was apparent that there were no valuable copper or other mineral deposits on the property. Bryan owned it until his death at "Mount Eagle" in 1802, at which time it passed by will to the third owner, Bryan's son, Thomas the Ninth Lord Fairfax, of Ash Grove.

Years later, in 1843, Thomas and his wife, Margaret "for and in consideration of the natural love and affection which they have for their Son Reginald," gave to him a large portion of the Great Falls Manor. It included over 8,600 acres on Colville's Branch (now called Colvin Run) and Lawyer's Road. This land, technically, went out of the Fairfax family when Reginald, who was on duty in the U.S. Navy in the Cape Verde Islands, sold the land through his attorney to Benjamin Thornton of Orange County, Virginia, in 1852. It was a sale he was to regret a hundred times in the years to come.

Coat-of-Arms of Thomas, Sixth Lord Fairfax.
Courtesy of Fairfax County History Commission

Leeds Castle in Kent, England, the family home where Thomas, Sixth Lord Fairfax, was born and grew to young manhood.
Courtesy of Virginia State Library

Bryan, Eighth Lord Fairfax, once owner of the Great Falls Manor, shown in his collar as an Anglican minister.
Courtesy of the Virginia Room, Fairfax County Public Library

The Armorial Bearings of

BRYAN FAIRFAX

EIGHTH LORD FAIRFAX OF CAMERON
CLERK IN HOLY ORDERS
(Born 1737, died 1802)

College of Arms
London, March 1982

Rodney Dennys
Somerset
Somerset Herald of Arms

Coat-of-Arms of Bryan, Eighth Lord Fairfax.
Courtesy of Montebello Associates

Fairfax hunting with Washington. A conjectural nineteenth-century painting by H. B. Hall.
Courtesy of the Virginia Room, Fairfax County Public Library

The "mansion house" built by Joseph Thornton prior to the Civil War, across the railroad tracks from the later Sunset Hills mansion and station. The structure burned in 1955.
   Courtesy of A. Smith Bowman Distillery

2

The Thornton Period: Logging and Litigation

In looking at some of the properties Benjamin Thornton purchased in Virginia which had formerly belonged to President James Madison, the Lords Fairfax, and Robert "King" Carter, one realizes that this Englishman had a knowledge of and interest in American history, to say the least. Like many land speculators before and after him, however, his reach was longer than his grasp.

Thornton had come to Orange County and purchased the James and Dolley Madison estate, Montpelier, in 1848. He was from Gomersale, near Leeds in the County of York, England, and owned considerable personal property including horses and "plate"—the tax records do not specify whether it was gold or silver.

He contracted for the Reginald Fairfax portion of Great Falls Manor in 1852, two parcels totaling 8,663 acres, at a cost of $43,300 or approximately $5 per acre. The next year, appearing in the court records as being "of the City of Richmond," he authorized his brother, Joseph Thornton of Montpelier, to act on his behalf in matters concerning real or personal property. Joseph moved to the Great Falls Manor property and shortly thereafter built the fourteen-room Gothic Revival-style house, which stood until 1955 on land just south of the railway right-of-way.

The westward expansion of the railroads was under way and it was to affect the Thornton prop-

erty. Alexandria had been an important seaport in the eighteenth century and its merchants and businessmen were striving in the 1840s to restore its economic health, seriously impaired by Baltimore's strong competition. Building of railroads to the western interior in the 1830s had enabled the Maryland metropolis to strengthen its position, already surpassing the Virginia port as a result of an excellent harbor and favorable tariffs to encourage international commerce.

In order to minimize the new threat to Alexandria's business interests, a group of prominent citizens, with financial assistance from the Commonwealth of Virginia, built their own railroad to the west, hoping to reach the interior farmlands and the rich Hampshire County coal fields. The Alexandria, Loudoun and Hampshire Railroad was chartered in 1853, and as the right-of-way purchase moved west from Alexandria, it took more than forty-five acres of the Thornton tract, splitting the estate into two fairly equal portions. The compensation was $2,140 or about $46 per acre, not a bad appreciation in value for the three years of the Englishman's ownership. Many years later this right-of-way was purchased by the Virginia Electric Power Company (VEPCO) for transmission lines, and for use as a linear park for the Washington and Old Dominion (W&OD) trail, administered by the Northern Virginia Regional Park Authority (NVRPA).

The first passenger service between Alexandria and Leesburg was inaugurated in 1860, the same year the Thornton estate acquired both a railroad station and a post office designation. It was for more than a quarter of a century referred to variously as Thornton's Depot, Thornton's Station, or Thornton's Mills. The hardest stretch of the railroad construction was yet to come—the climb up the Piedmont, tunnelling through the Blue Ridge, and the laying of track into the Shenandoah Valley. Construction never was completed beyond the Blue Ridge.

Plans for further expansion were abruptly halted with the outbreak of the Civil War. Reports of activities around Thornton's Station described reconnaissance parties from both sides of the conflict in the official records of the war. Dispatches mentioned Thornton's Mills, local streams, bridle paths, woods, roads, bridges, fords, pickets, and cavalry.

In September 1862, after the Battle of Chantilly, Gen. Robert E. Lee and his army came up the old Ox Road and the Ridge Road (Route 602, now Reston Parkway) through Thornton's Mills, reaching the Alexandria-Leesburg Turnpike near Dranesville. His troops crossed the Potomac River at White's Ford and entered Maryland on their way to Antietam. Before he withdrew from Northern Virginia, Lee destroyed most of the AL&H Railroad's western half between the Vienna and Leesburg stations. Rails were removed, heated, twisted, and scattered in the woods near the right-of-way. Ties and bridges were burned. Union Gen. Herman Haupt, whose particular responsibility was keeping the U.S. Military Railroad operating, reported to Gen. George B. McClellan in November 1863:

Camps had been established near the road and near the stations. Soldiers would tear up sidings, break switch-stands, burn the wood provided for the engines, wash clothes and persons with soap in the springs and streams which supplied the water stations, and many engines were stopped on the road by foaming boilers caused by soapy water.

When the war was ended, efforts were begun to pick up the scattered pieces, especially where the railroads were concerned. Joseph Thornton was appointed as an agent for the Commonwealth of Virginia by the State Board of Public Works in 1865 to look after the affairs of the AL&H. Bridges had to be rebuilt, tracks replaced and na-

ture had to be pushed back in the places where she was rapidly reclaiming the right-of-way with saplings and shrubs. When the railroad was again functioning, President U.S. Grant and members of his cabinet went on a day-long junket past Thornton's Station on the line, by then known as the Washington and Ohio Railroad, to visit Leesburg and the exhibition of the Agricultural Society at the Fair Grounds, to listen to the town band, and to have dinner with Col. John W. Fairfax.

The name of the rail line was changed again in 1883, reflecting even greater optimism on the part of its promoters, this time a group of New Yorkers who had purchased it out of bankruptcy receivership and dubbed it the Washington, Ohio and Western. A modernization program was inaugurated which included new engines and other rolling stock, as well as replacement of the old iron rails with new heavier steel and the old wooden bridges with iron. Plans to extend the railroad over the Blue Ridge Mountains to link up with the Norfolk and Western or the Baltimore and Ohio never materialized.

The railroad was not alone in its suffering of financial reverses. As early as 1857, law suits had been brought and attachments made for debts owed by both Benjamin, "who is a non-resident," and Joseph Thornton. After the Civil War, Joseph, a British subject, sued his brother, Benjamin, for £10,000 sterling for money owed to him for property management. He attached the acreage purchased from Reginald Fairfax in 1852, which had never been paid for in full. There were many other debtors including Joseph Thorp of Leeds, England, to whom the Thorntons owed $30,000, and William H. Davis and Andrew Pringle were owed back salary for their services as resident and managing proprietors of the "Thornton Manor Improvement Company." With two large steam-powered saws, the company had been logging thousands of acres of valuable timber for years and selling cross ties, cord wood, rails, and poles. The tract was also used for cutting firewood during the war by both armies.

For a while the property was in the hands of a court-appointed receiver, O. E. Hine, who had advertised the property and attributed the difficulties of selling it to the "unenviable reputation it had in connection with the long litigation and the name of Thornton."

Hine favored breaking it up in smaller parcels. The Circuit Court of the City of Alexandria decided instead to have court-appointed commissioners offer it through an advertisement in June 1885, reading in part:

SALE OF THE LARGE AND VALUABLE TRACT OF TIMBER AND AGRICULTURAL LAND IN FAIRFAX COUNTY, VIRGINIA, CONTAINING ABOUT 6,450 ACRES, WITHIN TWENTY MILES OF THE CITIES OF WASHINGTON AND ALEXANDRIA, TRAVERSED BY THE WASHINGTON, OHIO AND WESTERN RAILROAD, AND KNOWN AS "THE THORNTON TRACT."

THE SAID TRACT IS WELL WATERED, AND IS IMPROVED BY A SUBSTANTIAL MANSION HOUSE AND SEVERAL SMALLER HOUSES OCCUPIED BY TENANTS. TWO PASSENGER TRAINS A DAY PASS EACH WAY THROUGH THE TRACT.

Less than a year later, two gentlemen who had made separate bids for the property agreed to buy it together and partition it. One of the new owners was Dr. Carl Adolph Max Wiehle of Washington, late from a medical practice in Philadelphia. The other one was William McKee Dunn, a well-to-do land speculator. He served in the Northern Army's Judge Advocate General Department during the Civil War and lived in Maplewood, near Tysons Corner.

TIME TABLE--NO. 1,

Alexandria, Loudoun, and Hampshire Railroad Company,

To take effect on and after MONDAY, January 16, 1860.

TRAIN GOING WEST.	Fares.	NAMES OF STATIONS.	Distances	TRAIN GOING EAST.
Leave at 10 A. M.		..ALEXANDRIA..		Arrive at 2.30 p.m.
		3		
" " 10.9 "	15	.... Old Factory	3	" " 2.21 "
		2¼		
" " 10.15 "	25	... Arlington Mills ...	5½	" " 2.15 "
		1¼		
" · 10.25 "	30	..... Carlinville	6¾	" " 2.10 "
		3½		
" " 10.35 "	50	.... Falls Church	10¼	" " 1.55 "
		4½		
" " 10.55 "	75	...... Vienna	15	" " 1.35 "
		3		
" " 11.08 "	90	.... Hunter's Mill	18	" " 1.20 "
		3		
" " 11.20 "	1.00	...... Thornton	21	" " 1.10 "
		2¼		
" " 11.30 "	1.10	.... Herndon.....	23½	" " 1.00 "
		3¾		
" " 11.45 "	1.25	...... Guilford	27	" " 12.45 "
		4		
Arrive at 12.00 M.	1.40	.. FARMWELL ..	31	Leave at 12.30 PM.

An Alexandria, Loudoun and Hampshire Railroad Company timetable of 1860, from The Washington and Old Dominion Railroad *by Ames Williams.*
Courtesy of the author

MAIL LINE.
NEW ARRANGEMENT, MAY 21. 1860.

ALEXANDRIA, LOUDOUN, AND HAMPSHIRE RAILROAD.

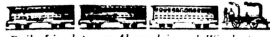

Daily Line between Alexandria and Winchester.

(Sundays excepted.)
Via Fall's Church, Vienna, Hunter's Mill, Thornton, Herndon, Guilford, Farmville, Leesburg, Hamilton, Purcellville, Snickersville, Castleman's Ferry, and Berryville, by the Alexandria, Loudoun, and Hampshire Railroad and Means & Fawcett's first class Mail Coaches.
On and after Monday, 21st instant, will leave the Depot, at Alexandria, at 8 A. M., and arrive at Winchester at 5 P. M.
Leave Winchester at 5 A. M. and Leesburg at 11¼ A. M., arriving at Alexandria 2 P. M., in time for immediate connexion with Winchester and Baltimore.

FARE:
To and from Winchester, $3.25; Berryville, $3. Leesburg, $1 50. Intermediate points in proportion.
W. BLYTHE,
may 18—d tf
General Superintendent.

An advertisement dated 1860 for the AL&H, from Rails to the Blue Ridge *by H. H. Harwood.*
Courtesy of the author

The Clarke *was one of three such loco-motives purchased by the AL&H in 1859 and taken over by the U.S. Military Rail-roads in 1861. Mathew Brady photograph from* The Washington and Old Dominion Railroad *by Ames Williams.*
Courtesy of the author

A wreck on the AL&H, then the U.S. Mil-itary Railroad, in 1863. Herman Haupt is standing on the train's truck inspecting damage. Photograph by Mathew Brady from The Washington and Old Dominion Railroad, *by Ames Williams.*
Courtesy of the author

Letter from Joseph Thornton regarding the Alexandria, Loudoun and Hampshire Railroad in 1865.
Courtesy of the Virginia State Archives

Alexandria. Va
Nov 16th 1865,

To the Board of
Public Works
Richmond, I beg to acknowledge the
receipt of the order, passed by the Board of Public
Works on the 11th Inst. appointing me one of the Agents
on the part of the State of Virginia, to look after &
temporarily manage the Affairs of the Alexandria
Loudoun & Hampshire Railroad, until your
honorable Board, or the Legislative authority
of the State, shall order otherwise,
I respectfully accept the position and
trust, conferred on me in said order, and
will endeavour to discharge its duties to the
best of my ability,
Respectfully,
Your Obedient Servant
Joseph Thornton

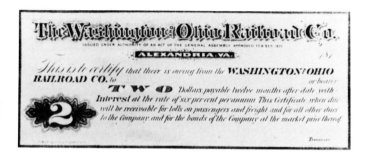

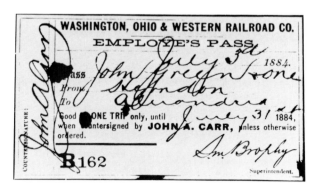

A certificate for the Washington and Ohio Railroad Company and a pass for the Washington, Ohio and Western Railroad Company, which was taken over by the Southern Railway. The Southern in turn leased this "Bluemont Branch," which was then named the Washington and Old Dominion Railroad. From Rails to the Blue Ridge *by H. H. Harwood.*
Courtesy of the author

Section of an 1878 map showing Herndon, the Thornton's Mills, and Ridge Road, now Reston Parkway. From G. M. Hopkins' Atlas of Fifteen Miles Around Washington.
Courtesy of the Virginia Room, Fairfax County Public Library

A "large tract for a colony" newspaper advertisement found in the Circuit Court papers of Thorpe v. Hine *concerning the Thornton land sold to Dunn and Wiehle in 1886.*
Courtesy of the Archives Room, Fairfax County Judicial Center

*The bridge which carried the county road
across the lakes at Wiehle, about 1900.
Courtesy of A. Smith Bowman Distillery*

3

Wiehle: A Little Town in the Woods

When the lengthy court suit was finally settled involving delinquent state and local taxes and the interests of many parties including Fairfax, Thornton, Thorp, Hine, and Kent, the land involved was still a sizable parcel. Some of the acreage had been sold off but the majority of the portion of Great Falls Manor which Benjamin Thornton had contracted to buy from Reginald Fairfax was still there, albeit much cut over by years of commercial logging.

After discussing the alternatives, the two bidders, Dr. C. A. Max Wiehle and Gen. William McKee Dunn, agreed to pay the court commissioners $20,000, a little over $3 for each of the remaining 6,449 acres. Within six months, in November 1886, the land had been partitioned between the two buyers, Dunn taking 3,221 acres south of the tracks of the Washington, Ohio and Western Railroad and Dr. Wiehle taking 3,228 acres principally on the north.

Dunn also acquired over 700 acres of land in an area called Lee Woods just west of Falls Church on the same railroad. He planned and laid out a subdivision in 1887, one of his partners in the venture being a friend, George B. Loring of Salem, Massachusetts. They planned to build a resort hotel there eventually, but Dunn died at his home, Maplewood, the same year, while the first two houses were still under construction in Dunn

Loring. The development languished thereafter since he had been the guiding force behind it. His share of the Thornton tract purchased with Wiehle was left by will to his wife, Elizabeth Lanier Dunn, who sold it to the Fairfax Lumber Company after the turn of the century.

Dr. Carl Adolph Max Wiehle was born in Germany, the son of a German Reformed Church minister. The family moved to Philadelphia when young Max was two years old. He was well-educated, graduated from the medical school of the University of Pennsylvania and successfully practiced medicine in the City of Brotherly Love. He married, had seven children, and eventually moved his family to Washington in 1881, where he built a residence at 1621 Connecticut Avenue.

After his purchase of part of the Thornton estate in 1886, Dr. Wiehle dreamed of building a town and engaged a city planner-architect to lay out a scheme for a community which would carry his name. Streets, curved avenues, parks, lakes, home building sites, a school, and an industrial area were all part of the grand plan.

The U.S. Post Office Department approved his request for a name change from Thornton's Mills to Wiehle in 1887. Dr. Wiehle soon built a large and ornate wooden summer home near the existing spring house and the railroad.

After the plat for the town had been drawn by Joseph Berry, surveyor, in 1892, Dr. Wiehle seems to have contracted a case of corporate hiccups. Three companies were formed in rapid succession, proposing to extract products from the land, to merchandise, and to acquire, hold, own, subdivide, and control real estate and to make loans. Family members made up the boards of directors of the corporations. The Thornton land, now called Wiehle, was placed under the control of the third company, Virginia Lumber and Manufacturing Company.

A variety of activities went into the effort to establish the town. Three small lakes were dug by hand. A bridge was built over the largest lake to carry Route 602 across it. A thirty-foot square brick icehouse was constructed, the largest for miles around. In it were stored in sawdust the large blocks of ice cut from the lakes each winter. The ice-cutting ceremony was always enjoyed by the Wiehles and their neighbors. A dozen residences were built of clapboard painted white. A one-room schoolhouse was constructed in what is now the Golf Course Island area. It was heated by a large wood stove and Bertie Poston, who lived most of her life in one of the original Wiehle houses, recalls that the school's ceiling was well-plastered with spitballs.

The commercial and industrial buildings consisted of a combination post office and general merchandise store, a lumber mill specializing in the manufacture of window frames and wagon spokes made from logs cut in the Wiehle woods, a talc and asbestos mill, and a brickyard. A brick building in which there was a hardware store was constructed with two stories and a steeple with a bell so the upper room could be used for holding Reformed Church services. Most of the town's residents walked to work in the mills or in the woods cutting logs. There were boardwalks between many of the residences and other buildings.

Sometime during the 1890s, after winning a lawsuit against a railroad because of an injury to his wife, Dr. Wiehle built the Aesculapian Hotel, named for the Roman god of medicine and healing, Aesculapius. It was built near the healthful springs, a large building with wide porches and a cupola, very stylish for the times. It became a mecca for Washingtonians seeking rest and relaxation—mostly U.S. government employees —for a number of years. By this time, the old WO&W Railroad had been consolidated with other lines into the Southern Railway system and provided convenient transportation for vacationers from Washington. At Wiehle, they enjoyed good meals, tennis, a bowling alley, and boating and fishing on the lakes.

Part of the Wiehle fortune had come from Mrs. Wiehle's family, who owned a brewery in Philadelphia. Dr. Wiehle was himself, however, strongly opposed to alcoholic beverages. He had deed forms printed up for the Virginia Lumber and Manufacturing Company with the following provision for all land transactions:

This conveyance is made upon the express condition that no alcoholic or malt liquor, or wine, or other intoxicating beverage of any kind whatsoever shall be manufactured, sold or kept for sale on the land hereby conveyed at any time or time in the future by the party of the second part . . . in case of any violation or breach of this condition, or any branch of it, the title to and possession of the said land shall forthwith revert to the party of the first part, its successors or assigns.

Application for a town charter was made to the Virginia General Assembly and it was formally granted in 1898. The next year, Erskin M. Sunderland, a Washington architect, completed plans for a substantial twenty-five-room brick mansion for the Wiehles, to be built in the newly established town between the wooden summer house and the Aesculapian Hotel. It had twenty-four-inch thick walls, large rooms, high ceilings and surrounding galleries. When construction was to begin, the Wiehles brought in a flock of goats to clear the underbrush and as the building progressed, goats could occasionally be seen peering out of the attic windows of the uncompleted house.

The entire country was experiencing financially difficult times at the turn of the century brought on by controversies over the price of silver, the gold standard, the Spanish-American War, and a general depression affecting land values. Before his fine new abode was finished, Dr. Wiehle died of pneumonia at his home in Washington, a victim also of the conditions of the times which contributed to the failure of his dream of a town and a small measure of immortality. The Wiehle town charter was revoked by the Virginia legislature in February 1989.

Dr. Wiehle's wife and children held on to the land for a few years, but like his short-time partner in the Thornton tract purchase (and developer of Dunn Loring), William McKee Dunn, Wiehle was the guiding force behind the project and it died with him. In 1908, the Wiehle family sold approximately thirty-five hundred acres of land for $80,000, or about $23 per acre, to Dr. Hugh B. Hutchison and William Crighton of Herndon, who had other plans for the use of the land.

Dr. C. A. Max Wiehle was the first developer to propose a planned community on the land holdings at Thornton's Mills in the 1890s. The same land is now the location of the twentieth-century "new town" of Reston. Portrait published in the Washington Sunday Star, *August 31, 1952.*
Courtesy of A. Smith Bowman Distillery

The Wiehle family at their summer home and spring house about 1895.
Courtesy of A. Smith Bowman Distillery

The Wiehle summer home, built about 1888. The gazebo was built over the early spring house about 1900.
Courtesy of A. Smith Bowman Distillery

Wiehle was surveyed and mapped by Joseph Berry in 1892. Note the area by the railroad and lake reserved for manufacturing sites. The town's charter was granted in 1898. It was revoked in 1989.
Courtesy of A. Smith Bowman Distillery

Bertie Poston, who lived for most of her life in one of the old frame Wiehle houses, remembers the Wiehle family with fondness.

Photograph taken in 1982.
Courtesy of Bertie Poston

The Town of Wiehle about 1900. From left to right: the bridge over the lakes, the gazebo, cousin Robert Wiehle's home, Dr. Max Wiehle's summer home, outbuildings and stable, town hall/church (with steeple), superintendent's office, and a private residence. The steeple was removed when the old town hall was in use as a whiskey warehouse.
Courtesy of A. Smith Bowman Distillery

The Aesculapian Hotel, built by Dr. Max Wiehle as part of his health resort. The building was demolished in 1956.
Courtesy of A. Smith Bowman Distillery

The front veranda of the Wiehle/Hutchison mansion at Sunset Hills in 1927.
Courtesy of A. Smith Bowman Distillery

A sextet with milking machines, ready for the evening milking on the Hutchison estate in 1927.
Courtesy of A. Smith Bowman Distillery

4

The Hutchison Period: Husbanding Farm and Forest

Dr. Hugh Barbour Hutchison was born in Herndon. He was a dentist by profession but was also interested in local land speculation and large scale farming. Agricultural practices since the Civil War, particularly in the western part of Fairfax County, had increasingly favored use of commercial and farmyard manures, more than doubling the productive capacity and therefore the value of farm lands. Dairying and poultry raising were becoming lucrative operations because of the needs of the growing populations of Washington and Baltimore and accessibility to those markets through the railroad system. The interest in scientific farming, which was experiencing rapid growth all over the United States, was also fostered by Virginia's Agriculture Experiment Station. Several of Virginia's colleges began to reach out early in the twentieth century into farm communities, with useful courses and demonstrations.

The charter for the Cuthbert Land and Development Company, which received the Wiehle land purchased by Hutchison and Crighton in 1908, had a very broad purpose. It was empowered to subdivide real estate, mine, erect buildings, and to aid or induce the construction and operations of institutions, establishments, and plants "which in the judgment of the directors of this company will enhance the value of the real or personal estate, or promote the health, happiness or well-being of those living on its property, or engaged in enterprises conducted thereon or in proximity thereto." The principal office of the company was at Wiehle and Dr. Hutchison moved into the "Big House," as the Wiehle's brick mansion was referred to locally. Later it was called Sunset Hills during the Bowman ownership.

The Southern Railway, Bluemont Branch, was an important factor in the commercial success of the owners of both the old Dunn and Wiehle properties. Little engines chugged through the scenic countryside pulling wooden cars which carried local passengers, mail, packages, and milk cans for the growing dairy business around Wiehle and Herndon. Usually one freight a day was all that was needed to haul the timber, brick, fertilizer, grain, and livestock needed for the largely agricultural pursuits of the area. The railroad line changed hands and name in 1911-1912. John R. McLean, owner of the *Washington Post* and the *Cincinnati Enquirer*, and Senator Stephen B. Elkins of West Virginia with his coal, lumber, and railroad interests, had been very successful entrepreneurs and had parlayed the electric trolley line from Washington to the Great Falls Park into a highly profitable venture. They looked around for another local investment. The Bluemont Branch of the Southern was just what they wanted, so they arranged for a long-term lease and renamed the line the "Washington and Old

Dominion Railway." Both men died soon after the transfer was made, so the running of the line fell to the lot of the heirs and their attorneys, who did not have the same degree of interest in it. The railroad went through periods of electrification, steam and diesel-powered locomotives, and eventually became a victim of the internal combustion engine in automobiles and trucks. For the period that Hutchison owned the old Wiehle estate, however, the train was a very necessary part of the farm operation.

The Cuthbert Company cleared five-hundred acres of land for cultivation and built a number of farm buildings, including a two-hundred-cow dairy barn and a two-thousand-hen poultry plant. As had been the case during the Thornton and Wiehle ownerships, the cutting of timber continued to be a lucrative business in the early twentieth century for a variety of purposes including railroad ties, fence posts, firewood, pulpwood, and lumber.

Another product which was very profitable appeared on the scene after the Eighteenth Amendment was passed. Prohibition created a demand which was supplied by bootleg stills in Fairfax County, particularly around Great Falls and the Wiehle woods. The alcoholic beverages produced (apparently without the knowledge of the Cuthbert Company) were easily disposed of in Washington with regular customers, as easily as were the milk and other dairy and farm products marketed by the legitimate producers.

The Wiehle woods had other local associations. They were a favorite haunt for people who enjoyed riding horses and walking, for there were many bridle paths and logging roads lacing back and forth across the extensive property. The forest was beautiful most times of the year, and peaceful, full of wild animals only occasionally sought by hunters who invaded the serenity of the place. Clear streams coursed along, their springs feeding into Colvin Run and Sugarland Run. Neighborhood children would come year after year from Herndon, Navy, and other nearby communities on hayrides or to enjoy community skating parties on the frozen lake.

After World War I, Crighton sold out his interests in the Cuthbert Company to Dr. Hutchison, who dissolved the company and continued to run the business himself even though he was in failing health. Probably in the interest of appealing to future investors, he applied to have the post office name changed from Wiehle and in 1923, the post office department approved the new designation of Sunset Hills, with Robert Wiehle, a cousin of the late Dr. Max Wiehle, as postmaster.

Because of heart trouble and illness, Dr. Hutchison decided to take an ocean trip for his health in the summer of 1924. When the ship put in at Boston, he was taken to a hospital where he died on July 14, at age fifty-four. His wife Ina and three sons, Hugh, Cuthbert, and Gilbert, survived him. The Washington *Evening Star* obituary mentioned that he was believed to have owned much of the land bought by the U.S. government for the Quantico Marine Base as well as his estate at Wiehle. Dr. Hutchison was a man of stature in his community. He had also owned a home in Washington and had been a member of the Masonic Lodge in Herndon, the Washington Board of Trade, and the Washington Golf and Country Club.

The heirs decided not to break up the Hutchison property into smaller parcels which might have made them more quickly and easily marketable to settle the estate. Instead, they prepared an illustrated brochure which was widely circulated, describing the property in detail. It was at the time the largest estate of its kind in the Washington area, and the publication suggested a variety of uses: a large private school, sanitarium, suburban development, or a club interested in agricultural development, outdoor life, or a game preserve.

The property was also advertised in various newspapers; one of the ads was seen by the Bowman family who lived in Indianapolis, Indiana. Intrigued by the farm's size, location, history, and potential, A. Smith Bowman lost little time in arranging to purchase the entire estate.

*The saw and planing mill on the Hutchi-
son estate at Sunset Hills about 1927.
Courtesy of A. Smith Bowman Distillery*

*Barns and silos on the Hutchison estate
at Sunset Hills about 1927.
Courtesy of A. Smith Bowman Distillery*

*Cows in the milking parlor at Sunset
Hills, the Hutchison estate, in 1927.
Courtesy of A. Smith Bowman Distillery*

Beef and dairy cattle on Sunset Hills farm after the Bowmans purchased it. The beef cattle later thrived on sour mash from the distillery and furnished the filet mignon.
Courtesy of A. Smith Bowman Distillery

5

The Bowman Period: Filet Mignon and Stirrup Cup

A. Smith Bowman, Sr., had already had several successful business careers before he purchased the Hutchison estate at Sunset Hills, Virginia. He had operated a highly mechanized wheat farm of eight thousand acres in Alberta, Canada, and during the First World War, he had owned a distillery in Louisiana which manufactured alcohol for the war effort. In 1920, he moved his family to Indianapolis, Indiana, where he instituted the first city-wide, coordinated bus system in the entire country, in direct competition with the existing street railway. After seven years of operation, he sold out to the street railway for a half million dollars, a satisfactory return for his initial investment of $65,000.

Bowman and his wife Katherine were natives of Kentucky. Following the sale of the bus line, they saw a financial opportunity to return to their home state and buy a large farm. In the interest of seeing what might be available, their younger son was sent out to buy a newsstand copy of the *Louisville Courier-Journal* in order to see the farms for sale ads. DeLong Bowman returned instead with a copy of the *Cincinnati Enquirer*. In this paper there was an ad for the four-thousand-acre farm in Fairfax County, Virginia, which had been part of an original grant to ancestors of Lord Fairfax. On September 30, 1927, Bowman bought Sunset Hills for cash—thirty-eight hundred acres "for $10 and other valuable considerations."

Considerable more cash changed hands.

It is ironic in light of later events that the deed for the land purchased from Gilbert M. Hutchison's heirs contained a provision whereby Bowman agreed never to manufacture or keep for sale any alcoholic or malt liquor or any other intoxicating beverage of any kind whatsoever. This stipulation, which ran with several parcels within the estate, had subsequently to be renegotiated.

Originally, the business on the Bowman estate at Sunset Hills was to be the growing of dairy and beef cattle, horses, and grain. When national Prohibition was repealed in 1933, however, Bowman decided to establish a distillery using his own home-grown corn, barley, and rye to manufacture "Fairfax County," "Virginia Gentleman," and several "special label" bourbons. The steeple was removed from the brick building which had in the early Wiehle days been used for German Reformed Church services, and the structure was then used for a distillery warehouse. By 1937, when the bottled-in-bond beverages were ready for the market, they were available to mix in the "stirrup cup" punch which was traditionally served at the meeting of the Fairfax Hunt. This was an organization founded by Bowman himself in 1928.

During World War II, the Bowmans distilled alcohol for the government's war effort, with a daily output of about eighteen hundred gallons. Most of the distillery employees lived on the estate and cultivated "victory gardens" as well, on land the Bowmans provided for the purpose. A profit-sharing trust based on length of service added a further incentive to employees to remain with the company. Expansion of the Sunset Hills estate was made right after the war when in 1947, the Bowmans purchased the former Dunn property south of the W&OD Railroad and reunited it with much of the old Wiehle/Thornton/Fairfax tract on the north side. The transaction, recorded April 26, 1948, was for 3,140 acres from the Willsboro Realty Company (formerly NYPEN Corporation) to A. Smith Bowman and Sons.

Katherine Bowman died in 1951 and Smith Bowman, Sr., in 1952. Their two sons, A. Smith Bowman, Jr., and E. DeLong Bowman, took over the family business and decided to expand it. Hundreds of additional acres of forest were cleared each year in order to establish pasture for larger numbers of grazing beef and dairy herds. The grass diet was augmented by protein-rich mash, a by-product from the distillery.

As farm lands in Fairfax County were converted to residential subdivisions for the expanding housing market in the 1950s, the Bowman brothers began to think about developing their large tract to its best potential. With the acquisition of the Dunn tract, they now had the largest single tract in the county and one of the largest working farms in the Commonwealth of Virginia, over seven thousand acres in all.

For five years, the Bowmans made a standing offer, to the Board of Visitors of the University of Virginia, of 250 acres of choice land at Sunset Hills for a branch of the University in Northern Virginia. Although the Visitors voted to accept the offer, the governing bodies of Arlington, Alexandria, Fairfax, and Falls Church were unwilling for a protracted period of time to vote on the matter. The Bowmans had great hopes for the future of the northwestern segment of Fairfax County, which had not yet been significantly affected by the housing boom. "When we are," said Smith Bowman, who had been formally trained as an architect, "I think we'll think more of planning than they have elsewhere in the County. That's why the University of Virginia belongs right here." The Bowmans were understandably disappointed when the impasse over the location of the branch was finally broken with a gift of land in 1959 from the town of Fairfax, whereon George Mason University was later built.

Meanwhile, subdivision of farm land for residential, commercial, and industrial uses was proceeding at an ever-increasing pace. Fairfax County was rapidly urbanizing into the southern end of the "megalopolis" between Boston and Washington—and beyond. Plans were made by the Bowmans to convert the seven-thousand-acre Bowman farm into a satellite city. Seward H. Mott and Associates of Washington, in charge of preparing the plans for development, stated that the Sunset Hills property was one of the largest parcels in one ownership near any large metropolitan area in the United States. Mott's plan included fifteen hundred acres of parks, bridle paths, wildlife refuge, swimming pools, and fish ponds. There would be an industrial area, shopping centers, churches, and other facilities which would create a "self-contained community." Homes would be built on variously-sized lots from urban to five-to-ten-acre rural parcels. The water supply would possibly be available from the Goose Creek reservoir proposed by the town of Fairfax and sewage disposal was to be accommodated through the Herndon town plant or by the construction of a private plant to be built by the developers.

Several unfavorable factors affected the implementation of this ambitious plan. It would be difficult to get the necessary zoning under existing county ordinances. The Sunset Hills property lay between two watersheds, Difficult and Sugarland runs, both of which flowed into the Potomac River above the Washington water supply intake. This last factor was of primary concern to the Fairfax County Board of Supervisors who were determined to protect the vital water resource. A third impediment of major proportions appeared on the scene in 1958 when General E. R. Quesada, chairman of a national study committee, selected the Chantilly area as the 12,500-acre site for a second metropolitan Washington airport. To service this new facility, the Federal Aviation Administration decided to build a limited access highway to the airport, initially from the Tysons Corner area west through Sunset Hills, splitting the seven-thousand-acre property into two distinct and separated parcels. Only Route 602 (now Reston Parkway) would be carried across the semi-depressed airport highway on a narrow, two-lane overpass.

Airport construction moved rapidly forward. Construction materials were carried on the W&OD Railroad to a siding near Sterling for delivery to the building site. Most of the railroad's 11,464 carloads hauled in 1959 rolled through Sunset Hills. The Chantilly Airport terminal, designed by internationally known architect Eero Saarinen, soon became a reality.

In April 1960, the Bowmans decided to sell their property for $19,750,000, including the bourbon distillery, to Lefcourt Realty. This firm had been involved in the development of numerous subdivisions in Florida. The new buyer was apparently not fully aware of the difficult situations regarding the airport limited access road or the sewer problems. Furthermore, when Lefcourt did realize some of the difficulties ahead of them, they were already overextended financially and felt that prompt resale was necessary. In less than a year, Lefcourt Realty was able to sell the Sunset Hills property (minus the distillery, which reverted to the Bowmans) to Palindrome, a corporation owned by Robert E. Simon, Jr., of New York City. A *palindrome* is a word or phrase that reads the same backward or forward. Simon's nickname was "Bob" and his wife Anne's was "Nan," hence the significance of the corporation name.

The Bowmans continued to operate their distillery for twenty-seven years after the Simon sale. But after fifty-five years of successful production since the end of Prohibition in 1933, real estate values soared and the land became too expensive to age whiskey on. The family business was moved to a new site of twenty acres, south of Fredericksburg. The motivating force was the favorable offer made for the remaining land that the owners could not refuse. In June 1988, the last barrel of aged Virginia Gentleman bourbon was transported from the old Sunset Hills site to the new location in Spotsylvania County, Virginia.

The Fairfax Hunt's first ride to the hounds, in 1928, began in front of the Wiehle/Hutchison/Bowman mansion. Courtesy of the Fairfax Hunt

THE FAIRFAX HUNT

ESTABLISHED 1928   RECOGNIZED 1933

A. Smith Bowman, Founder
ORIGINAL MEMBERS

A. Smith Bowman, M.F.H.	John F. Finerty
John S. Barbour	Robert D. Graham
A. Smith Bowman, Jr.	Nancy P. Hanna
E. DeLong Bowman	Major Hobart H. Hawkins
Margo Couzens Bryant	Anna F. Hedrick
Guy Church	Thomas C. Henderson
Roland Dawson	Estler M. Palmer
Colonel H.W.T. Eglin	Mrs. Arthur A. Snyder
Marshall Exnicios	Joseph Wheeler

By: Board of Governors 1971

Courtesy of the Fairfax Hunt

Barrels for the bonded warehouse made of oak staves cut from the woods.
  Courtesy of A. Smith Bowman Distillery

The structures were demolished in 1989 to prepare a building site. Distillery buildings about 1960.
  Courtesy of A. Smith Bowman Distillery

Imitation is thought to be the sincerest form of flattery.
Cartoon courtesy of A. Smith Bowman Distillery

Completed in 1902, this imposing brick mansion of twenty-five rooms was first the home of the Wiehle family and later, from 1927 to 1978, the home of the A. Smith Bowmans. In 1983, Prison Fellowship International purchased the mansion and grounds for use as a conference center and administrative offices. The organization is an evangelical group involved in Bible study and leadership training.
Courtesy of Reston Land Corporation

"What'll we make today? Cream of Kentucky or Virginia Gentleman?"

A Smith Bowman, Sr., in the portrait; A. Smith Bowman, Jr., standing; and E. DeLong Bowman, seated, about 1970.
Courtesy of A. Smith Bowman Distillery

Washington and Old Dominion freight train westbound through Sunset Hills in June 1958.

Courtesy of H. H. Harwood

A Washington and Old Dominion freight eastbound at the Sunset Hills station in December 1966. The gazebo, pool, and Sunset Hills mansion are in the background.

Courtesy of H. H. Harwood

Carnegie Hall in New York City was sold by Robert Simon, Jr., in 1960. The proceeds were invested in the land at Sunset Hills which became Reston.
Courtesy of Carnegie Hall

6

Reston: Inventing a New Town in Exurbia

From the time he first saw the Sunset Hills estate to the end of the initial phases of the development of his New Town of Reston, Robert E. Simon, Jr., was deeply involved with every detail of the emerging community. In addition to fostering a moneymaking venture, his was a personal and passionate commitment to the creative utilization of the land, which was at the time beyond the fringe of intensive suburban development in Fairfax County, Virginia.

Robert E. Simon, Jr., was born in New York City in 1914. When he was eleven years old, his father, a real estate manager and developer, purchased Carnegie Hall with a group of friends. The investors fully expected that a new concert hall would soon be built elsewhere, that the old building would be torn down, and they would develop their property in some other way. However the new hall was not built until 1960. Bob Simon made the remarkable discovery in his youth that 75 percent of the people who had studios in Carnegie Hall also lived there, an unusual arrangement which made a lasting impression on him.

His father's many real estate ventures included participation in financing America's first modern garden city, Radburn, New Jersey, in 1928. Later Simon would remember this as, in the 1940s and 1950s, he watched the impacts of the new technology. The proliferation of highways to serve the increase of motor vehicles pulled apart the monopoly of economic, social and cultural opportunities that American cities had enjoyed when he was growing up. He saw, also, that the suburbs of the 1950s were not designed to serve as adequate substitutes for these earlier communities.

His father died just after Simon had graduated from Harvard and as a young man of twenty-one, he took over the family business which initially consisted mostly of property management, including Carnegie Hall. Gradually, he became interested in designing and building regional shopping centers in various cities throughout the country as a solution to the problems of providing attractive and efficient shopping facilities. He found that the traditional centers had two major flaws. One was that shoppers had to do a lot of walking in order to complete their tasks. The other was that the large centers required tremendous blacktopped parking areas which resulted in visual pollution for the residential neighbors in the immediate surrounding areas. He was later to experiment in Reston with improvements in these commercial parking lot designs.

Shortly after Simon's first marriage, he moved his young family to a lovely wooded place in the country near Syosset, Long Island. Besides having a deep interest in the arts, the Simons also enjoyed all kinds of recreational activities such as tennis, swimming, boating, horseback riding, and gardening. Because they were isolated among houses built far apart on small estates, Simon's wife became the chauffeur, driving family members here and there, bridging distances too great for walking. On Sunday drives, the family often saw subdivisions of houses built closely together with large child populations who lived, played, and attended schools together. As their children reached school age, the Simon family moved to one such subdivision on Long Island. It was fine for the children and their playmates, but hard on family life. The working parents were all commuters. Simon spent over two hours each day going back and forth to his office in New York City. Socializing for adults with family, friends, and neighbors was limited to weekends because of the long work days.

In June 1960 Simon sold one of his properties, Carnegie Hall, to a quasi-public body which had received funds from the city of New York for the purchase of the famous concert hall. In order to postpone payment of capital gains taxes from this sale, Simon had to reinvest the proceeds no later than the summer of 1962. So the word went out to the business community that he was looking for an attractive real estate investment. Henry Rice of the firm of James Felt and Company first called Simon's attention to the Lefcourt/Sunset Hills property in November 1960 at which time Simon visited Virginia to see it and "fell in love with the property as an opportunity, as a location, as a physical phenomenon." At the time, neither Rice nor he knew the full extent of the problems which the Bowmans and Lefcourt had discovered regarding sewer, water, and the Federal Aviation Administration's Dulles limited access highway situations. Numerous real estate brokers and would-be brokers became involved with the sale before it was finally consummated in March 1961. The price of the purchase of 6,750 acres was $13,150,000 or about $2,000 per acre. Several smaller parcels were purchased later, making a total of 7,419 acres.

The property lay entirely within the boundaries of Fairfax County and consisted largely of meadows, woods, stream valleys, and low rising hills typical of Virginia's Piedmont. It was criss-crossed with old woods roads and trails and bisected by both the Washington and Old Dominion Railroad and the new Dulles access road. The Blue Ridge Mountains were easily visible from the northern elevations of the property.

The county itself had experienced phenomenal population growth since A. Smith Bowman had

purchased Sunset Hills from the Hutchison heirs in 1927. The number of inhabitants had been 25,264 in 1930; the 1960 census tally was 248,897. Most of the people had come to the Washington area to work for the government or to provide services for the burgeoning population. An unprecedented demand was thus created for government and other services as well as for the increasingly valuable land and other resources needed for residential and business uses. The pressures had dramatic impact on lifestyle and tax base, and on forest, field, and stream in an area where only three hundred years before, Indian tribes from both the north and south had lived, hunted, fished, farmed, and fought.

As he studied the land he had purchased and its proximity to the new Dulles International Airport, which was under construction at the time, Simon decided to implement the New Town concept on his land. In addition to familiarity with his father's involvement with Radburn, Simon had seen the British New Towns movement develop after World War II. Scandinavia, Russia, Israel, and other countries had begun building New Towns as well, and he had read of and visited British new towns and Tapiola, Finland. His personal experiences with real estate development and problems of his active, growing family guided him. He would attempt a new town. The idea was untested in the U.S. marketplace, but he was convinced that its superiority would stimulate the necessary demand which would make it successful.

Before Robert Simon engaged his first planner, architect, economist, or sociologist to begin the designing of Reston, he set down the personal philosophy he had evolved as his goals for the New Town:

1. That the widest choice of opportunities be made available for the full use of leisure time. This means that the New Town should provide a wide range of recreational and cultural facilities as well as an environment for privacy.

2. That it be possible for anyone to remain in a single neighborhood throughout his life, uprooting being neither inevitable nor always desirable. By providing the fullest range of housing styles and prices—from high rise efficiencies to six-bedroom townhouses and detached houses—housing needs can be met at a variety of income levels, and at different stages of family life. This kind of mixture

Robert E. Simon, Jr., in about 1962. The founder of Reston looks over contour maps of the eleven square miles of Fairfax County which were to be developed as a planned New Town in Virginia.
Courtesy of Reston Regional Branch, Fairfax County Public Library

The Dulles International Airport Terminal designed by architect Eero Saarinen.
Department of Transportation photograph. Courtesy of Reston Land Corporation

E. A. Prichard, graduate of the University of Virginia Law School and member of the Virginia, D.C., and Supreme Court Bars. He is a partner in the firm of McGuire, Woods, Battle and Boothe in McLean and is on the Board of Visitors of George Mason University.
Photograph about 1980. Courtesy of E. A. Prichard

permits residents to remain rooted in the community—if they so choose—as their particular housing needs change. As a by-product, this also results in the heterogeneity that spells a lively and varied community.

3. That the importance and dignity of each individual be the focal point for all planning, and take precedence over large scale concepts.

4. That people may be able to live and work in the same community.

5. That commercial, cultural and recreational facilities be made available to the residents from the outset of the development—not years later.

6. That beauty—structural and natural—is a necessity of the good life and should be fostered.

7. That Reston be a financial success.

Arthur D. Little, Inc. of Cambridge, Massachusetts, was the first consulting firm engaged by Simon to do a land-use feasibility study of the property in April 1961. Because Simon did not at this time have a clearly defined conception of what he wanted, and because some of the things he did want could not be produced in the time available, Simon and the firm soon came to a parting of the ways. A. D. Little did provide, at Simon's request, a list of possible master planners with comments on their qualifications and an emphasis on experience and ability to handle large projects.

Harland Bartholomew and Associates of St. Louis was one of Simon's two final choices for his master planners. They were the oldest and largest private planning consultant firm in the United States, with broad experience and technical skills in preparing plans for over 150 cities with populations ranging from 10,000 to over 250,000. The firm had a branch office in Washington and Bartholomew had himself served as chairman of the Maryland-National Capital Park and Planning Commission when it was assisting with work on the Year 2000 Plan for Metropolitan Washington.

The other group was Whittlesey and Conklin of New York, a small firm with an emphasis on architectural design and experience with large-scale housing projects. Julian Whittlesey had in the late

1920s been associated with Radburn's development and later the firm had been involved in developing the greenbelt towns for the federal government's Resettlement Administration during the 1930s and defense housing during World War II. In the 1950s, the firm had accepted worldwide assignments for both industrial and governmental clients involving all kinds of land uses. The firm had demonstrated imaginative architectural ability.

Ultimately, Simon engaged both firms: Harland Bartholomew to develop the first master plan and propose a change in the zoning ordinance, and Whittlesey and Conklin for the architectural design of the first village center around a man-made lake and an eighteen-hole golf course. The new town was to be developed by private enterprise, establishing concepts by the trial and error method as work progressed. Simon was able initially to provide the planners with impressions and goals which he had evolved through his own experiences and evaluations. His ultimate plan for the new town "Reston"—an acronym formed from his name's initials plus the English suffix for "town"—was that it be a satellite city with mixed land uses not solely devoted to single-family homes. He wanted to emphasize the use of modern concepts in urban design and current planning ideas. There were to be clusters with mixtures of housing types and sizes and cooperative land holding devices like condominiums in neighborhood village centers of approximately ten thousand people. Low density areas were designed on the periphery rather than having a greenbelt.

Both planning consultant firms recognized the tight restriction imposed on their planning process by existing building and zoning restrictions in Fairfax County. By December 1961, Bartholomew proposed to the county's planning office that zoning ordinance changes be made. The new regulations were based on an Urban Land Institute model ordinance which had been proposed by members of the Harland Bartholomew firm.

Realizing the importance of expert advice within Fairfax County, Simon, an "outsider" from New York, selected local attorneys who were willing and able to coordinate his efforts with county departments and elected officials. Armistead Boothe, then in the state legislature, and Lytton Gibson, a prominent zoning attorney, were engaged. Attorney E. A. Prichard then worked directly with Rosser Payne and William Burrage of the county's planning office, as well as the members of the Board of Supervisors, to draw up a new county

Footings and walls being poured for the Lake Anne Village Center, October 1963.
Courtesy of Reston Land Corporation

Lake Anne Village Center, Washington Plaza Cluster, Heron House, and Hickory Cluster, in the foreground, all under construction in the summer of 1964. Lake Anne had not yet filled behind the earthen dam.
Courtesy of Reston Land Corporation

zoning ordinance proposal which would provide the best opportunity for orderly, planned, and controlled growth in the county for projects which involved large developers like Simon. It came at a time when the Board of Supervisors had lost an important court case in their attempt to control growth in the western portion of the county by means of the ill-fated Freehill Zoning Amendment calling, among other things, for five-acre minimum lot sizes. The result was a speedy passage of the Residential Planned Community (RPC) Zoning Amendment by the board on July 18, 1962, and the approval of Reston's master plan. An important and expensive last-minute change was made just prior to ordinance approval. On the advice of Dr. Harold Kennedy, Fairfax County health officer, the approval for septic systems for the Hunters Woods single family dwellings was withdrawn, and Robert Simon was required to provide a central sewerage system for Hunters Woods. The central water system was to be installed by Reston and supplied by the Fairfax County Water Authority.

Whittlesey and Conklin had been given the Bartholomew master plan in December 1961 for the architectural design phase and implementation. Conklin designed clustered village centers connected by high-density sinews which would lace the whole composition together. This plan would avoid monotony in repetition of clusters and would give a single structural design to the entire community. There were to be grade level separations of the pedestrian and automobile rights-of-way. The population base for each village was to be ten thousand, the practical size then desired as a service area by supermarkets. Conklin proposed the creation of a man-made lake around which to design the first high-density village center. Individual lots were to be sold to private builders for detached houses on the lake and surrounding the nearby eighteen hole golf course. This would raise income for the first village venture. In this way, the land itself became the estate's "cash crop" previously represented by timber, beef, milk, chickens, eggs, and bourbon.

The simplest way to take care of the rules and regulations necessitated by all of the planned community's jointly owned open space and clustered residences would have been to incorporate the project as a town or city. The Reston land was a part of Fairfax County and directly under its jurisdiction. Much of the community would be developed in advance of the residents moving in, and it could not be granted separate governing

status without residents and without a state charter. Therefore it was agreed that Fairfax County would furnish the community with needed services and Simon would not try to incorporate. The protective covenants made possible by the RPC Zoning Amendment to some extent made up for Reston's lack of legal authority to exercise zoning powers separate from Fairfax County's control. The proper upkeep and permanent maintenance of the extensive public space would be provided for in the covenants within the deeds to the individual property owners.

Public space, amounting to 42 percent of the entire tract, was to be owned by purchasers of residential property in Reston. Generally, all park and public lands within the Reston boundaries were to belong to the First and Second Homeowners Associations; the First was to serve the area north of the Dulles access road, initially Lake Anne (named for Simon's wife); the Second to serve the area south of Dulles road, initially Hunters Woods. Deeds of dedication and bylaws were drawn up for these two associations by Simon's legal consultants and they assumed their final form in the spring of 1963.

In Hunters Woods, Simon planned to sell lots for detached, single-family homes in case the townhouse cluster concept at Lake Anne Village was not acceptable to the Washington metropolitan area housing market.

The Homeowners Associations in both areas were to care for the land and facilities in common ownership: open spaces, parking areas, pathways, streets, and other public properties. The associations were incorporated and given power to assess annual dues to meet expenses. The swimming pools, tennis courts, and golf courses were to be maintained separately by fees from the users of those facilities.

In the areas immediately adjacent to the clusters, open space was reserved for inhabitants of the clusters and the control of this property was to be exercised by each cluster's association, provided with the same powers as the Homeowners Associations, membership of which would be composed of the property owners within each cluster.

There were many protective covenants formulated relative to the use of all property. Proposed changes in the physical appearance of the community were to be scrutinized by an Architectural Board of Review (ABR) to assure an attractive atmosphere throughout. Several of the covenants provided that clothing, laundry, and washing

Artist Gonzales Fonseca works on
Washington Plaza Cluster sculpture
across from Quayside Apartments and
Washington Plaza in October 1964.
Courtesy of Peter L. McCandless

A young Restonian enjoys Gonzales
Fonseca's sculptured "sunboat" near
Heron House on Lake Anne.
Photograph by William A. Graham.
Courtesy of Reston Land Corporation

Gonzales Fonseca's tree sculpture near
Hickory Cluster in Lake Anne Village,
about 1966.
Courtesy of Reston Land Corporation

were not to be aired or dried in areas exposed to view and that antennas, fences, plantings, signs, etc. were to be subject to regulation. The ABR was also empowered to review all non-developer construction. The attractive appearance of the community had been aided initially by the decision to put utilities underground.

Construction of the Lake Anne dam was begun in the spring of 1963 to create the twenty-seven-acre lake for the first village center. The dam was forty-five feet high and five hundred feet long when it was completed, with a road across the top. Forester Lew Lewis was hired, a Reston nursery area was designated by Simon, and native hollys and dogwoods were removed from the future lake bed to be used later in landscaping the community. The waters of Colvin Run began to fill the basin behind the dam. Rules were established for use of water craft upon it, prohibiting all engines except for small electric motors. Other recreational facilities—swimming pools and tennis courts—were designed and built.

Many of the artistic embellishments which were early put in place continue to intrigue and delight residents and visitors alike. There were several individual designers. David Aaron, an expert on playgrounds, did small play spots within sight of houses. Street signs and graphics were designed by the firm of Chermayeff and Geismar. Lighting was conceived by Seymour Evans Associates. Gonzales Fonseca's sculptures graced three areas: the stone pyramid playhouse on the Washington Plaza, the stone boat near Heron House, and the sculptural composition near the Hickory Cluster pedestrian underpass. James Rossant of the Whittlesey and Conklin firm designed the sculptured fountain on the Plaza, the designs for the storefronts, and the water jet fountain in Lake Anne patterned after a similar one at Geneva, Switzerland. Rossant succinctly expressed the goal of his firm in their plan for the center at Lake Anne.

We wanted to create the village center with a sense of the past. We felt that the location was a dramatic one, adding depth to the European coastal town feeling we were striving for in our overall design.

The novelty of the endeavor in which Simon was involved had created all kinds of problems from the very beginning. Since his plan for the New Town was constantly evolving as he and others saw more clearly the direction in which he

wished to go, it was difficult in the early months to tell consultants and staff exactly what he wanted. He himself frequently lost sight of the larger picture when he got bogged down in daily minutiae.

After having worked with consultants entirely for the first year, Simon realized that he had to move from reliance on them to the development of a permanent staff. The Bartholomew firm had located his first project manager, Ira "Dutch" Willard, a man with management experience and a familiarity with the workings of local government in Virginia. The latter was a particularly desirable attribute since so many of the plans and facilities depended for their success and availability upon a cooperative working relationship with the Fairfax County government. Willard hired Glenn Saunders as project engineer because of his experience and contacts with the local governments and business community. These had developed when Saunders was manager of the town, later city, of Fairfax. Saunders had interest, vision, and the courage to associate himself with a very precarious project which had an uncertain future. When Willard and Simon were unable to establish a satisfactory working relationship, the project manager left and Saunders remained on the staff as the principal local representative and vice president of planning, engineering, and construction of the Reston project. Saunders hired, early in 1962, Donald Cummings as director, later vice president of engineering and design, in which capacity he worked until 1978. David McKinley was signed on as vice president of construction and was replaced in 1964 by Hans Schultz, who remained until 1967.

Two new staff members were hired by Simon in the spring of 1962. Peter Clow had experience with land development in England and was to handle the residential division including sale and rental of the yet unbuilt residential structures. There was, however, much to do to get the buildings planned, in the ground, completed, and priced as well. Livingston Goddard, who had been president of the Waterman Pen Company, was a lawyer by training. He was hired and put in charge of general services; greatly varied were the tasks he was expected to accomplish. For a variety of reasons, neither of the two was able to gain adequate control of his responsibilities. The difficulty of getting on with the building of the New Town with the myriad details attendant thereto moved Simon to look around for someone who showed promise of ability to deal with political realities,

On top of James Rossant's pyramid at Lake Anne Village Center about 1964 are Norman Rowland, construction superintendent; Ardee Ames, special assistant to Robert E. Simon, Jr.; and James Rossant, architect and designer.
Courtesy of Reston Land Corporation

For a few months in 1963, these men headed Reston's development. From the left, Livingston Goddard, director of the General Services Division; Michael V. DiSalle, chief executive officer; and L. Peter Clow, director of the Residential Division.
Courtesy of Reston Land Corporation

Glenn Saunders, project engineer when he joined Robert Simon at Reston's beginnings in 1961, was executive vice president of Gulf Reston, Inc., from 1968 to 1971, and executive vice president of Gulf Oil Real Estate Development Company (GOREDCO) from 1971 to 1978. Since then he has been president of International Real Estate Associates, Limited, involved in development and management of various projects.
Photograph about 1975. Courtesy of Reston Land Corporation

James B. Selonick joined Simon Enterprises in New York in 1961 and shortly thereafter became executive vice president of Reston, Va., Inc. He left Reston in the fall of 1968.
Photograph by Rob Paris Studios of Cincinnati. Courtesy of James Selonick

particularly those concerning the Federal government. He wanted to accomplish three objectives: access to the Dulles Airport road, funding for housing programs, and the location of a Federal agency in Reston.

In the spring of 1963, Simon decided to hire Ohio's ex-Governor Michael Vincent DiSalle as administrator and president of Reston operations. Action was urgently needed to begin actual construction. DiSalle had had administrative experience as director of the Federal government's Office of Price Stabilization and was a Democrat who might be useful in dealing with the administration under President John F. Kennedy. DiSalle did not move to Virginia but as a condition of hiring engaged as his assistant James Maloon, a public administration specialist. DiSalle and Maloon were expected to alleviate much of the pressure on Simon of the day-to-day decision making, and also to pull the entire unwieldy project under one administration on site. The skills required for such a job were enormous and there was a constant need for new skills and new concepts.

The two men arrived on the scene when there were no encouraging signs that there would be future access to the Dulles limited access highway; prospects looked poor for federally assisted housing construction in Reston; and the Federal government was not looking with favor upon the proposal to establish a government agency employment center out in the wilderness before any residents had moved into the new community. Simon hoped that DiSalle would be influential in turning the negative situation around with positive action.

Simon was unwilling to delegate, to relinquish his own control over financial arrangements or future planning for Reston to DiSalle. In an effort to form a strong organization, DiSalle insisted on a strict hierarchical office and organization structure with each employee adhering to the chain of command. This technique interfered with what was formerly freedom of direct communications between Simon and all of his staff. The resulting friction eventually precipitated DiSalle's departure in the fall of 1963, eight months after he had been hired. He left a new complex of administrative offices which in September was established in an undistinguished old remodeled farmhouse surrounded by office trailers, near the Bowman distillery. It was an inappropriate setting for an organization striving to create the atmosphere of a New Town of architectural excellence.

When DiSalle left, there was a "general house cleaning and rearrangement of the furniture." He left a report for Simon with certain recommendations, one of them being that there be an economic study made with projections to 1980, the estimated year of completion for the project. He had often advised this step during his brief administration. With him went Maloon, Goddard, and Clow.

A new effort was made to get the organization moving ahead, and James B. Selonick was brought down from the New York offices of Simon Enterprises, where he was executive vice president. He was made president in charge of the industrial and commercial division at Reston. Selonick was a lawyer and had had considerable experience as a commercial business and real estate manager. He was a dedicated employee whom Simon trusted and he and Simon continued to manage the project until Gulf Oil took it over in October 1967.

After a few brief abortive attempts at delegating partial but not complete authority, Simon sized up his management problems and realized that he must make a total commitment to manage the Reston development until he was assured that the project was on secure footing. There was a built-in plus—a big one. He had a loyal and competent staff in the New York offices of Simon Enterprises to whom he could delegate his other business affairs and also count on them to bridge the gap with important matters while he hired dozens of people to strengthen and fill out the staff in Reston. By May 1964, there were 126 employees, and important projects were nearing completion. The Reston North Golf Course, designed by golf course architect Edmund B. Ault, opened. An underground irrigation system was installed, using water from Lake Anne. During the first season, an average of one thousand rounds of golf were played each week. Another significant amenity was in place despite problems in many other areas of development. The forty-stall South Riding Center in Hunters Woods began to make its appearance as walls of single-family dwellings rose above their foundations within sight of it.

Quite early in the history of the Reston project, Simon had begun to implement one of his basic goals for the New Town; the creation of a balanced social community. He hired as a consultant Carol Lubin, a lawyer who had had many years of varied experience in social, economic, and urban studies. She was enthusiastic about the Reston plans and had a few ideas of her own regarding the comprehensive social facilities which should

The Reston Golf and Country Club, on North Shore and Fairway Drives, opened in 1964. It was purchased in 1983 by new owners and renamed the Hidden Creek Country Club.
Photograph by William A. Graham.
Courtesy of Reston Land Corporation

Consultant Carol Lubin, who planned social programs for the New Town.
Courtesy of Reston Land Corporation

Redeemer Methodist, the first church to open in Reston, began its services during the Christmas season, 1966. As a United Methodist Church, it became a member of the United Christian Parish of Reston in June 1973, when four denominations granted a charter for the purpose. The other churches are Christian Church (Disciples of Christ), Presbyterian Church (USA), and the United Church of Christ.
Photograph by William A. Graham.
Courtesy of Reston Land Corporation

be included among the amenities of the new community. James Rouse, just getting established as the developer of the new town of Columbia, Maryland, between Washington and Baltimore, hired thirteen consultants to deal with different aspects of his community's social development; local government and administration, social structure, economics, education, recreation, health, transportation, communication, and community problems, including the emerging role of women in contemporary society. Mrs. Lubin had all of these program-planning responsibilities by herself in Reston. In January, May, and August 1962, she held brainstorming sessions with numerous representatives of local government, schools, parks, libraries, and various agencies, planning groups, churches, and community organizations in order to determine how each group might assist with Reston's social programs. At the same time, through close study of those same programs in British New Towns she found out about the adverse effect of early overplanning that made residents feel that they had no part in the planning process in their own communities.

A nonprofit corporation was proposed to operate the program until neighborhood councils could be formed as residents gradually moved in. In January 1963, the Reston Communities Fund was established to receive funds and grants and to operate programs. An initial donation of five hundred dollars was made by Simon. Mrs. Lubin was the executive secretary. The name of the organization was later changed to the Reston, Virginia Foundation for Community Programs, Inc.

The Council of Churches and their associates met to discuss the role that they were to play in Reston. The first two churches to be built were Methodist and Baptist.

With the approval of a county-wide bond issue in May 1963, money for the first three elementary schools was made available. Cooperating with the Fairfax County School Board, Mrs. Lubin was able to obtain a small grant from the Ford Foundation to fund an innovative design for the first school, incorporating knowledge of modern technology and the teaching tools which would be utilized. The hope was that a school would be open by the time the first family moved in in 1964, but it was not ready until 1966. Intermediate and high schools, and college level programs for Reston were frequently discussed but came along much later.

A library had been projected in the county's capital improvements budget and a temporary branch was arranged for in rent-free quarters of the Lake Anne Village Center, courtesy of Reston. This was later named the Carter Glass Branch Library.

Not all plans were successfully implemented initially. Health facilities planning was much more complicated and dependent on many factors extraneous to Reston itself. After much effort, partial medical service was ascertained and would be in place for the new residents in a medical professionals building.

These detailed arrangements and the setting aside of land parcels for the associated buildings were in direct contrast to the common practice of builders in the 1950s and early 1960s who put up subdivisions without any allowances being made for public facilities. This created a situation which made it difficult if not impossible to find convenient, reasonably priced land later for public uses. Reston was setting a good example.

Simon was interested in encouraging the Federal government to use Reston as a "guinea pig" for new and experimental programs involving Federal aid to the development of new communities. For instance, more highway overpasses were needed to join the north and south segments of Reston across the Dulles access road. Simon wanted Reston to have access to the Dulles highway by access ramps to the road or to parallel lanes which could be built by the Commonwealth of Virginia on the same right-of-way. The second alternative possibility would be that the median strip of the airport road could be utilized by a regional transit system, probably on rails. But despite numerous conferences with Federal and state agencies, planners and politicians, Simon and his staff were unable to move the solution to the Dulles road problem forward.

Under President Kennedy's directive of October 1962 respecting the decentralization and dispersal of government agencies, Simon and his staff hoped to persuade the Patent Office, Coast and Geodetic Survey, or some other similar agency to make a commitment to build a facility in Reston, thereby offering employment for future residents of the new town. There was strong government objection to even considering the location of an agency "in a wilderness," and without registered voters already in place, it was impossible to have political clout in Reston. Further, there was a certain amount of antipathy on the part of the Federal government toward New Towns and private developers' economic benefits from them. On the contrary, government money had been appropriated to rehabilitate old cities and towns in the urban renewal programs of the 1950s.

The Reston situation was quite different from that of the European New Towns. In the first place, the European countries are small in area and population. Secondly, the Europeans have for centuries had a respect for tradition and national government leadership which has never existed in the United States. Without exception, they have adopted official policies for dispersing population, a national growth policy which the United States has not established. Because of this lack, planners and developers do not have government incentives which might encourage private investors to go into new areas.

International guests who visited Reston were amazed that a financial undertaking of such magnitude could succeed under one man who acted within the American private enterprise system of financing. The leaders in the fields of finance, mortgage banking, and real estate watched the process of growth closely and doubted that Simon's "townhouses in the boondocks" would succeed.

There were three major reasons for the slow development of Simon's program for attracting construction and long-term financing. The size and scope of Reston were far greater than the majority of real estate ventures. The amenities concept meant a great outlay of "front end money" before houses could be built or sold. Examples were the initial construction of the dam for Lake Anne, the entire Lake Anne Village Center, the eighteen-hole golf course and riding stable, and the pathways, bridges, and underpasses. Finally, because the Sunset Hills estate had been principally undeveloped farmland and forest, land improvements such as installation of roads and utilities had to be made. Simon's concept and design involved an urban statement in the building of the fifteen-story Heron House and groups of townhouses rather than the usual and more economical subdivision method of the initial erection of several separate model homes from which others would be sold and built.

The Sunset Hills property had been purchased from Lefcourt Realty in 1961 for $13,150,000, but relatively little cash had changed hands. The debt service for the mortgage loans and other carrying costs mounted as planning and construction schedules were repeatedly delayed. The conservative attitude of lenders, due in great part to his innovative designs thus far untested in the local

The Washington Plaza Baptist Church at Lake Anne Village Center was dedicated in July 1968 and has received a number of architectural awards.
Photograph by Daniels. Courtesy of Reston Land Corporation

market place, made Simon's job of raising additional funds extremely difficult. Added to these problems was his inability to predict when income would begin to exceed disbursements on the project.

Delays caused by the inability to manage the outside construction contractors led to Simon's establishment of Reston's own construction company, but even the conversion to independent operation took longer than anticipated. The county's various permit departments were also sources of delay. Money shortage became an acute problem. Nevertheless, in spring 1964, the Lake Anne Village Center, designed by planners Conklin and Rossant, was well under way. (Whittlesey had retired from the firm). Waterview Cluster, 90 townhouse units designed by Cloethiel W. Smith, 90 townhouses in Hickory Cluster, designed by Charles M. Goodman, and 47 units of Chimney House Cluster designed by Conklin and Rossant, were also under construction. The first development phase included 227 townhouses, 133 rental apartments and fifty thousand square feet of commercial space. The Lake Anne Village Center was a unique design, reminiscent of the Old World in the New, apartments over shops, all grouped around an open plaza with a sculptured fountain, the whole composition on a human scale with a comfortable feeling of enclosure.

The financial arrangements which Simon had made from the beginning of his venture on the New Town were complex. From part of the proceeds of the sale of Carnegie Hall in June 1960, he invested $800,000 to purchase the Sunset Hills estate from Lefcourt Realty in March 1961, financing the remainder of the purchase price of $13,150,000 with mortgages. By 1964, Simon's annual interest payments on the loans amounted to approximately $1,000,000. In addition, he estimated he would need $7,800,000 for the construction of the first units for sale and rental. In May 1963, an outside appraisal had put the value of the Reston tract at $23,400,000 with an anticipated increase by several millions when the sewer lines were in, the land having almost doubled in value in two years. The Palindrome Corporation therefore had an equity in the property of over $11,000,000. The New York Life Insurance Company was approached but declined to "pioneer" in an innovative plan which included a high-rise apartment building in the midst of vacant land out in the country beyond the suburbs in exurbia. Their policy was a conservative one, investing in proven markets with known variables.

A study for a large New York financial company, White-Weld, which was interested in the possibility of financing the venture, revealed that Reston's architecture was not that of the known preferences of residents of the Northern Virginia area for "colonial styling." The first townhouses in still-rural Fairfax County were alarmingly innovative. Other studies saw at best a long-range success as the demand for housing in the Washington metropolitan area increased.

The general field of real estate financing experienced a weakening of investor confidence with the bankruptcy of entrepreneur William Zeckendorff. In mid-1964, good real estate investments were hard to find for savings and loan companies and mortgage bankers because of an excess of caution. This had an effect on Simon's difficulties although it was only indirectly related to the probable future success of his Reston venture. He contemplated selling stock to raise money, or even selling the property to another developer.

Simon made fifty-six contacts with various financial prospects between 1961 and 1964. His negotiations with oil companies began in 1962 in the form of talks with Cities Service, Humble, and Gulf. Inducements were preferential access for retailing gasoline, the possibility of a community-wide oil-heating system, and a 10 percent limited-equity participation in the project. Esso, Shell, American Oil, Atlantic, and Mobil were approached, but most declined participation early. Several discussions were held with Gulf Oil, which demonstrated the greatest interest in participation with investment capital.

In February 1964 Gulf closed a deal with Simon which included a loan of $15 million, secured by a first deed of trust on Reston acreage owned by Simon, at 5.5 percent interest to be repaid in ten years, an option to purchase forty service station sites and an option to buy 25 percent of Palindrome's outstanding stock. This money was soon entirely disbursed. Approximately $10 million went to pay off the several mortgages. Almost $3 million went to the Hercer Corporation, a Simon family firm holding other properties which had loaned the project money. This left only $2 million for development. Soon money was again needed, this time to pay for the actual construction of the houses and the first industrial center buildings, already under way.

Simon was able to get a commitment of $2.4 million from Empire Trust of New York City in April 1964 to finance the high-rise Heron House.

A group of hikers and boaters enjoy the "Van Gogh" bridge near Lake Anne, a link in the Reston pathways system.
Courtesy of the photographer, Abbie Edwards

The South Riding Center in Hunters Woods was completed by 1966 with a forty-stall stable and inside and outside riding rings. The stable collapsed in January 1980.
Courtesy of Reston Land Corporation

Frank Slattery, stablemaster of the first South Riding Center in Hunters Woods. He was from Ireland and had been a steeple-chase and flat rider in England.
Photograph by William A. Graham.
Courtesy of Reston Land Corporation

It took longer to get loans for house construction and short-term financial arrangements. First Chase Manhattan turned him down, and then Morgan Guaranty Trust. Those two financial firms later joined other investors in James Rouse's New Town, Columbia, a more conservative, market-oriented venture in nearby Maryland. In early November, the State Planters Bank of Commerce in Richmond agreed to come to Simon's rescue with a loan of $6 to 8 million. Now the project was really underway. The first industrial firm, Air Survey Corporation, moved into the Group Facilities complex (later named Isaac Newton Square) across from the Bowman distillery in November. Townhouses were completed and the first family, Mr. and Mrs. Samuel Furcron, moved into a unit of the Waterview Cluster on Lake Anne in December 1964. By February 1965, the entire commercial space available in the Lake Anne Village Center had been leased.

Sensitivity to the marketplace had made it desirable to establish four alternatives for companies or government agencies contemplating a location in Reston. The organization could purchase land and build an architecturally approved structure; Hunter Laboratories was an early example of this option. A second choice included site selection and building design by the buyer, with construction done by Reston; Motorola chose this method. Third, Reston could build a custom-designed facility and rent it; H R B - Singer chose this option. The fourth alternative was rental space in Isaac Newton Square designed by Reston where each building accommodated five or six companies.

The occupancy of the first industrial and commercial units and the first dwelling units were the culmination of more than three years of intense innovative planning and designing. It was hard and at times frustrating work, dealing with the political process, pleading with conservative financial institutions and never giving up on an unusually creative idea "which Bob Simon thought deserved a world-class implementation effort." The future looked good. He felt that the enthusiastic home buyers demonstrated belief in his philosophy that "Modern man with leisure is restless within the confines of conformity. With time to do what he chooses and to live where he wishes, he will search out a setting which gives him freedom to expand his capacities."

From the first occupancy, Reston residents enjoyed the new adventure. There was a great deal of "pioneering spirit" among the early settlers. They knew they were participating in an unusual experiment and most of them enjoyed being a part of it. Simon enjoyed knowing this about the people who shared his dream. When the water-spout fountain was turned on for the first time in Lake Anne in the spring of 1965, he announced that everyone who lived in Reston at that time belonged to the "FFRs"—the First Families of Reston.

Other water-related activities some of the early residents enjoyed involved taking their electrically powered pontoon houseboats, a party of ten or twelve guests and a gallon of martinis out to the middle of Lake Anne, anchoring, and not coming ashore until the party was over and the martinis were gone. There were no reports of collisions at sea, or incidents of passengers or crew lost overboard. Because this became such a popular tradition, the watercraft were nicknamed "booze barges." The lake was stocked and fishing was enjoyed particularly by the young. Occasional water regattas were fine excuses for everyone to launch everything that was seaworthy.

Simon's dream included simultaneous innovations in social, architectural, and land-use development. The entire concept was too new for most of the buying public to accept readily. Lenders were conservative—they didn't know what the effect the documents relating to the home-owners and cluster associations would have on initial sales and later resales, and whether or not the real estate values would remain high. Most were unwilling to take the risk. One lender who did believe in the community and supplied a great deal of money in the early days was Martin L. Schnider, president of Northern Virginia Savings and Loan. With low down payments and competitive interest rates for mortgages for home buyers, his firm made it possible for many of the early residents to move in—with long-term benefits for all.

Some of the "growing pains" experienced by the developer are remembered vividly by Charles "Chuck" Veatch, first "postmaster" of Reston and one of the first salesmen, now himself a developer and president of the Environmental Concepts firm. The Simon organization was plagued with late deliveries, inexperienced interior construction personnel and the resulting faulty workmanship. Poorly fastened cabinets full of fine crystal and china fell off walls in one new townhouse and broke everything to pieces shortly after the owners moved in. Hot and cold waterlines were reversed during early construction of townhouses at Lake Anne. The first time the main water

The site of Wiehle/Sunset Hills from the air, showing Lake Anne and Heron House in the background, in 1965.
Photograph by Fred M. Hublitz, Courtesy of Reston Land Corporation

valves were turned on, all the hot water tanks in the model houses blew out under excessively high pressure, flooding wall-to-wall carpets and requiring forty-eight hours of working day and night to dry everything out before the scheduled official opening of the models in 1964. There was excellent media coverage and ten thousand people came to see Reston the first weekend, but not one unit sold.

Prospective buyers received certain unfortunate impressions. Sales conditions actually couldn't have been worse. Most roads were not paved, so there was either mud or dust with which to contend. Construction equipment often blocked the way to sites in which early prospective buyers were interested. One large earth mover backed over and crushed a small car waiting to get by it; the occupants escaped with only seconds to spare by jumping out of the car and running to the side of the road. While construction was proceeding, the dam was finished but the spillway was left

open while Lake Anne Plaza foundations were under construction. This meant there was a large muddy depression in the middle of Lake Anne Village with a trickling stream running down the middle. It was difficult for visitors to imagine that when the system was closed, beautiful Lake Anne would very quickly fill up behind the dam.

Although many thousands of interested prospective home buyers came to look at the new town growing in the wilderness, few bought. Simon's hope that the dynamic new concept would create its own market was slow in taking hold. It was probably ahead of its time. Perhaps the architecture and the cluster concept departed too far from the normal single-family dwelling designs potential buyers were accustomed to thinking of as "home." Sales of the townhouses were slow. They were the first to be built in Fairfax County and revealed a new life-style to most who came to view them with the idea of possible purchase.

A Sunday morning volleyball game at Hickory Cluster.
            Courtesy of the photographer,
                        Arvil Daniels

Breezing up on Lake Anne near Washington Plaza Cluster.
            Courtesy of the photographer,
                        Arvil Daniels

Boys chatting on the quay at Lake Anne near Washington Plaza Cluster.
            Courtesy of the photographer,
                        Arvil Daniel

*Rafting on Lake Anne in front of
Waterview Cluster.
Courtesy of the photographer,
Arvil Daniels*

*A moment of relaxation at Waterview
Cluster in Lake Anne Village about 1967.
Photograph by William A. Graham.
Courtesy of Reston Land Corporation*

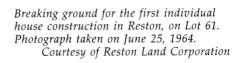

The Air Survey Corporation occupied
their building on Sunset Hills Road in
November 1964, ten days ahead of the
first residents in Reston. The company is
an aerial photographic and photogramme-
tric engineering firm still in operation in
Reston.
    Courtesy of Reston Land Corporation

Breaking ground for the first individual
house construction in Reston, on Lot 61.
Photograph taken on June 25, 1964.
    Courtesy of Reston Land Corporation

Mr. and Mrs. Samuel A. Furcron became the first residents in Reston, Virginia, on December 9, 1964. The Furcrons chose a townhouse in Waterview Cluster designed by Chloethiel Smith, with a balcony overlooking Lake Anne, the scenic focal point of the first village center.
Courtesy of Reston Land Corporation

An early view of Lake Anne with an oriental feeling, looking toward Waterview and Washington Plaza Clusters, Heron House, and the Plaza. Photograph by William A. Graham in the spring of 1966.
Courtesy of Reston Land Corporation

View of the Fountain, the Van Gogh Bridge, Heron House, and the Washington Plaza Cluster. Seen from the Hong Kong swing on an inlet of Lake Anne, in 1966.
Courtesy of Reston Land Corporation

Recreation barge on Lake Anne in 1982. Watercraft of this type, with electric motors, have floated on the lake since it filled behind the earthen dam.
Photograph by James Kirby. Courtesy of Reston Homeowners Association

Charles A. Veatch, president, Environmental Concepts, Incorporated. He was one of Reston's first salesmen and sales managers. His company built The Atrium, Virginia's first condominium office building, in 1976, in Reston.
Photograph by William A. Graham.
Courtesy of Reston Land Corporation

The Van Gogh Bridge viewed from above.
Photograph by William A. Graham.
Courtesy of Reston Land Corporation

Chuck Veatch, as Reston's first rural postmaster, received a one dollar check in July 1965 from the treasurer of the United States.
Courtesy of Charles Veatch

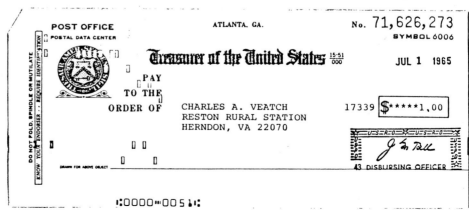

View from the east side of Lake Anne Village Center with Heron House, in 1967. Hickory Cluster is at the upper right and the white roofs of Lake Anne Elementary School can be seen upper left.
Photograph by William A. Graham.
Courtesy of Reston Land Corporation.

*Lake Anne seen from the north about
1970. Fellowship House I is under
construction in the right foreground.
Cameron Crescent Apartments appear in
the left foreground, and Isaac Newton
Square is top left.*
        Courtesy of Reston Land Corporation

Reston's first community swimming pool overlooks Heron House from Waterview Cluster.

Courtesy of Peter L. McCandless

7

A Dream Becomes a Nightmare

As work progressed on the development of America's first major post-World War II New Town, Reston was studied and commented upon by students, planners, architectural critics, sociologists, authors, residents, visitors, and real estate people from around the world. Reston made the front page of the *New York Times*. A lengthy illustrated essay appeared in *Look* magazine. Virtually every news, home, and architectural magazine carried articles and pictures on the developing New Town. Urban planner Frederick Gutheim wrote in the *Washington Post* that "Reston seeks to break with [the suburban] pattern and meet many of the criticisms of low-density 'slurbs' and the headaches local governments have found in providing community services." Robert Murray wrote in *House and Home* that "Reston more than almost any other town comes closest to being a self-contained city .... The new towns will inevitably awaken the public to the possibilities for better housing and environments, unlike suburbia's monotonous whelping grounds." Architectural critic Wolf Von Eckardt waxed poetic and likened his experience of coming onto the Plaza at Lake Anne Village to the discovery of the Piazza San Marco in Venice: " ... it is not a mere square but a grand hall with the open sky its ceiling and the lake providing an ever-changing dimension and well-framed kinetic mural."

The first shops in the Washington Plaza of Lake Anne Village Center were leased by the Vienna Trust Company (a bank), a small Safeway supermarket, Cardwright Book Shop, the Quay Club, the Mooring restaurant, Gallagher's Dry Cleaning, Tom's Barber Shop, Meenehan's Hardware, Jules Hairstylists, the Scandinavian Decorator Studio, the Community Hall, the Carter Glass Branch of the Fairfax County Public Library, and the Lakeside Pharmacy. Added features were the boat rental service provided by Meenehan's, and outdoor dining with colorful tables and umbrellas on the plaza in front of the restaurant.

By the time of the official opening of Lake Anne Village Center on December 4, 1965, the list of amenities already in place in Reston was imposing. There were two community swimming pools, four tennis courts, a volleyball court, numerous playgrounds, outdoor sculpture, a pedestrian underpass and several miles of pedestrian pathways, the first eighteen-hole golf course, a riding center, a fifteen-story high rise, 227 townhouses, 133 apartments, and approximately 100 single-family detached homes.

The official opening was a fine celebration. It took the form of "A Salute to the Arts," and was an all-day affair. Guest speaker August Heckscher, director of the Twentieth Century Fund, summed up his ideas, impressions and hopes for Reston:

First, we see here a brave and deliberate design to create a community out of whole cloth. That is not an easy or a commonplace thing. There is a mystery at the heart of it and I dare say not one, not even Mr. Simon, is quite sure of all the answers. You take good land, and the power of wealth brought together from diverse sources and many skills, and toil and a sense of beauty; you add people, and you sit by hoping that the result will be the marvelously complex and subtle creation of a living organism . . . . Will it work: Does it represent in its fulfillment what men and women have really desired? . . . . We are recapturing here something which the modern world tends to erode and dissipate: the sense of pace, the feeling that men's lives exist within a frame which helps give meaning to what they do and plan . . . . Reston stands for the ascendancy of the human element over the technological. This is a place: it is a place made for men and women—shaped to satisfy their needs and desires. Opportunities for employment will develop here . . . [but] Reston is not for work only, but for the growth of the human personality in its variety and fullness—through recreation, through the arts, through civic activities, through contact with an unspoiled environment.

Architectural critic Ada Louise Huxtable wrote the next day in the *New York Times* that Reston had been the dream of Robert E. Simon, Jr., a real estate developer with ideas and thousands of acres of gently rolling, wooded Virginia land, collaborating with a county with growth problems. She succinctly summed up the venture to date and put it in an international perspective:

Mr. Simon's dream was for a coordinated, creatively designed community that would start with over-all planning of landscape, recreation, culture, commerce, and industry as well as housing, conceived as a distinctive, total environment. At a time when the American landscape is being plowed under at the rate of one million acres a year, his efforts are being recognized by critics on conventional suburbs as the American answer to the European planned new towns.

Another amenity had to do with education of the very young. There were no public kindergar-

tens in Fairfax County at the time. Simon, who believed the developer should support educational activities, wanted to provide a meaningful and useful preschool experience for both children and parents. He gave an initial subsidy and quarters at a low rental fee to get the private Lake Anne Nursery School and Kindergarten (LANK) started. It was located in the Lake Anne Village Center above the Safeway when it opened in 1965; later the LANK board of directors decided to buy their own property and build a specially designed facility. From its inception until it became an independent operation in 1967, Jane Gilmer Wilhelm, director of the Reston Community Relations Department from the time of her appointment in 1964, was organizer and supervisor.

Industries were beginning to move into the area set aside for them. Seven had signed leases for space in the Industrial Center and four, with over 250 employees, were already functioning.

All of this tangible evidence of success resulted in a new source of funding from the John Hancock Mutual Life Insurance Company, which had been watching Reston's progress closely for two years. In 1966, the company announced that it would invest $20 million in permanent financing for the orderly long-term development of Reston. The undeveloped land was to be titled in the name of John Hancock, and parcels were to be purchased by Simon as development progressed. In spite of this financial boost, Reston was to run into major problems in less than two years, partly due to poor management and undercapitalization for the size and scope of the project.

Reston did not lack for observers and commentators as it developed. It was viewed through microscope and telescope, measured with carpenter's rule and calipers, written about, talked about and filmed for nationwide and worldwide audiences. Simon and his architects were said in one architectural publication "to exemplify the trend toward designing cities for people—not gods, kings, or automobiles."

As was astutely pointed out by researcher Dr. Carl Norcross of the Urban Land Institute in 1966, the test of a new community is not how writers and editors like it, but how the people who live there like it. His trained interviewers sampled seventy-one families asking why they had moved there and what they thought of Reston. They found the buyers "exuberantly enthusiastic;" they loved Reston. To some, it was like a new religion, using all the planned facilities, a wonderful adventure, "the most delightful experience of our

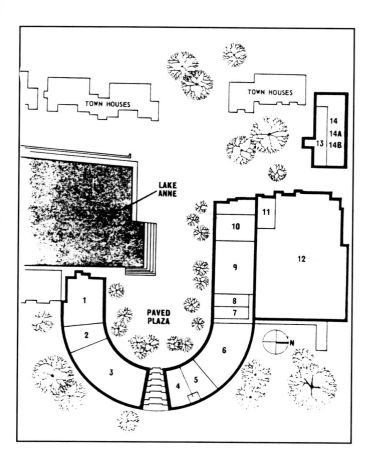

This is a diagram of Lake Anne Village Center. Its 1965 tenants are:

1. Lakeside Pharmacy—and old-fashioned corner drugstore
2. Fairfax County Public Library—Carter Glass Branch
3. Community Center—lectures, adult education courses, university extension courses, concerts, community meetings, Rathskeller for teens
4. Scandinavian Decorator Studio—furniture, furnishings, gift items
5. Jule's Hair Stylists—women's hairdresser
6. Meenehan's Hardware—hardware and garden supplies, boat concession for Lake Anne
7. Tom's Barber Shop—four chairs
8. Gallagher Dry Cleaning
9. The Mooring Restaurant
10. The Quay Club—private social club
11. Cardwright books, stationery and gift shop
12. Safeway supermarket
13. Youngland—children's specialty store
14. Vienna Trust Company—bank
14a Life insurance company
14b Lawyer's offices

Above the Safeway was a nursery school (LANK) with its own rooftop playground. Above the crescent-shaped building's first floor were thirty-four rental apartments.
            Courtesy of Reston Land Corporation

Five little girls enjoy a chat in front of the Lakeside Pharmacy at Lake Anne Village Center.
            Photograph by Arvil Daniels

lives." Those who had already purchased were busy promoting the community and its developers and builders to their families, friends, relatives, and acquaintances. "We'd recommend it because they paid attention to quality in the planning. They kept their word. But above all, they saved the trees." Mothers appreciated not having to jump into the family car whenever their children wanted to go somewhere. Parents and children had many opportunities for recreation: swimming, sailing, tennis, playgrounds, horseback riding, walking, biking, dancing, ice skating, sledding, scouts, music lessons, and golf. The cultural activities, the community hall at Lake Anne, the lake itself, and the out-of-doors were all great assets to the enjoyment of life in Reston. One of the buyers expressed his strong opinion that Simon was a genius.

The managers of a number of the "smokeless industries" which moved into Reston's Isaac Newton Square complex were also pleased to express their opinions on their new town environment. Richard Delmas, vice president of Air Survey Corporation, the first tenant to move in, was optimistic about the community concept as a pleasant environment for his employees. Robert L. Riddle, technical vice president of HRB-Singer, Reston's second industrial resident, commented on the environment which would not only be conducive to a more effective individual performance but that eventually the industrial park with other new industries would be a fine development. Dr. M. Dean Bavron, president of Human Sciences Research, praised the planned community for its exceptionally good environment for both living and working. It was pointed out that Reston was ten minutes from Dulles Airport, thirty-five minutes from National Airport, and right on the Washington and Old Dominion Railroad, which was then still running one freight train a day between Purcellville and Washington.

Even tourists had interesting comments to make about the new town. Reston's visitors center had a tour book, a guest register, which was kept for a number of years beginning in August 1963. By December 1965, 270 scheduled tours of official visitors from all over the world had been recorded, representing more than two thousand guests. P. J. Butler, principal planning officer for the Housing Commission of New South Wales, Australia, stated that he had come to the United States principally to see Reston. Selwin B. Myers, general manager of the Garden Cities Association, Capetown, South Africa, said his visit to Reston was the highlight of his visit to the United States. Thirty students and the faculty of engineering from the University of Vera Cruz, Mexico, came. Takayuki Kuwahara, secretary of Japan's Socialist Party, was impressed by the recreational facilities close to residential areas. Dr. Harma Walz, a social scientist from Frankfurt, West Germany, was enthusiastic about the facilities for the arts and the trained staffs for painting and pottery lessons, dance and ballet classes, discussion groups, concerts, lectures, and film series. Marko Slajmer, director of the urban planning office for the Standing Conference of New Towns, Ljubljana, Yugoslavia, thought Reston had "all the charms of the best hamlets and cities in Europe."

The antipathy which many critics felt toward postwar subdivision building contrasted with Reston's plan was expressed with a vitriolic pen by designer Vladimir Kagan:

Taken in perspective of other American communities that have sprouted in virgin countrysides, Reston is a mecca, an oasis in a wilderness of ugliness. It heralds a new renaissance of collaboration of the arts, architecture and culture . . . .

Objects and things are aesthetic and beautiful because there is no reason for them to be mundane and pedestrian. This is one of the charms of Reston: somebody cared all the way . . . . There is welcome new thought in this village in Virginia, an attempt has been made to break the shackles of thousands of soleless macadam strips and split-level communities that have dotted our countryside like fly-droppings. Will Reston spell the end of the Bulldozitis that has flattened millions of acres of woodlands, hills and natural landscape?

For some time, Simon had indeed been concerned about the preservation and interpretation of the open spaces which had been reserved by his clustering and variable density planning concept. By the time Kagan wrote his critique, Simon had hired an employee whose responsibility it was to oversee a program for the natural amenities, even though the money situation was beginning to be desperate in the Reston development offices. Vernon Walker, who had had over ten years of experience with various outdoor environmental education programs in camps and schools in New Jersey, was brought in under the sponsorship of the Reston Foundation in March

In the Simon years, Lake Anne Nursery and Kindergarten (LANK) was located in the Lake Anne Village Center in quarters especially designed for it over the supermarket. The fifteen-story Heron House can be seen in the background.
Photograph by William A. Graham.
Courtesy of Reston Land Corporation

Jane G. Wilhelm was director of community and social programs during the Simon years. In this 1965 photograph by William A. Graham, she is shown in Reston's first Community Center, on Washington Plaza.
Courtesy Reston Land Corporation

These damp residents are meandering home after a swim in a Reston pool.
Photograph by Abbie Edwards

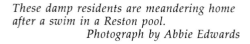

1966. There were eighteen hundred people in the community at the time. He set up two environmental management committees, one in Lake Anne Village and one in Hunters Woods. A community action program was then established which pleased a majority of the residents of both areas.

The Reston community was officially dedicated on May 21, 1966. Guest speakers at the Dedication Day program included Stewart L. Udall, Secretary of the Department of Interior, and Robert C. Weaver, Secretary of the Department of Housing and Urban Development (HUD). Mills E. Godwin, Jr. Governor of the Commonwealth of Virginia, gave the dedication address. Robert Simon was awarded HUD's first Urban Pioneer Award. A telegram from President Lyndon Johnson extended greetings and said, in part, "In this age of ever-mounting urban growth . . . the birth of a new town such as Reston is a living influence which invigorates our concepts of urban planning . . . ."

Representatives came to the ceremonies from the following New Town countries throughout the world: Algeria, Argentina, Australia, Brazil, Bulgaria, Canada, Ceylon, Czechoslovakia, Finland, France, Germany, Ghana, Great Britain, Greece, Guinea, Hungary, India, Indonesia, Israel, Italy, Japan, Libya, Malaysia, Mexico, Netherlands, Nigeria, Norway, Pakistan, Poland, Romania, Sudan, Sweden, Thailand, Union of Soviet Socialist Republics, United Arab Republic, and Venezuela.

During the program, Secretary Udall announced that after a ten-year search for a central home for the U.S. Geological Survey (USGS), it had been decided that the new $50 million headquarters would be built on a one-hundred-acre site in the Reston Center for Government and Industry. The architects for the one-million-plus square foot building were to be Skidmore, Owings and Merrill. A further example of Simon's openhandedness when times were tough and he could ill afford the gesture, was his outright gift of eighty-five acres of land for the USGS building site. The government bought only fifteen acres of the total of one hundred.

The Interior Secretary also brought up an important problem which Simon had not yet been able to solve. "A true 'New Town,' " he said, "must be a cross section of America or it must be deemed a failure despite the brilliance of its design and the insight of its community planning. In this land of equal opportunity, *no* town can claim to be truly American if it is an enclave of the

well-to-do or the private preserve of any single ethnic or racial group."

Simon promised to build a variety of reasonably priced housing units for the USGS employees. It was a pledge in keeping with the stated policy of encouraging all who work in the community to live there, regardless of race or level of income. A HUD-financed low interest loan had been promised and Simon was soon to construct the first two hundred units of low-cost housing.

Although it was not apparent to the outside world and not openly discussed within Simon's Reston organization, it was obvious to the staff by the end of 1966 that the project was in deep trouble. For the first time since its inception, the employees did not receive a Christmas bonus. They knew Simon would have given them one if he could possibly have done so.

The tremendous burden of overall development cost had by early 1967 all but exhausted Simon's resources. Still new amenities were added: Fairfax County's Lake Anne Elementary School was opened in January; Simon had paid to have all the earth moving work done so that the school could be built within the county's budgeted amount. All spring and summer, preparations, classes and programs were carried out for the Reston Music Center under the direction of James Christian Pfohl; that program, too, was operating on a shoestring. The summer music camp for orchestral students and professionals from all over the country, sponsored by the Reston Foundation, and subsidized by Simon, was a musical success but a financial disaster. By the summer of 1967, Bill Henry, executive vice president of Gulf Oil had a plane standing by to fly to Richmond to pick up a loan from State Planters Bank.

Time schedules for sales and development did not keep pace with the carrying costs of the Reston project. By fall of 1967, the residential population was only twenty-five hundred. There were about 370 townhouses, 400 apartments, and 325 home sites sold or rented. Gulf Oil Corporation decided it would have to step in and protect its unsecured loan by taking over the management of Reston. The alternative seemed to be to accept as a total loss the investment of the $15 million advanced in 1964. John Hancock Life Insurance Company, which had the undeveloped land as security for its loan, was not prepared to complete the development of the New Town—the land would probably have been broken into large chunks and sold.

The fears of many Reston-watchers throughout

A tennis lesson progresses on one of
Reston's courts.
Photograph by Burtnett Studios
of Silver Spring. Courtesy of
Reston Land Corporation

A couple pause on the bike-hike trail on
their way to nearby tennis courts.
Courtesy of Reston Land Corporation

Several times during each winter, ice
freezes thick enough for skating on this
spur of Lake Anne.
Photograph by Peter L. McCandless,
in 1965. Courtesy of
Reston Land Corporation

79

the world who thought that the New Town idea would be abandoned were expressed by *New York Times* architectural critic Ada Louise Huxtable in September. After noting that Simon and Gulf had signed an agreement creating Gulf Reston, Inc., in September 1967, she was of the opinion that Simon's community had "changed from one man's dream to a corporate subsidiary." She went on to say:

Reston may have been one man's dream (even its name is built out of his initials) but in six years it has become the nation's model. In those six years it ran on faith, hope and desperate, last-minute injections of cash. It also ran counter to every standard practice and procedure of conventional real estate development.

Standard practice means the sleazy subdivision and the asphalted shopping center, the familiar fast-buck operation, composed of short-term, quick profit, in-and-out financing and instant obsolescence. Reston is a long-range capital investment. It coordinates sociology and design, nature and building, to create a sensitive, extremely handsome small world and a way of life formed and molded with high art and sophistication by some of the country's best talents. Its plan promoted townhouses, cluster zoning, communal open land and amenity programs, all of which meant hard crusading for local reforms and bitter battles for financing. Reston has been a combination of a tenacious personal vision and an obstacle course to excellence.

The architects themselves were vocal. The president of the American Institute of Architects, Robert L. Durham, outlined the problems faced by Simon and anyone else who wanted to build, from the ground up, a community which included social institutions. He thought that Simon's problems were neither the result of the failure of the New Town movement nor of Reston's design. Durham wrote:

They reflect the fact that in the U.S. we have not yet faced up to the special kind of financing needed by New Towns. Contrary to other kinds of construction projects, a New Town by its nature must provide for a long lead-time between investment and returns—a time when costly community facilities and amenities, plus payments, taxes and land carrying cost in gen-

eral will deplete early capital and there will be insufficient income to replace it.

Gulf Reston's new chief executive officer was Robert H. Ryan, a real estate consultant who had been involved in many development projects from New England to the West Coast and south to Florida. Ryan was frank to state that Gulf did not consider Reston a particularly good investment but that his employer had the "patient" money and the long view that the success of this kind of community required.

Numerous observers commented on the doubtful future of Reston and feared it would not long remain "Simon-pure." Wolf Von Eckardt predicted that it would "soon become en-Gulfed in mediocre urban sprawl, as were Radburn, New Jersey, the green belt towns of the New Deal and several other noble attempts to build good total communities in this country. 'For Gulf Oil,' said Ryan, 'will henceforth listen to the market.' " To this, one angry Restonian replied that the trouble with that approach was that "until 1492 the market said the earth was flat."

The land on which Reston was being developed had great natural beauty and the utilization of it had been well worked out to preserve that beauty. On the other hand, the market had been misjudged from the product point of view. All house designs were contemporary, inside and out, in the Lake Anne area. Some were poorly constructed, with poor family livability. They were also overpriced. Traditional designs were selling in the Washington area housing market and none were offered by Simon's organization.

The project's personnel had been numerous and costly. Bob Simon always wanted to get the best for Reston—the best consultants, the best managers, the best of everything. He picked thoroughbreds for his stable, but because of the lack of a good overall management structure, they were mostly just milling around instead of running a race in the same direction. He never put together a system that made them all work together. Design goals were not consistent with the marketplace. Too many decisions were based on emotional rather than economic considerations. Simon was a dreamer and a father figure. His was a gamble, a deep commitment to a new and better lifestyle.

The first group of residents in Reston admired Simon's grand plan, his taste, his zeal, his imagination, and his energy. They had all been "pioneers" together, and this experience had

In 1965, Bob Simon leased prime space on ground level in Heron House at a nominal fee in order to provide an exhibit hall and teaching space for Reston's early graphics arts group. The Greater Reston Arts Center (GRACE) was incorporated and gave art shows and classes in the gallery until the rent was raised under Gulf Reston's administration. In temporary quarters, GRACE is waiting for permanent space in a Bowman whiskey warehouse, which must be remodelled for their use.
Courtesy of Reston Land Corporation

Vernon Walker gives an illustrated nature talk to a group of young people on the quay at Lake Anne.
Photograph by Arvil Daniels

Vernon Walker, naturalist, shows a snake to an absorbed group of Reston kids.
Courtesy of Elfriede Walker

Isaac Newton Square, the first industrial/commercial complex in Reston, is bounded by Wiehle Avenue and Sunset Hills Road. Offices of RHOA, now called the Reston Association, occupy the central building in the complex.
Courtesy of Reston Land Corporation

Hickory Cluster townhouses designed by Charles Goodman at Lake Anne Village. Photograph by William A. Graham. Courtesy of Reston Land Corporation

engendered a fierce loyalty toward Simon on the part of the early Restonians. They did not think that anyone could take his place and doubted that the new town concept could survive under the ownership of a large oil corporation.

The Carter Glass branch of the Fairfax County public library opened in a small storefront on Washington Plaza in April 1966.

Courtesy of Fairfax County Public Library

At Reston's formal dedication ceremony, while Secretary of the Interior Stewart Udall watched, Secretary of Housing and Urban Development Robert Weaver conferred upon Robert E. Simon, Jr., HUD's first Urban Pioneer Award, in May 1966. It was at this ceremony that Secretary Udall announced that Reston had been selected as the site for a new United States Geological Survey headquarters building complex.

Photograph by William A. Graham. Courtesy of Reston Land Corporation

Also at the dedication ceremony, Virginia Governor Mills Godwin gave an address. He compared the future importance of Reston with the historical worth of Williamsburg.

Photograph by William A. Graham. Courtesy of Reston Land Corporation

Lake Anne Elementary School is shown here about 1968. Built in part with a grant from the Ford Foundation, this was Reston's first elementary school. The building to the right was the Redeemer Methodist Church, now part of the United Christian Parish of Reston. Photograph by Blue Ridge Aerial Surveys. Courtesy of Reston Land Corporation

83

The Atrium, designed by Environmental Concepts, Inc., was Virginia's first commercial condominium, completed in 1976 on Roger Bacon Drive. Photograph by the William C. Pflaum Company.
   Courtesy of Reston Land Corporation

Scope, Incorporated, opened in the Reston Business Center on Michael Faraday Drive. It was an architectural award winner in 1967.
   Courtesy of Reston Land Corporation

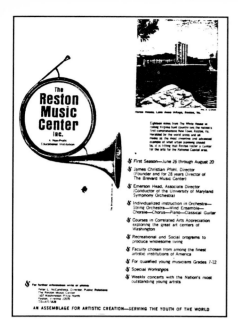

An advertisement in the Music Journal of January 1967 announced the Reston Music Center's summer program for "qualified young musicians" nationwide.
Courtesy of Peter L. McCandless

The Reston Music Center operated a music camp in Reston during the summer of 1967, under the direction of Dr. James Christian Pfohl of Brevard, North Carolina. Gifted high school music students and artists came from all over the United States as well as from foreign countries to play together under the guidance of noted professional musicians. The large striped tent for rehearsals and concerts was set up in the field behind the present location of Brown's Chapel on Baron Cameron Avenue.
Courtesy of the author

THE RESTON MUSIC CENTER 1967 PERSONNEL DIRECTORY

A young resident expresses the exuberance felt by many Restonians of all ages who live in the New Town.
Photograph by William A. Graham.
Courtesy of Reston Land Corporation

Robert Simon, left, and Vernon Walker, right, escorted Lady Bird Johnson along the Reston pathways. They gave her a tour of the new town when she visited in July 1967. She also visited the Reston Music Center and saw how students from all over the country were working at the summer music camp.
Courtesy of Mrs. Robert H. Walker

*Reston's first gasoline station, built by
Gulf, was winner of an architectural
award in 1967.*
Courtesy of Reston Land Corporation

8

Gulf Reston: Oil on Troubled Waters

In a little more than a decade of ownership Gulf Oil not only put the financial operation of the growing New Town on a sound basis but in the early 1970s was able to survive a severe international oil crisis and a locally imposed sewer moratorium against new hookups. The community which had enjoyed its infancy under Bob Simon's administration matured. Responsible individuals within it began to plan and provide for some of the amenities which initially had been expected from the builder. The new town began to show a healthy growth not only in residential building of all kinds, but in the gratifying expansion of interest in and development of commercial and industrial enterprises which provided employment centers.

The Gulf Oil Corporation took over control of the development of Reston in September 1967, forming the subsidiary company, Gulf Reston, Inc. It was a period in the nation's development when large, "impersonal" corporations were beginning to feel the need to demonstrate positive community involvement. The company moved in to protect its initial investment of $15 million made in 1964, knowing that additional millions would be needed to get construction moving again. The Board of Directors of Gulf Oil was interested in seeing if good management practices would improve productivity, and the quality of American life and society as experienced in the New Town. Reston

was not alone in its floundering condition. Other real estate developments from coast to coast were having rough times or in some cases had actually failed because of insufficient financial backing or poor management. In the fall of 1967, Reston owed $6 million to New York banks and $10 million to John Hancock Life Insurance Company in addition to the $15 million Gulf Oil debt, plus accrued interest.

There were those who had watched Reston's development during the Bob Simon years who felt that the New Town was designed more to reflect his own tastes than to appeal to buyers. The executive director of the Urban Land Institute, Max S. Wehrly opined, "Simon let himself fall into the hands of his architects and designers and made mistakes that a seasoned developer wouldn't have." It was a commonly held opinion by the Reston staff as well as outsiders that "Bob Simon had too many architects and not enough accountants."

The town was not the utopia that many had expected a brand-spanking-new planned town to be. Some disenchantment of the residents had occurred when there was a wave of juvenile vandalism in Reston during the summer of 1966. Just a few weeks before the Gulf takeover, arrests had been made of two residents charged with possessing and selling marijuana. The liberalism and permissiveness of many of the community's parents were blamed in part for the situation.

Still another problem plagued the new town: the business people did not find Reston profitable. The townspeople were not interested in patronizing their own local merchants. Dr. George Zacko, a local dentist who served as president of the Reston Business and Professional Association, thought that two of the reasons were that the small stores had limited selections of merchandise and their prices were high compared with stores in nearby Herndon. This problem did not directly affect the dentist and the local doctor who were the only persons who benefitted immediately because they provided services that were in demand.

Gulf's consultant, Bob Ryan, had a master's degree in business administration from Harvard and an aim to combine good planning and design with "economic feasibility." Prior to coming to Reston, Ryan had wide experience with housing and urban development and some knowledge of what a new town could be with adequate financial and management backing. The question in the minds of everyone, particularly Reston residents, was whether or not he could accomplish Gulf's purposes without compromising Reston's original master plan and standards in future development.

Ryan was immediately labelled with a number of descriptive names, most of them uncomplimentary. "Hatchet man," "hired gun," "energizer," and "quick fixer," were some of them. They indicated the high level of emotion with which both Simon's employees and the residents of Simon's new town reacted to the new order of things and the fears generally held that the whole wonderful plan was going down the drain.

When he had first been asked by Gulf Oil to take a look at Reston's books and the entire physical operation, Ryan was not sure the project could succeed. The alternative was for Gulf to drop out, take the loss, and let John Hancock Mutual Life Insurance Company, which had no interest in the new town concept, take the land and sell it off in large parcels to individual developers. Gulf gave Ryan a vote of confidence and hired him as a consultant. "With the boat dead in the water and leaking," said the former Naval officer, "I was the one who grabbed ahold of what was there and got it moving again." The project was out of funds and heavily in debt at this point.

The first thing Ryan did was to cut back drastically on the staff, believing that there were too many people around to get things done. He talked to each employee to see if he or she would fit into his plan for future economic feasibility. He

rearranged priorities and put Simon's last of seven goals—the community's financial success—at the top of his list, followed by good value for the money in buildings and sites offered for sale. Ryan looked at the amenities as "the little bonus" after economic feasibility and good value had been achieved.

In these respects and others, Ryan's theories agreed with two of the employees who left when Gulf took over—Bernard Norwitch and Edward Eichler. They had worked for Simon's organization for less than two years on advertising and residential construction. Both had extensive experience in their fields and had built reputations in them. They had repeatedly advised Simon of problems they found in the development of Reston: he had missed the market from the product point of view; some of the buildings were poorly constructed and overpriced; there were not enough designs from which prospective buyers might choose—all contemporary, no traditional, inside or out. The houses were perceived to have poor livability by most of the potential buyers who came to look. Despite repeated advice, Simon had refused to recognize that there was a serious need on his staff for marketing expertise.

Ryan's aggressive tactics were not popular with the residents, many of whom were fiercely loyal to Simon and his ideals. They were sure that Gulf was not going to continue with the plans of the new town's founder. Some of the fun went out of living in Reston. Ryan discovered that the Quay Club, a private membership bottle club for Reston residents located next to the restaurant at Lake Anne, had been heavily subsidized by Simon. Ryan moved quickly to close it. It had been established as a sociable neighborhood "watering place" before the day when local option had been approved in Virginia, allowing commercial purveyors to sell liquor by the drink. The club members were very unhappy. The night the Quay Club was closed, some of the members brought a life-size effigy of Bob Ryan and sat it in a chair while they cleaned the bottles out of their lockers. Although the effigy was not burned that night in true revolutionary fashion, it was stuck full of pins.

On October 26, the first meeting of the Board of Directors of Gulf Reston was held. Ryan took control of the meeting. He showed slides, including views of unkempt lawns in front of the model homes and a large Reston directional billboard on Route 7 located beside an Esso station. Observers noted that the slides tended to belittle past management. A three-man executive committee of Gulf representatives was formed to oversee Ryan's decisions. Simon strongly objected because he was not included and he wanted an active role in management, not wishing merely to serve as a figurehead. The controversy was not resolved; after the meeting, Simon was asked to resign, he refused, and was fired.

Bob Simon had built a strong sense of community and purpose at Reston. He was a visionary, in many ways fifteen to twenty years ahead of his time, who refused to develop strong management practices. He laid the groundwork for the post-industrial, high technology age which was coming in the future. The Gulf gasoline station at Lake Anne Village Center was in operation at this time and after the firing of Simon, many unhappy Reston citizens were seen publicly burning their Gulf credit cards. Then, what was the last straw for many fiercely loyal and traumatized Restonians happened, it seemed, overnight. Suddenly, all of the signs, company trucks and equipment which had been painted symbolic "Simon green" partly to signify his deep concern about the environment, had a nice fresh coat of "Ryan blue" Gulf Reston paint.

Although Ryan constantly assured the residents that he would continue to follow Simon's master plan, they were nervous about his reordering of priorities, placing financial success at the top of the list. They disliked his changing of a group of planned townhouses in Hunters Woods to detached dwellings. They thought the future completion of the pathway system was in doubt —after all, wasn't Gulf in the business of selling gas?

After Simon was fired as chairman of the board in late October due to differences with Ryan over "the whole range of policies, plans and priorities," Restonians rallied 'round and gave Simon a gala farewell party at Lake Anne's Washington Plaza. Dr. George Zacko was master of ceremonies. It was a time of great sadness. The man who developed the dream community with a little touch of Venice was gone.

Citizens decided to take positive action. The Reston Community Association (RCA) was formed in November 1967 as an independent organization "to promote Reston's growth as a new town within the framework of county government and to help foster a community spirit,"—and to keep a watchful eye on the new developer. The membership, open to all residents, both owner and tenant, grew to nine hundred in a few months. Joseph R.

Stowers, later president of RCA, 1969-1970, "saw it as the beginning evolution of a democratic government for the new town . . . . " It has since then operated as an issue and crisis-oriented group of volunteers which serves as adviser, watchdog, agitator, and advocate in dealing with the county government.

Meanwhile, Ryan was setting about the business of tightening up management procedures and accelerating development. He let many of the high-priced consultants go and fired many of the staff members. This shake-up of the organization was not a happy experience for Ryan, but severe cutbacks were necessary.

More industrial development was needed; a larger number of dwellings had to be sold each year to enable Gulf Reston to operate at a profit. Mortgage financing obtained at 90 percent of the market price was a step in the right direction, and some of the townhouse models were redesigned for better value. In 1968, seven hundred units of all types of housing sold for $10 million, triple the sales of 1967. Reston's population went over the five thousand mark. Ten major industries were added to the Industrial Center and over 100,000 square feet of lease space were added in Isaac Newton Square, including the 30,000 square feet Newton Building in the center of the complex. The long-awaited housing funds from HUD finally became available and, for the first time in Reston, moderate income housing construction began on the Cedar Ridge apartments. Another goal of the fiftyish Ryan was to provide housing for the elderly. Financial assistance was so long in coming that he often said in despair, "I'm going to be ready to *live* in Fellowship House [for senior citizens] before this thing gets off the ground!"

James Barker, manager of Gulf Reston's industrial and commercial development and a former Simon employee, attended an early meeting of the Reston Community Association's transportation committee in December 1967. Invited by the chairman, Karl Ingebritsen, he told the group of the developer's attempt to save the W&OD right-of-way for rapid transit. The inauguration of express bus service to and from Washington was also discussed with enthusiasm. After the meeting, Ingebritsen and Pierce Gaver began to look into the possibilities of express bus service. The Washington, Virginia and Maryland Bus Company required a minimum guarantee for an experimental time period, so the two decided upon a system of advance sale of tickets since financial assistance was not readily available. Barker was called at

Gulf Reston; Glenn Saunders, executive vice president, agreed to underwrite losses up to $150 for the first two weeks of the experiment. The plan was successful and received national attention as a citizen-sponsored, regularly scheduled means of commuting between Reston and Washington. The new transportation system had a positive influence on the marketability of Reston. To Karl Ingebritsen must go major credit for resourcefulness, imagination, persistence, and energy in carrying the idea through until the procedures and regular patrons for the Reston Commuter Bus (RCB) were firmly established.

Local lore was enriched by certain activities of the Reston Commuter Bus riders in the early days. Some of the amusing folk-tales and legends of the new town revolve around the "bus meisters," (individual bus directors), their inventiveness in finding new and shorter routes for the buses to take in and out of Washington and the famous—or infamous—bus partying around special holidays. The happy Friday afternoon mobile cocktail hour eventually had to be discontinued for the sake of propriety.

The streamlining of Gulf Reston's development continued under Bob Ryan's administration until April 1969. An example of his stern commitment to economizing is the case of the grand piano in the Bowman house—Simon's official guest house—which Ryan took delight in playing. When he discovered it was rented, he had it picked up by the rental agency.

He operated on a strictly structured planning and production schedule, week by week. Outstanding in his memory was the fact that at weekly meetings, one staff member—Fran Steinbauer—had always prepared his assignments from the previous meeting. It was cooperation like that which enabled Ryan to repair the "leaky boat" and get moving forward again. Steinbauer had been engineer-supervisor of construction for the Federal Aviation Administration (FAA) at Dulles Airport in 1959, after graduation from the University of Maryland. When the airport was near completion in April 1964, he was hired as an engineer for Reston, in charge of all the in-house design for site plans, roads, utilities, all the ground elements—everything except for the actual buildings. Within a few months, he had set up a working organization which included over forty people. Steinbauer felt that he had been "present at the creation"—there was only a dry lake bed taking shape where Lake Anne was soon to be—when he first began carrying rolls of Reston

development plans around under his arm.

Another staff member who represented value to Ryan and the Gulf Reston organization was Vernon Walker, director of the nature center. Not only was Walker a competent professional, he represented continuity from the Simon days, keeping the nature center going as a commitment to ecology and the environment on the part of the new developer and the community.

Eventually, Gulf Oil Corporation executives decided that it was time to put a company man in charge of the Reston project. In April 1969, Ryan returned to his consulting firm in Pittsburgh and William Magness, who had gradually been working into the organization structure since November 1967, became the chief operating officer of Gulf Reston. He had had extensive experience since the mid-1950s in developing company towns abroad for Gulf Oil workers in South America and the Middle East. As a resident of Reston and president of Gulf Reston, Magness' primary goals were three: building a middle management team, encouraging residents to assume a more active role in providing their own services and amenities, and reducing the prices of housing so that people of moderate means really could live in Reston. The new town was "coming of age in Virginia." Its infancy had been lived out under a paternalistic, talented, and benevolent dreamer; it now faced adolescence and the need to start taking charge of its own life.

The corporate developers were determined to turn Simon's dream into a reality in as businesslike a manner as possible. After Gulf Oil had written off $7 million of its initial $15 million investment, the company put in some $35 million more for a total book investment by mid-1969 of $43 million. The rate of sales by that time was almost enough to carry the costs.

Joseph Stowers had an overview of the situation from his position as president of RCA. He saw a pattern emerging. He admitted that, contrary to residents' initial fears, both Ryan and Magness had continued to follow the Simon master plan, with recognizable exceptions in social perspectives. There was too little construction by the developer of community facilities, for example, youth centers, and a relaxing of the original efforts to implement a racial and economic mix in Reston. These problems were not easily solved and it was to take a number of years before the community and its organizations were able to deal with many of them.

An idea which was well-received as cultural

Robert H. Ryan was a consultant hired in 1967 by Gulf Oil to accelerate development and protect Gulf's earlier investment in the new town. He was Gulf Reston's first chief operations officer and had experience with the problems of housing development.
From the Reston Times. Courtesy of Reston Regional Library

By car, on foot, by boat, barge and bicycle, Restonians converged on Washington Plaza in a festive mood in 1967.
Photograph by William A. Graham. Courtesy of Reston Land Corporation

Lake Anne's Washington Plaza about 1967. The design combines residential, commercial, religious, and community facilities and separates pedestrian and vehicular traffic.
Photograph by William A. Graham. Courtesy of Reston Land Corporation

enrichment was Simon's establishment of a cable television system with dual cables to each residence. He wanted to avoid having antennas on all the roofs because of the visual pollution, so he inaugurated the original cable system with all cables underground. Construction work was continued when Gulf Reston took over development of Reston and the system was later purchased by Reston Transmission Company in 1969. Continental Telephone operated the facilities in 1971-1972, and Warner Cable Television purchased it in 1972. Reston cable television has included a community service channel since its inception, with a built-in live programming capability from each village center. Local Reston programming has won a number of national awards for Warner Cable.

Gulf Reston markedly accelerated the new town's building program. By the end of 1969, twelve hundred residential units had been completed. The community's population was 7,500, a jump of 5,000 since Gulf's take-over twenty-seven months before. It was distributed among apartments, town and patio houses, and single-family dwellings. Thirty industries were in place in the Industrial Center with a working population of 2,000, up 600 from the previous year. A graduate school extension program had been inaugurated by the Virginia Polytechnic Institute (VPI). Classes first met in 1969 at the old farmhouse which was also used for Reston's business offices. Later VPI moved to Isaac Newton Square, where their graduate extension facilities remained until 1977. A branch bank and a 300-seat cafeteria had opened at Isaac Newton Square and the first few USGS employees had begun work in rental quarters on Isaac Newton Square. Hunters Woods Elementary, Reston's second school, had opened. There were more than ten miles of paved pathways, with seven pedestrian underpasses, five swimming pools and eight tennis courts. The second eighteen-hole golf course was nearly completed and plans for the construction of the Sheraton Inn and Reston International Center had been announced. It was to have three hundred guest rooms, a twin cinema, retail shops, and a fifteen-story office tower. Preparations were also being made to construct the Hunters Woods Village Center. The improvement in the financial picture brought about by Gulf Reston's strong fiscal management policy prompted the Metropolitan Life Insurance Company to sign a long-term mortgage agreement in October, for existing, income-producing property, in the amount of $14 million. It had been an eventful year in construction and

increased population.

There were other changes in process. Magness moved to bring about a consolidation and assumption of responsibilities on the part of the residents for some of the services and amenities they wished to have. Since the original deeds of dedication had been filed by Palindrome Corporation in 1964, there had been two home owners' associations in Reston to manage open space and to provide services. The facilities were maintained by Reston residents from annual dues assessments at no cost to the county, and it was anticipated that the plans would eventually provide for almost one thousand acres of open space and park land. Simon's initial reason for having two rather than one association was to protect the more conventional Hunters Woods section from financial failure should the innovative Lake Anne area not appeal to the market. It was his intention eventually to merge the two if Lake Anne Village was a success.

Most owner-residents of the new town were members of their cluster associations and either the First Home Owners Association (FHOA) or the Second Home Owners Association (SHOA) which had been developer-controlled organizations, with little member activity. Glenn Saunders had acted as president for both in addition to his position first as Simon's and then as Gulf Reston's executive vice president. But as the community grew and more and more open space was designated as common land, the need for one executive officer to serve both associations became more and more apparent.

Saunders decided to hire Karl Ingebritsen, who had high community visibility and acceptance as a result of his mammoth and successful effort in organizing the Reston Commuter Bus system in 1967-1968 under the newly organized Reston Community Association. The new executive director of FHOA and SHOA recommended during his first day on the job that the two separate associations be made one. Bill Magness, on staff and soon to replace Ryan as chief operations officer of Gulf Reston, also strongly favored the merger.

On the opposite side of the merger question, among many others, was Michael Healy, a resident president of SHOA, who was certain that this form of centralization would kill committee work, lose valuable volunteer time, and jeopardize fair leadership and funding for each village. There was also the danger of losing the benefit of new ideas from numerous individuals within the community.

Because the majority of the Reston land had not yet been developed, it was in the interest of the developer to retain control over FHOA and SHOA but, in the interest of increased citizen involvement, it was desirable to open positions on the nine-man board of directors to residents, replacing some of the developer's board members. Three resident board members who would begin having a direct involvement in the management of their own affairs would also relieve several Gulf Reston employees from the tremendous amount of time spent on home owners' activities which was increasing weekly as the community continued to grow.

Karl Ingebritsen plunged into the new executive job for FHOA and SHOA with characteristic zeal and energy in February 1969. He was dismayed to find the state of affairs with existing records which were totally inadequate for efficient billing and accounting procedures. He immediately set about the task of consolidation of accounts and administrative responsibilities.

For the next year, heated discussions were held in the community which included individual public name calling and unveiled references to a "banana government." The emotional issue was spread across the pages of the *Reston Times* regarding the pros and cons of the merging of the two associations. In August, Magness engaged Booz-Allen and Hamilton, management consultants, to prepare a study of the two homeowners' associations with an analysis recommending improvements to meet future growth.

When the Booz-Allen study had been completed, the recommendations included merging of the two associations, an increase in the professional staff, a ten-member board of directors including residents as well as developer's representatives and a town council composed largely of vice presidents from each village. There was a recommendation that volunteers be utilized on committees and in the operation of local village programs and projects.

Just before the consolidation of the First and Second Home Owners Associations by Gulf Reston in 1970, a public board of directors meeting was held with over two hundred residents in attendance. Feelings were running pretty high because of the citizen opposition to the merger and their perception of its inevitability because the developer wished it to come about. Resident James Ridgill was in the midst of delivering a long statement opposing the merger when he looked up from his prepared text in frustration and accused Gulf's Bill

It was the Quay Club in the Moorings Restaurant at the Lake Anne Village Center that Robert Ryan of Gulf Reston promptly closed as part of his drastic measures to get the development on a sound financial basis.
Courtesy of Reston Land Corporation

This is the sign that irritated Robert Ryan, Gulf Reston's consultant, with a competitive oil company's name prominently displayed.
Courtesy of Reston Land Corporation

Magness, a member of the board, of espousing the "mushroom theory" when it came to his high-handed treatment of the democratic process. When asked what that theory was, Ridgill replied, "Mr. Magness, that's where you keep them in the dark and every once in a while throw some manure on them." The hearty laughter which filled the meeting hall eased the tensions of the moment.

Gulf Reston implemented the merger in April 1970 forming the Reston Home Owners Association (RHOA). No elections were held. The developer appointed three residents to the nine-member board, retaining for the developer a majority of the association's votes. From the former First Home Owners Association, the president, a developer's representative, Robert Perce, and treasurer Fred Naef were appointed. Former Second Home Owners Association president Michael Healy was the third appointee to the RHOA board. After the new organizations took effect, Gulf Reston deeded $600,000 worth of debt-free recreational facilities, pathways, bridges, parks, lakes and open space, and the pedestrian overpass at North Shore Drive and Wiehle Avenue to RHOA.

Following the merger, a lawsuit was brought by several Hunters Woods residents against the developer. It ended with a decision by Federal District Court Judge Albert V. Bryan, Jr., in July 1970, finding that there was no evident plan or conspiracy on the part of the developer to wrongfully maintain control over SHOA. The judge ruled that home purchasers should be aware of the by-laws, articles of incorporation, and deeds of dedication. He appraised Hunters Woods petitioner Charles Baker's role as that of a gadfly but observed that there was "a suggestion of arrogance on the part of Magness." With rueful humor, board member Healy later presented Magness with a handsome and substantial toy "Reston steamroller" as a symbol of the tactics which the recipient had used to prevail in the RHOA situation.

The good faith and determination on the part of the developer to be cooperative with the residents and to do some solid future planning was evident in a long letter written by Magness in December 1970 to Gene S. Bergoffen, president of the Reston Community Association. It was in reply to an open letter to Magness which Bergoffen had sent to the *Reston Times* and the paper had published. In the *Times* letter, the RCA president complained that Gulf Reston had periodic talks with the RHOA

town council without including RCA. Magness countered that there were many organizations—too many for his staff to meet with regularly or even periodically. He clearly expressed his willingness to communicate, as well as his conception of a number of working relationships and goals for Gulf and Reston. He stated, in part:

It is our strong conviction that it is extremely important that Gulf Reston have a permanent group through which we can channel information and receive appropriate feedback from our residents. It is important that this group be in contact with all organizations in Reston. The Town Council is a representative body that is charged with and by organization has the channels of communication to discharge this responsibility. As you know, the Village Councils are elected by all residents, including renters and teenagers 16 years and older. The Village Councils each have representation on the Town Council. The Town Council also has a direct line of communication with the RHOA Board, which is the financially responsible body for the Reston residents . . . .

I am sure that RCA will continue to be one of the major resident organizations that will be involved in Reston's future. I feel, however, that it is a two way street. All parties must remain open-minded and willing to look at all sides of a particular problem . . . .

Karl Ingebritsen had been appointed director of RHOA after the merger. There were still hard feelings in the community over continued moves by the developer to consolidate services and functions under the RHOA structure where the residents would be paying for them through assessments. In a disagreement over the professional chain of command when the nature center program was placed under RHOA, Ingebritsen was fired in March 1971. In looking back years later on the sometimes traumatic experience as the first executive director of RHOA, he intoned somewhat ruefully, "It was like being dropped into Lake Anne with a set of oars but no boat. And I rowed very, very vigorously for about two and a half years before I sank."

When Ingebritsen left RHOA, the board of directors appointed RHOA's treasurer, Joyce Pfeffer, a Hunters Woods resident and professional accountant, to the position of acting executive director. Mrs. Pfeffer handled the routine business of the association from August 1971 until February 1972. During this time she also produced a ten-page proposed RHOA operating budget for 1972 reflecting the growth of the association's responsibilities since 1968, when the total budget had been presented to the governing board on one page.

Changes in the RHOA procedures and executive director's responsibilities were effected largely through a thorough report made by an RCA study team early in 1972. Titled "Toward New Town Governance," it was written by a team of highly respected residents who as professionals in various fields brought their knowledge and experience to bear on the many problems related to both RHOA and the matter of ultimate governmental structure for Reston.

A new executive director, Thomas J. Burgess, was hired by the RHOA Board of Directors, after many candidate interviews, on March 13, 1972. At this time the board pointed out that RHOA was not set up as a governmental body but as a land and facilities-oriented maintenance corporation.

An advisory committee was formed consisting of the RHOA board president, the two RHOA resident board members, the chairmen of the Lake Anne, Hunters Woods, and Tall Oaks village councils, and the RHOA executive director to review and make recommendations for RHOA solutions of community problems. This organization replaced the more political town council system previously in operation.

Somewhat parallel to RHOA in administrative responsibilities, but actually separate microcosms of local government in extremely close quarters, are the incorporated cluster associations in Reston. The cluster associations have legal power, derived from Reston's covenants running with the land, to maintain the cluster, assess residents in order to do so, and enforce covenants. It is sometimes difficult for the self-governing cluster boards of directors to decide the complex problems which arise in relation to day-to-day maintenance and physical improvements of the townhouses and the land as well as the social conflicts which arise. Boards have unlimited power to set annual dues, which amount to a form of taxation. The directors are elected by the owners' resident in the cluster; generally, neither absentee landlords nor tenants may vote. The board of directors can vote to amend the articles of incorporation and by-laws. The cluster association is responsible for short and long-term maintenance including everything from mowing grass in the common areas and snow

The Reston Community Association was formed in 1967 as a reaction by Reston residents to the change in developers and fear of future lack of planning. The RCA has since played a significant role in assisting with the planning of a community which would provide for the needs and some of the wants of its inhabitants. These included a commuter bus, community health plan, a planning and zoning committee, the RIBS internal bus system, the Community Center, and cable television. The original Board of Directors of the Reston Community Association is shown here in 1968. Front row: Joseph Stowers, Marian Secundy, Carol Arnold, and Jeffrey Wellborn. Middle row: William Newbold, Carolyn Lindberg, Vernon George, and Patrick Kane. Top row: Walter Prybyla, ArDee Ames, Richard Hays, and Henry Greene.
Photograph by Daniels. Courtesy of Dick Hays

removal to roofing and painting carports, and repairing private roads and sidewalks. The political aspects of administration involve many sensitive issues including covenant enforcement, mowing of individual patches of lawn, and individual or cluster disagreements over pets and children. It is very much like living with a large extended family, and like families, some clusters get along very amicably and others less so.

Reston controls have been tested in the courts. The first court test of the Reston deed of dedication concerned land in a single family development. The case was decided in favor of RHOA in June 1971. A family had erected a chicken wire fence enclosure, without Architectural Board of Review (ABR) approval, to keep balls hit from their paddle tennis court from disappearing into the woods. This act was in direct violation of the covenant which prohibited erection of a fence or wall of any kind without ABR approval. Judge Albert V. Bryan, Jr., ruled that "taking the covenants as a whole, they project a scheme for an orderly and eye-pleasing development. This structure (the backstop) could be just as much an eyesore whether its purpose was tennis ball retention, cattle retention, or purely ornamental. The covenant delegates to the ABR the right to approve its design and placement."

Not all services within Reston were provided by RHOA or the cluster associations. Among the services provided by the Fairfax County government were police and fire protection. Reston posed a unique set of problems from the standpoint of effective police work. Lands held by the cluster associations were actually group-owned private property. Beautiful Washington Plaza on Lake Anne, so celebrated in the New Town literature, was found to be a natural gathering place for both good and other purposes. The village center had a mixture of shops, offices, and residences so that loitering laws which applied to suburban shopping centers were not applicable.

Two major developments which were to have positive far-reaching effects took place in 1970. The National Education Association (NEA), the nation's largest association of educators, finding their facilities in Washington, D.C., to be inadequate, purchased fifty-six acres, with ten national affiliates, to establish the Reston Center for Educational Associations near the inn and conference center site on Reston Avenue. The proximity to that site and to Dulles Airport, and the housing availability, the open space, community facilities, and concern with the environment were all strong factors in the decision. The second influential decision was made by the directors of the American Newspaper Publishers Association (ANPA) to purchase ten acres adjacent to NEA's center acreage in order to move their headquarters to the Washington Metropolitan area from New York City. Many other associations were to follow their example in the next few years.

The Fairfax County Board of Supervisors presented three awards to Reston in 1970. Lake Anne Village Center received a beautification award for design; Bill Magness received a bronze plaque for the industrial beautification of Reston; and the Newton Building in Isaac Newton Square and the Professional Building at Lake Anne were especially recognized for environmental design enhancement.

A long-awaited financial recovery was experienced in 1971 when a positive cash flow was established and the operating budget began to show a margin of profit. In forty-eight months, Gulf Reston had been able to put the New Town development on a firm footing. The Board of Directors of Gulf Oil were so impressed with the strong pattern of growth in Reston over their four years of operation of it that they decided real estate was a good investment. The formation of a new subsidiary was announced— Gulf Oil Real Estate Development Company (GOREDCO) to be headquartered in Reston with Bill Magness, president and chairman of the board, and Glenn W. Saunders, Jr., executive vice president. John W. Guinee, Jr., was then appointed executive vice president for Gulf Reston. Guinee hired James Todd as marketing vice president. He had been a marketing expert at the Yeonas real estate organization and was a graduate of the University of Virginia with both BS and MBA degrees. Gulf Oil planned to utilize its extensive land holdings throughout the world, with expert management and marketing, to their optimum profit potential, tempered with a feeling of responsibility "for the well-being of society." Success continued in 1972 with a healthy national economy, and Gulf Reston was able to repay all Gulf Oil monies advanced to develop Reston. By the end of the year, 5,244 dwelling units had been completed, the population exceeded twenty thousand, and over 170 businesses and associations, providing twenty-five hundred jobs, were operating in the New Town. Commuting had improved for those who had jobs in Washington. The FAA had given permission for use of the Dulles access road by the Reston commuter bus system and

Gulf Reston Secretary Edith Keenan posed at Lake Anne in 1967. She had also worked for Bob Simon.
            Courtesy of Edith Keenan

Cameron Crescent, Reston's first apartment complex, was completed in 1967.
            Courtesy of Reston Land Corporation

Fellowship House I, at Lake Anne Village Center, was ready for its first senior citizen occupants in May 1971.
            Courtesy of Reston Land Corporation

Cedar Ridge apartments, moderate-income housing, were partially funded by HUD.
            Photograph by Daniels.
Courtesy of Reston Land Corporation

Gulf Reston had built the highway ramps for ingress and egress to Washington. The Common Ground community action group's intra-Reston mini-bus service, later Reston Internal Bus System (RIBS), had been inaugurated with two routes, one in Lake Anne and one in Hunters Woods.

The extent to which the county provided services to Reston, like schools and police protection, was the subject of a Booz-Allen and Hamilton study made for Gulf Reston. The study examined revenues to and services from the county and found that revenues exceeded expenditures by the county in the community by about $1.5 million in fiscal year (FY) 1972, with projections for year by year revenue increases in the future in excess of $16 million by FY 1980.

The Booz-Allen study with its positive picture of Reston's financial situation relative to county taxes came out in a year—1973—which was marked by both boom and gloom for the New Town's development. It started out with record-breaking residential sales (135 in the month of March alone) and an announcement that Gulf Reston was for the first time operating in the black. Its cumulative negative cash flow of $33 million had been turned around and with the project really rolling, and a potential total profit of $200 million possible, Gulf Oil Corporation's Chairman of the Board B. R. Dorsey stated jubilantly, "Gulf will be remembered more for developing Reston and making it profitable than for anything else."

It was the year of the Watergate scandal, the Arab oil embargo, rising inflation and the first double-digit prime interest rate. The hardest hit of all industries was housing, with an unprecedented residential sales downturn in the second half of the year. Meantime, comprehensive health programs which had been hoped for, discussed, planned and awaited for almost ten years began to be implemented that year in Reston. The Georgetown University Community Health Plan, a non-profit health care program affiliated with the University, opened a two-story medical building in April 1973. It was in the Hunters Woods Village Center which had itself enjoyed a grandiose Renaissance-style opening the previous December.

Another professional building was completed in Reston at the fifty-six-acre Reston Center for Educational Associations. The headquarters for the National Council of Teachers of Mathematics was dedicated in May 1973. This organization publishes the *Mathematics Teacher* and *Arithmetic Teacher* journals and other publications. Their principal goal is that K-14 teachers "have available supplemental materials ranging from the metric system to the latest technology."

Two areas in Reston made news that summer and fall. The USGS headquarters employees began to move into their partially completed building in September 1973. It had been constructed by Gulf Reston and was turned over to USGS on a twenty-year lease-purchase agreement. A few weeks later, a formal dedication ceremony was held at the end of September at the $10 million Reston International Center in the presence of ambassadors and representatives of eighteen nations with New Town programs. A bronze plaque was unveiled dedicating the plaza to Dag Hammarskjold, former secretary general of the United Nations. Bob Simon's dream was flowering under strong management and financial responsibility.

Since the Booz-Allen report on Reston's economic impact on Fairfax County government had proven so useful, Gulf Reston decided to make a study on the social impact of the New Town on the county. The study revealed that Reston had indeed helped to improve planning, implementation, construction, and development activities with the adoption of planned unit development (PUD) zoning for mixed land use in 1969. This new procedure was based on Reston's 1962 RPC zoning. It was a better alternative for dealing with explosive growth than earlier subdivision zoning. Developers had found that community planning could be profitable and more attractive subdivisions were now being planned throughout Northern Virginia with clustered densities, parks and open space, pathways and other amenities.

Immediately following the Arab oil embargo in the Middle East, which was to have a long-range effect on the entire world economy, including Reston, world-renowned anthropologist Margaret Mead visited Reston in November 1973. She pointed out that the New Towns were important if for no other reason than "the chance to try new things." New Towns were ahead of the rest of the country, she thought, in regard to accommodating different lifestyles. Viability of such a community was assured by housing "for at least three generations (not just families) providing enough for all to do; and it must be a place which you can leave and come back to or live in forever." Certainly there were many families who had left for a while and eagerly returned who could verify the fact that Reston *was* such a community.

An interesting accounting of Gulf Reston's ap-

Karl Ingebritsen, an early resident of Hickory Cluster, was appointed Reston Homeowners Association's first executive director. He was a prime mover behind Reston's commuter bus system as well as the establishment of Reston's Board of Commerce.

Courtesy of Karl Ingebritsen

Just as the Reston Commuter Bus was providing a significant service to Reston residents who worked in Washington, D.C., the Washington and Old Dominion Railroad, which once had provided the same service for residents of Thornton's Station, Wiehle, and Sunset Hills, ceased to run. The last passengers on the W&OD were these two men, Mel Marcey of Falls Church, and Alan Pennell of Leesburg, who built this gasoline-operated track car for exploring abandoned railroad lines, both standard and narrow gauge, in 1969. From The Washington and Old Dominion Railroad by Ames Williams.

Courtesy of the author

Gulf Reston paid for the moving of Brown's Chapel, in 1968, from the intersection of the Leesburg Pike (Route 7) and Baron Cameron Avenue (Route 606) to a hillside overlooking Lake Anne Village Center on Baron Cameron Avenue.

Photograph by William Edmund Barrett

propriation of monies for housing and amenities while operating at a profit was provided during 1973. Working with the Fairfax County Board of Supervisors on provisions for a low and moderate income housing mix, subsidizing of land costs in excess of $1 million had been provided. Recreational facilities and open space valued in excess of $1 million had been deeded to RHOA. These facilities, maintained by Reston residents on annual dues assessments, amounted in 1973 alone to a total value of approximately $746,000. About 330 acres of land had been set aside at a value of over $16 million for schools and fire stations, etc. Cash contributions and subsidies for community facilities had amounted to $885,000 and $281,000 had been given to the Virginia Department of Highways for construction of commuter bus ramps at the Reston interchange of the Dulles access road.

In June 1974, a major problem for Reston development was resolved. An unfortunate situation had developed in 1972. The Fairfax County Board of Supervisors, faced with runaway growth and building, had decided to slow them down by imposing a sewer moratorium on any new taps requested for buildings not yet under construction in Fairfax County in May 1972. There was a question of whether or not there would be sufficient capacity at the sewage treatment plants for additional Reston users as time passed. Gulf Reston filed a suit for sewer taps against the county in January 1973. Robert Simon, who had regularly read the *Reston Times* since his departure in 1967, wrote a letter to the Board of Supervisors which was published in the *Times* in August 1973. He pointed out that Gulf Reston was following the spirit of the original master plan; their revisions did not violate but followed the original principles. In fact, he himself had contemplated a revision of the master plan before his departure in 1967. He urged the Board to keep the commitment they had made to him in 1962 when the original master plan was approved so that Reston development could proceed at a steady pace. He believed this should be done partly because "Planners all over the world have studied Reston since its beginning and are following its progress." Centreville Supervisor Martha Pennino was impressed with the concept of building a total community from scratch and she wanted to be a strong motivating force behind the completion of the New Town. At times, however, the overall needs of the county as perceived by board members from other districts took precedence over the needs, however great, of one community within it.

The county supervisor-imposed sewer moratorium threatened Reston's future as the permits for new buildings already issued were used up. At the annual Fairfax County Chamber of Commerce dinner on June 27, 1974, Gulf Reston Board Chairman Magness told the assembled members and guests that the Board of Supervisors' "slow-growth" and "no-growth" policies had virtually spelled doom for the New Town of Reston. Along the same line, Reston public relations man Peter McCandless published an article in *Realtor* magazine which evidenced frustration peppered with wry good humor. He wrote in part: "Aided by the constipation of Blue Plains [sewage treatment plant] and with glowing euphemisms of better planning, more effective controls, preserving the natural environment and quality of life in Fairfax County, we are being asked to perform an unnatural act: hold our breath for 18 months!"

Approximately one quarter of Fairfax County including Reston was again opened up for development by action of the Board of Supervisors three days after Magness' speech. The court case was decided in Reston's favor and sewer taps slowly became available for new construction.

A new commercial enterprise was launched later that year. Tall Oaks, the third village center, was opened in November 1974. It was after it had been open for only a few months that the center's merchants realized that the old formula of ten thousand residents for each village center designed did not produce the needed traffic and income.

Another effort on a much larger scale also proved to be a disappointment. Because Reston, Virginia, and Columbia, Maryland, and other privately financed New Towns in the United States had high visibility and promise of success in the long term, Congress had passed legislation in 1968 and 1970 authorizing New Towns to be developed under HUD sponsorship. The goals for the new communities were economic self-sufficiency, racial integration, and ecological integrity. Yet in January 1975, HUD announced that their failing program was to be phased out and aid to developers of New Towns would no longer be available. Some urban planners believed that HUD had lacked full commitment or willingness to spend monies properly, others felt that the plan was undercapitalized, mismanaged and a victim of "economic hard times, unrealistic expectations and bureaucratic bickering." Another major cause of failure of these "Title VII" New Towns was bad locations with limited growth po-

William Magness was chief executive
officer for Gulf Reston, Inc., from 1969 to
1976.
Courtesy of Reston Land Corporation

These are the award-winning Louis Sauer
Golf Course Island townhouses. The first
section was completed in 1967.
Courtesy of Reston Land Corporation

tential. Neither Reston nor Columbia had received any of these HUD New Town funds, so the abandonment of the government program did not impede their continued growth.

An invaluable demographic profile of Reston was prepared in 1975 by George Hickey, director of budget and research for RHOA. It analyzed statistics from the period 1970 to 1975 ostensibly to guide RHOA's delivery of services to the community based on citizens' needs and demands. It showed an increasingly heterogeneity of the population with an increase in the number of blacks, poor, rich, singles, female head of household families, and the elderly. As the family unit was losing its primacy nationally, so it was in Reston. There was a widening gap between rich and poor, a polarization of family incomes at each end of the scale.

Six important changes had occurred in population characteristics during the five-year study period. First, there had been an increase in the percentage of black population mainly due to the availability of low and moderate income housing. Second, family units were growing larger, wealthier, and older. Because of the increased costs in the housing market, older families with higher incomes were staying or moving in, and the younger, lower-income families were moving out. Third, the total population in families had dropped as, fourth, the number of non-family households represented a larger percentage of all households. Fifth, the percentage of elderly had increased greatly, in part because of the special housing facilities built for them and the increase in subsidized housing. Also, the higher income families tended to include one or more grandparents. Sixth, there had been a large increase in number and percentage of female head of household families who came to Reston with the expectation of being accepted in the sophisticated community and having facilities and activities provided for their children. Subsidized housing was also a factor in this grouping. All in all, the profile presented an increasingly urbanized population. The changes reflected national population trends and had been influenced by Fairfax County housing programs, the marketing strategy of the developer and the housing market situation in general. Only a month after the report was completed, the *Ladies Home Journal* in August 1975 chose Reston as the best suburb in the Washington area and one of the fifteen best suburbs in the United States.

As it became more like a small city in its pop-ulation composition, Reston also acquired some of the problems of cities, well-publicized because the New Town was good media material. Some of the residents in Reston had come to the community with dreams of utopia, of a harmonious society. One of the several federally subsidized housing projects in the community, however, Fox Mill Apartments, suffered repeatedly from racial tensions, crime, vandalism, and disrepair due to poor property management policies and lack of tenant screening. Isolated by lack of money and distance from participating in many of Reston's recreational pursuits as well as daily observing the affluence so obviously surrounding them, some of the residents, particularly teenagers, lashed out in anti-social but understandable frustration. Lack of supervision and overcrowding created severe social difficulties. It was a rude awakening for many Restonians. Some of the big city problems had come to the community and solutions would not be simple. The change of the apartment project's name to Stonegate did not alter the basic problems.

The United States bicentennial year of 1976 was an interesting combination of the old and the new. Not only was there a long look back into the past with the anniversary observance, there was also a brief glimpse into the future. A controversy which had raged for several years was resolved in a fashion not to everyone's liking. The governments of Great Britain and France were given permission by the U.S. Department of Transportation for their supersonic Concorde passenger planes to serve Dulles International Airport. This was allowed for a limited trial period in order to test the impact the sound produced on residents and businesses in the vicinity of the airport—including Reston—before permanent landing rights were given for the innovative aircraft. Eventually, permanent approval was granted.

Another controversy with international ramifications was to have a major effect on Reston. Scandals linking the names of four of Gulf's executives to illegal contributions to Richard Nixon's presidential campaign and to bribes of foreign governments caused the dismissal of the four officials in 1976. Among them was Bill Henry, executive vice president of Gulf Oil, who had been a friend of Gulf Reston since its inception and favored the real estate operations in which Gulf Oil had been involved. That a decision had been made for a change in direction was apparent in Gulf Oil's 1977 annual report which simply stated that real estate investments "are not closely related to Gulf's basic business and have not made a meaningful contribution to corporate profits." The

The Armstrong Cork Concept House, one
of three showpiece houses under construction in 1970 at Reston's South Lakes,
was designed as a core "starter house."
Photograph by Warren Mattox. Courtesy
of Reston Land Corporation

Gulf Reston's first million dollar sales
team members were photographed with
their 1968 awards at a time when the average real estate sale was $30,000. Left to
right are Ed Carroll, Jim Cleveland, Tom
Cunningham, Chuck Veatch, Nancy
Charlton, and Paul Butterfield.
Courtesy of Jim Cleveland

Fairway Apartments, completed in 1969,
overlook the North Reston Golf Course,
now called Hidden Creek Country Club.
Courtesy of Reston Land Corporation

annual report went on to say that Gulf Oil would in the future be involved with the business of energy. The corporation then put all of its non-energy-related real estate holdings throughout the world on the market.

As part of this divestiture, Gulf Oil decided to sell its holdings in Reston. The company had had some good years and some bad with its Reston project. During his tenure as chief executive officer, Bill Magness had accomplished his three principal goals. He had built a middle management team with some of the personnel whose experience with the community's development dated back to the Simon days, as well as some new and capable people who had joined the staff later. He could with confidence leave them to carry on. The community had taken over responsibilities for many programs and Gulf Reston had constructed houses, apartment buildings, and low and moderate income housing units, as well as commercial and industrial complexes.

While Gulf looked for a buyer for Reston, building activities continued. Crime problems, sewer tap problems, the Simon-Gulf Oil controversy, the Arab oil embargo, national economic problems, the lack of traffic through Reston's sales center, and the need for new perspectives stimulated marketing director Lee Shur's sense of urgency. He had been on the staff since 1972 and had witnessed a steady decline in sales percentages and realized that all the elements of marketing had to be pulled together—opinion research, advertising, promotion, public relations, and publicity. The advertising firm of Siddall, Matus and Coughter (SMC) was engaged to research the problem and found clearly declining traffic and sales since the boom days of the early 1970s. They discovered that the outside community was full of the misconceptions that Reston had closed down, it was built out, there was nothing for sale. SMC recommended a major promotional "event" which would build awareness, renewed excitement, and traffic. They persuaded the newly opened Bloomingdale's department store at Tysons Corner to decorate a Reston townhouse, their first decorated and furnished rooms outside any store in their chain. A promotion campaign was launched in March 1977.

The results can only be described as dramatic. The first weekend, five thousand people stood in line in the rain to tour the house. Traffic to the Bloomingdale house during the three-month promotion period exceeded fifty thousand visitors—ten times the previous average annual number in

Reston. The daily sales rate increased almost 300 percent. The total creative marketing idea resulted, as well, in awards for Lee Shur, SMC, and annual Reston promotion programs thereafter. News of the success of the event reached the Yale University School of Business, which in 1979 began to use it as a classic case study for a total marketing program.

The success of the Bloomingdale house in 1977 led to the promotion of the Design House the following year. Designed by Washington architect Hugh Newell Jacobsen, the house's interior was decorated by Woodward and Lothrop. *House and Garden* magazine and the American Wood Council were sponsors of the promotion, again a sales success.

Another residence in Reston experienced quite the opposite—a sharp reduction in "traffic" in 1977. The E. DeLong Bowman House, which still stands on Reston Avenue, was "decommissioned" in an effort to effect economies. The event brought back memories to many a Reston "old timer." The house had been Simon's house when he came down from New York; it had been the only meeting place available until Lake Anne community hall was completed. The Fairfax County Friends of the Library had a local author's reception there. The Methodists held services there until their building was completed. The Reston Foundation met there; the Reston Music Center was born there and guest artists stayed there when they came to give performances. Foreign dignitaries were fed and housed there overnight; tennis tournament luncheons, Fairfax Hunt brunches, Christmas buffets, and Gulf Reston dinners were given there. Bob Simon and later Bob Ryan played classics and popular tunes on the rented piano. The house was on the spring church and garden club tours and at least one wedding was held there. Norris and Rudean Williams were the talented couple who kept the Bowman House operating as graciously as possible. It was a difficult house to heat and to maintain and carried lots of nicknames, not all of them printable, but including Reston's "White House" and its "White Elephant."

Major advances in health, education, and local transportation were culminations of years of work by the developer, the Reston citizens and the county. Health care was upgraded when "ACCESS"—Ambulatory Care Center-Emergency Service System—opened in May 1977, operated by Fairfax Hospital. There was another look at things to come when Terraset School opened in

September 1977. Reston was again the locus of innovative architectural design and thoughtful planning; the building was the first earth-sheltered elementary school with a solar heat reclamation system in the country.

Two major improvements in the transportation network within Reston itself tied the community together with sinews of concrete and steel. Reston Avenue was widened by Gulf Reston and a new bridge was built across the Dulles access road and opened in January 1978. The Wiehle Avenue bridge was opened on September 20, 1978; both bridges linked the two separated parts of Reston. Rather than waiting for the highway department to schedule the building of the bridges in the distant future, Martha Pennino, the Centreville District Supervisor, and the rest of the County Board members had agreed to let Gulf Reston advance $1,200,000 for the construction cost of the Wiehle Avenue bridge, the amount to be deducted from Reston's county tax bill at the rate of $400,000 per year for the following three years.

Gulf Oil Corporation had sent William Moyles from the Pittsburgh office in 1976 to take charge of the sale of Reston. The Mobil Corporation eventually heard through trade channels that Reston was for sale and approached Moyles about purchasing part of it. On July 13, 1978, the thirty-seven hundred acres of undeveloped land was conveyed to Mobil. Donatelli and Klein of Bethesda and the Mark Winkler Company of Alexandria later purchased the investment portfolio of buildings owned by Gulf Reston in January 1979.

Even as Gulf Reston was looking for a buyer, the Northern Virginia Chapter of the American Institute of Planners met at the Reston Golf and Country Club for a seminar entitled "Lessons Learned." Dorn McGrath, chairman of the housing and urban development department of George Washington University, cited eight factors wherein he felt that Reston had fallen short of its New Town goals. The low and moderate income housing was isolated from transportation and other services; there was a lack of consistency in policies and support from all levels of government; new residents wanted to "freeze" growth as soon as they arrived and not allow for changes; planning for parking at the Tall Oaks Village Center (the third village center, which had opened in November 1974) was poor; there was a lack of protection from urban sprawl on Reston's periphery; the population was mainly a homogenized middle class; and there was a "tendency to oversell New Towns as a cure for all of society's ills."

Reston South Golf Course Club House, on Sunrise Valley Drive near the International Center, first opened to the public in June 1970. An award was given later to the architects for the design. The community's two eighteen-hole courses provide large open areas of grass and trees around which residential and commercial structures have been built.
Courtesy of Reston Land Corporation

The Woodwinds condominiums offered a modern design nestled in trees beside the south golf course. They were built between 1977 and 1979.
Courtesy of Reston Land Corporation

Virginia Governor and Mrs. Linwood Holton toured the new town of Reston in April 1970. William H. Magness, left, president of Gulf Reston, Inc., and Glenn Saunders, right, executive vice president, were hosts. Governor Holton commented on the many economic and social levels working in the community side by side.
Photograph by William A. Graham.
Courtesy of Reston Land Corporation

At the time Gulf Oil Corporation sold the Reston land in 1978, the community's population was 30,100, a marked increase over the 2,500 in residence when Gulf Reston took over in 1967. The number of jobs totaled 8,856, about four times the figure eleven years before. There were 3,519 apartments, 1,522 condominiums, 4,132 patio homes and townhouses, and 2,292 single family homes. Prices ranged from $30,000 to $150,000. There were 324 commercial and industrial firms.

Amenities in place for the employees and residents included forty miles of paved pathways, forty-five tennis courts, fifteen swimming pools, nineteen baseball fields, five community buildings, six elementary schools, three lakes, two stables, three village centers, six churches, two golf courses, and five hundred acres of open space. The W&OD linear park trail, owned and operated by the Northern Virginia Regional Park Authority for the area's citizens, bisected the community. It was built on the same right-of-way where trains once chugged back and forth from Alexandria to the top of the Blue Ridge Mountains at Bluemont.

Restonians well knew that the economic crunch nationwide, in housing construction and sales particularly, might cause Gulf Reston to sell out to a less conscientious business concern at a time when half the property was still undeveloped. One of the prospective but unsuccessful buyers

had indeed planned to sell off the land north of Route 606 for regular subdivision development.

It was not just the potential of the thirty-seven hundred acres of land which attracted the Mobil Corporation to Reston. The company also "bought" key members of the staff which Magness had built into a strong team. In fact, out of over two hundred of the Gulf Reston staff, thirty-three people in management, marketing, finance, design, planning, engineering, and land development were retained. The organization had reached maturity: it had identity, balance, and was making a profit. The top men who moved to Mobil's Reston Land Corporation (RLC) were Jim Todd, president, the management and marketing expert who had risen steadily up through the ranks after being hired away from the Yeonas organization in 1970; Fran Steinbauer, executive vice president, the engineer who remembered the dry lake bed under construction in 1964 when he came to Reston after finishing the engineering job at Dulles Airport; and Lee Shur, who came over from Gulf to Reston Land Corporation as marketing vice president. It was a team who enjoyed working together—young, vigorous, and optimistic about the future of both Reston residential and industrial land sales and development until eventual build-out, sometime in the 1990s.

The Gulf Reston headquarters office
building was opened at Isaac Newton
Square in 1969.
Courtesy of Reston Land Corporation

*The Wiehle Avenue pedestrian overpass
was opened in 1970. Among those present were, left to right, Glenn Saunders
(hand on rail); Roland Clarke (in back),
William Magness (on left holding tape);*

*William Hoofnagle, chairman of the Fair-
fax County Board of Supervisors (snipping
tape); and Robert Perce, Gulf Reston
attorney.*
Courtesy of Peter L. McCandless

*Robert Perce, Jr., First Reston Homeown-
ers Association (FHOA) president and
Reston Players award winner, was a
member of the legal staff of Gulf Reston.*
Photograph by Lyn K. Daniels.
Courtesy of Reston Land Corporation

With the Hyatt Regency Hotel presently
under construction, as well as other
buildings which will form the urban core
of Town Center, it is difficult to imagine
that in 1972, when this photograph was
taken, cattle were grazing on the very
same spot. The Bowman family was still
operating the whiskey distillery and feeding the mash to their stock. Gulf Reston
was the developer at the time.

Courtesy of Reston Land Corporation

Conducting business in the drafty old
Patriarca farmhouse, surrounded by temporary house trailer offices, was a source
of embarrassment to early developers,
Robert E. Simon, Jr., and Gulf Reston. It
was an inappropriate setting from which
to try to market an ultramodern New
Town. Gulf Reston soon built a brick

headquarters in Isaac Newton Square after they assumed ownership of the project
from Simon in 1967. For a short time, the
branch of the Virginia Polytechnic Institute at Blacksburg held classes in the
ancient complex as well.

Courtesy of Reston Land Corporation

After the consolidation of FHOA and SHOA into one organization, RHOA, Michael Healy ruefully presented Bill Magness with this Reston steamroller as a symbol of the tactics which the recipient had used to prevail.
Courtesy of Michael Healy

Joyce Pfeffer, RHOA's treasurer and a professional accountant, was appointed acting executive director in August 1971. She served until Thomas Burgess was hired as executive director in March 1972, and has remained on the staff since. She is now assistant executive vice president.
Courtesy of Joyce Pfeffer

Thomas Burgess was appointed executive director of RHOA in March 1972 by the organization's board of directors. He administers a program with an annual budget in excess of $6.7 million.
Courtesy of the Reston Association

The Reston Center for Educational Associations, a twenty-seven-acre condominium park, includes national headquarters for, left to right, the Council for Exceptional Children, the Art Education Association (under construction in 1973) when this photograph was made), the Distributive Education Clubs of America, the National Council of Teachers of Mathematics, the National Association of Secondary School Principals, and the Music Educators National Conference.
Photograph by Lois Weissflog.
Courtesy of Reston Land Corporation

In January 1970, William Magness, left, of Gulf Reston, and Irving Wasserman, chief city planner for Reston, received a bronze plaque county Beautification Award for Reston from Mrs. Martha Peninno, Centreville District supervisor (left), and Mrs. John Pickett, chairman of the Fairfax County Beautification Committee (right).
Courtesy of Reston Land Corporation

Dedication ceremonies in February 1971 opened the Dulles Expressway ramps at Reston Avenue. Initially funded by Gulf Reston, the ramps were said to have signified the "End of an Old Fashioned Era."
Courtesy of Peter L. McCandless

In this aerial, Golf Course Island Cluster appears in the lower left foreground, the Reston Golf and Country Club course in the center, and the offices, laboratories, light industry, and racquet club of Isaac Newton Square, upper right.
Photograph by Lois Weissflog.
Courtesy of Reston Land Corporation

The Hunters Woods Village Center, on Glade Drive and Colts Neck Road, was completed in November 1972. It was designed by Cohen Haft Associates of Silver Spring and included shops, restaurants, the Hunters Woods Public Library, and professional offices. This view, looking west, shows the fountain pool/ice skating rink which proved to be too small and was converted into a garden.
Photograph by Robert Lautman. Courtesy of Reston Land Corporation

First opened in August 1970, this center, located adjacent to the club house of the Reston Golf and Country Club (now Hidden Creek), provided the first professional office space for dentists, an oral surgeon, a pediatrician, a podiatrist, an obstetrician, a gynecologist, and general practitioners.
Courtesy of Peter L. McCandless

111

Georgetown University Hospital opened a medical center at Hunters Woods in 1974. It later became Kaiser-Georgetown Community Health Plan and since 1979 has been expanded and relocated in the Lake Anne Village Office Building.
Courtesy of Reston Land Corporation

Designed by Skidmore, Owings and Merrill of Chicago, the national headquarters of the United States Geological Survey on Sunrise Valley Drive in Reston was completed in 1973. In its million square feet of space are housed the world's largest earth science library, geological and hydrological laboratories, and a topographic map division.
Photograph by Robert Lautman.
Courtesy of Reston Land Corporation

Reston's International Center, the Sheraton Inn, and Dag Hammarskjold Plaza, was completed in September 1973 near the Dulles Access Road, on Sunrise Valley Drive.
Photograph by Robert Lautman.
Courtesy of Reston Land Corporation

On September 23, 1973, the Reston International Center was dedicated to world leader Dag Hammarskjold, former secretary general of the United Nations and a man deeply respected for his tireless efforts to achieve world peace. Present were ambassadors and representatives of eighteen nations experienced in the building of new towns. Here a group of dignitaries is led across Dag Hammarskjold Plaza by Peter L. McCandless of Gulf Reston.
Courtesy of Reston Land Corporation

The designers of Tall Oaks Village Center, Collins and Kronstadt, received awards after it was opened in November 1974. But Reston citizens' community efforts to have the complex harmonize with the surroundings in a low-visibility setting with inward orientation meant that it was underutilized for many years.
Photograph by Lois Weissflog.
Courtesy of Reston Land Corporation.

This jungle gym at the Tall Oaks Village Center, now gone, was once the source of endless fascination for children who came to respond to the climbing challenges.
Photograph by Abbie Edwards.
Courtesy of Reston Land Corporation

Bentana Woods townhouses were winners
of design and planning awards. They are
located in Tall Oaks Village.
Courtesy of Reston Land Corporation

The First Virginia Regiment of the Continental Line (1776) marched in 1976 in a
very modern setting at the Bicentennial
Celebration at Lake Anne. The Lookout
sculpture (with stairs) is in the
background.
Photograph by Abbie Edwards

Both British Airways and Air France Con-
cordes began landing and taking off at
Dulles International Airport in 1976.
Aerial photograph by Bernie Boston

Centreville Supervisor Martha Pennino and Gulf Reston's William Magness held a symbolic plumbers' friend at his retirement party in 1977. The Board of Supervisors had lost a sewer moratorium suit to Gulf Reston and Mrs. Pennino presented the Golden Plunger Award to Magness as a farewell gift to help him unplug any sewer moratoriums he might encounter in retirement.
Courtesy of Reston Land Corporation

William Henry, Gulf Oil Corporation; William Magness, Gulf Reston; and Robert Dawson, editor of the Reston Times; celebrate Magness' selection by the Times as "Reston's Man of the Year," at the Magness farewell party on January 15, 1977.
Courtesy of Peter L. McCandless

Peter L. McCandless, public relations vice president, and Lee Shur, marketing vice president, set up and analyze Reston's marketing tools for Gulf Reston, Incorporated.
Courtesy of Peter McCandless

This Virginia Colonial-style mansion was built in 1941 for E. DeLong Bowman on what is now Reston Parkway. It served as a guest house and conference center for Robert Simon and for Gulf Reston, and is now the focal point of the Bowman Green business complex.
Courtesy of Reston Land Corporation

The ACCESS Emergency Care Center opened at the Town Center site in May 1977, with emergency care provided by staff members rotating from Fairfax Hospital, treating nearly two hundred patients per day.
Photograph by Warren Mattox.
Courtesy of Reston Land Corporation

The Wiehle Avenue Bridge was built over the Dulles Access Road in 1978. Together with the Reston Avenue Bridge, eight lanes became available for traffic between north and south Reston that year.
Photograph by Warren Mattox.
Courtesy of Reston Land Corporation

Fairfax County Board of Supervisors Chairman Jack Herrity and Centreville District Supervisor Martha Peninno waved from atop a County of Fairfax fire engine at the ceremony opening the Wiehle Avenue Bridge—dubbed "Martha's Bridge"—in September 1978.
Photograph by Warren Mattox.
Courtesy of Reston Land Corporation

Fran Steinbauer, president of Reston Land Corporation, watched Tom Burgess, executive director of the Reston Homeowners Association, drive a symbolic spike at the opening of the Wiehle Avenue Bridge.
Photograph by Warren Mattox.
Courtesy of Reston Land Corporation

The Colonial Green Cluster rises on the edge of Reston's South Golf Course.
Photograph by Phil Fraga.
Courtesy of Peter McCandless

Helpers and observors, both human and animal, watch a sailboat launching on Lake Audubon.
Courtesy of the Reston Association

This was just part of the crowd who gathered to celebrate the dedication of the new Reston Community Center at the Hunters Woods Village Center in May 1979. Robert Simon was one of the honored guests and speakers. The building, which cost $2.6 million, houses a 275-seat theater, an Olympic-size pool, arts and crafts areas, meeting rooms, a darkroom, and a woodworking shop.
Photography by Warren Mattox. Courtesy of Reston Land Corporation

9

Mobilization

The Gulf Oil Corporation was eager to divest itself of its Reston real estate and the Mobil Corporation was just as eager to acquire it. The new owner was bullish on real estate, especially the thirty-seven hundred acres of undeveloped Reston land for which it paid $31 million. Gulf Reston retained its interest in the income-producing properties until a buyer could be found. Mobil liked the strategic location and its obvious potential. The corporation had been very successful with "Mei Foo Sun Chuen" in Hong Kong, possibly the world's largest privately financed condominium project, begun in 1966. It had included 13,100 apartments, shops, restaurants, and schools. In 1970, Mobil had established a separate entity, Mobil Land Development Corporation (MLDC), a wholly owned subsidiary of Mobil Corporation with its own staff of experienced architects, planners, and developers.

Reston Land Corporation (RLC) was formed in 1978 as a subsidiary of the parent company, MLDC, which was already involved in real estate projects all over the United States. Mobil Corporation Chairman Rawleigh Warner, Jr., had issued a statement declaring MLDC's objective to be "utilization of long-range creative planning to provide attractive living and recreation areas consistent with protection of the environment." Jim Todd, who had succeeded Bill Magness as presi-

dent of Gulf Reston in 1976, became president of RLC. Having many of the same people in other staff positions who had also been with Gulf, the usual training period during the transition to Mobil was unnecessary. The staff already in place had had long experience with Reston, knew their community, cared about, and were deeply committed to the New Town concept, and most of them were Reston residents. They knew the County Supervisors, planners and department heads, and could continue working with established relationships. They had all found that a spirit of cooperation was far preferable to confrontation in working with the community.

RLC president Todd believed that "Mobil does not usually 'follow the pack' and is willing to go in new directions." He thought that the company understood the meaning of long-range planning. The role of RLC was to be exclusively that of a community developer, not competing in any way with the thirty-five or so homebuilders and office developers who are actively building in Reston. The community's attainment of "young adulthood" was under way as Mobil took over—the well-informed residents welcomed a new developer who had confidence in the future of the New Town of Reston.

In addition to the purchase of thousands of acres of undeveloped land, Mobil acquired the two operating golf courses; the Country Club of

Reston including its private golf course, and the public Reston South Golf Course. This step was taken to ensure that the two recreational properties would eventually pass to responsible owners.

Diplomacy was a key factor in the smooth acquisition of the large Reston land area. Even before the property was purchased in 1978, Mobil had asked Jim Todd and Fran Steinbauer to approach Jack Herrity, chairman of the Fairfax County Board of Supervisors, and Martha Pennino, the supervisor from the Centreville District who had long been a helpful friend to Reston. The Reston emissaries told them that Mobil was contemplating buying the land. Mobil promised to do two things. One was to stick to the basic master plan and the other was to put together a team of people familiar with the master plan to keep managing the development. The same assurances were given to the Reston Community Association.

A number of the people on the Reston staff who dated back to the Simon days and early Gulf days had through the years been heavily involved in a wide diversity of functions in the ongoing task of creating a new town. Just before Mobil acquired the project, the Gulf Reston staff conducted a critical evaluation of the job they had done as Reston's developer under Gulf and came to the conclusions that being involved in so many different activities did not allow time to do any of them as well as they would have liked. Particularly, they believed that the labor-intensive activities of homebuilding and operating village centers and apartments took too much management time away from the more important aspects of community planning. So when RLC was organized, a new business strategy was formulated that emphasized bringing in more quality homebuilders and already successful apartment and shopping center developers who could do a better job in these areas because they were specialists. RLC would concentrate on what it was best at doing: overall strategic community planning, market research, zoning, land development, comprehensive marketing, and land sales. RLC's developing of the "amenities package" was to continue, including the building of swimming pools, tennis courts, ballfields, and pathways.

The organization had matured after years of pioneering efforts—certainly there had been no ready-made plan or scheme available that could be applied to Reston development for guaranteed success. As Gulf Reston ended its eleven-year involvement with the new town's development, nu-

merous evaluations were made of the pluses and minuses during its tenure. There was general agreement that Gulf Reston had followed Bob Simon's master plan. Supervisor Martha Pennino acknowledged that adherence to the plan was one of Gulf Reston's major achievements. Todd said that Gulf never had wanted to scrap the master plan in which Restonians saw assurance that their community would be built differently from other suburbs. Steinbauer believed that the company had followed Simon's dream even though his master plan was not the most profitable way to develop the land.

Growth and development continued at an accelerated pace under RLC, but no longer as a "company town." A progressive step long-hoped-for by residents and developer alike was taken in early 1979. The Virginia General Assembly, largely through the diligent efforts of State Senator Omer Hirst, authorized the issuance of $57 million in revenue bonds to finance the building of a thirteen-mile Dulles toll road. Opened October 1, 1984, it was constructed in the same right-of-way with the Dulles Airport access road, taking the form of parallel outside lanes and ramps for local traffic from Route 123 near McLean, to Sully Road, Route 28, at Dulles International Airport. Even before it was completed, this proved to be of immediate marketing value for both residential and industrial land. Combined with aggressive promotion by the Fairfax County Economic Development Authority and RLC, the maturing of Reston as a community, and the strong residential and real estate markets in the Washington metropolitan area, the new road stimulated a healthy momentum in the community's development and sales. After fourteen years of uneven growth, Reston was no longer an island out in the middle of Fairfax County's hunt country but, because of other suburban building and road improvements, was in the heart of county growth.

On January 1, 1979, marketing vice president Lee Shur left. Jim Cleveland, who had begun his Reston career under Bob Simon as a real estate salesman in 1967, became the new marketing vice president.

Two important events occurred in the spring of 1979 which had required years of work by the developers and residents. Hunters Woods Fellowship House, the second Reston high rise for the elderly, was completed in the Hunters Woods Village Center and residents began to move in. Right beside it, the 53,000 square foot Reston Community Center, planned and built through the

Francis Steinbauer was project engineer from 1964 under Robert Simon, executive vice president for Gulf Reston, president of Reston Land Corporation, and later, president of the Eastern Division of Mobil Land Development Corporation. He resigned in February 1985.
Courtesy of Reston Land Corporation

Michael Was, vice president for marketing and executive vice president for Reston Land Corporation, resigned in June 1985 to organize his own company.
Courtesy of Reston Land Company

James Todd was once chief executive officer and president of Gulf Reston and Reston Land Corporation. He joined Gulf Reston in 1970 and became president of Mobil Land Development Corporation, Eastern Division, before he resigned in June 1984.
Courtesy of Reston Land Coporation

Gregory J. Friess is executive vice president and general manager of Reston Land Corporation in Fairfax County and Colonial Village, Inc., in Arlington County. He has been with Mobil Corporation since 1971 and involved with the real estate development group since 1974.
Courtesy of Reston Land Corporation

James Cleveland, with Reston's management since 1967, was director of sales with Gulf Reston, and marketing vice president and executive vice president of Reston Land Corporation before becoming their president. He is also president of the Virginia Region of Mobil Land Development Corporation.
Courtesy of Reston Land Corporation

initiative of Reston residents at a cost of $2.6 million, was dedicated on May 20 with a speech by Bob Simon at the ribbon-cutting ceremony. He noted his pleasure at seeing that his early goals were being fulfilled. He had planned as far back as 1963 to have a combination of housing for the elderly, shopping, and a recreation center at each village center. Simon hoped that the new edifice would be "a community center without walls, an institution. It's more than a building, it's an opportunity to reunite north and south Reston."

Following the sale of the undeveloped land and the two golf courses to Mobil, Gulf began to concentrate on the sale of its income-producing properties in which Mobil had no interest. Gulf Reston was successful in divesting itself of twenty Reston commercial properties on February 5, 1980. The new owners, Donatelli and Klein, Incorporated, a Bethesda, Maryland, investment firm, joined forces with Mark Winkler Management, Incorporated, of Alexandria, to purchase the properties for $40 million. One project, the Shadowood condominiums, was sold to the Stephen G. Yeonas Investment Company. The Donatelli-Klein-Winkler sale included the three village centers—Lake Anne, Hunters Woods, and Tall Oaks—the International Center complex, five apartment complexes, Isaac Newton Square, Triangle Park, and the Reston Air Conditioning Corporation which serves the Lake Anne Village Center. The new investment group promised to streamline management and maintenance procedures and tighten up significantly on the operation of the properties. It was the plan of the purchasers to spend a $1 million fund over a two-year period to repair mechanical systems, concrete work and leaky roofs, to paint, and to replace plantings. The Winkler organization installed its management offices in the Isaac Newton Square Gulf Reston office building.

The owners of the investment properties needed to use some innovative thinking and planning to rehabilitate at least one of their holdings. Lake Anne's Washington Plaza, praised and honored far and wide in the 1960s, had fallen on hard times and was aging by 1981. Tenants had moved out of some of the commercial spaces or some were at least temporarily closed for business because of interiors damaged by leaky roofs. Vandalized light fixtures had not been repaired. After dark, the plaza was deserted. The problems required a major effort to return the plaza to its strikingly beautiful appearance which still brings architects, planners, and government officials from all over the world to view and experience the

unique design. Donatelli and Klein changed the center to a mixed use condominium, units were sold, and rehabilitation is still under way. Later, the Fresh Value grocery store, Il Cigno Restaurant, and other businesses drew Restonians back to Washington Plaza. But even as citizens expressed dismay at the deterioration of the Lake Anne Village Center in 1981, the Board of Supervisors placed the complex in an historic district and the Fairfax County History Commission nominated it to the National Register of Historic Places as the most successful of the New Town concepts in the United States.

From the time of the early beginnings in the Simon days, Reston's "built-in" features had included many options for the conservation of energy in the area of transportation. This consideration again became important in 1979 as the price of imported oil rose rapidly. The situation brought back vivid memories of the gasoline shortages of 1973-1974. Reston offered over thirty-five miles of pathways and bicycle paths to keep pedestrians and riders safe from automobile traffic. The internal bus system, (RIBS) which had replaced the Common Ground bus in 1977, had two Mercedes Benz buses circulating through the residential, commercial, and employment areas to pick up and discharge passengers. Over seventy rush hour commuter buses carried almost three thousand riders daily to and from Washington employment centers.

Because of the national economic downturn during 1980, there were fewer housing starts; the entire housing industry countrywide was suffering from a shortage of money, excessively high mortgage interest rates and public resistance to purchasing houses because of both. Fortunately, as Jim Cleveland, vice president of marketing, observed in a company newsletter, condominiums and moderately priced townhouses were available in Reston and residential sales held their own. Despite the drab look of the economy, Reston's industrial areas sported the new look of several completed buildings constructed with an interesting variety of purposes. Sperry Systems Management opened a major research and development facility at Reston Avenue and Sunrise Valley Drive. Centec, an energy environment consulting firm, moved into their building across from Isaac Newton Square. The American Alliance for Health, Physical Education, Recreation and Dance occupied their building in the Education Park. The Mid-Atlantic Gift Center was completed on Sunrise Valley Drive across from the U.S. Geological

This aerial view of Hunters Woods
Village Center was taken after Hunters
Woods Fellowship House and the Reston
Community Center had been completed
in 1979.
Courtesy of Reston Land Corporation

Jean Balderson is the executive secretary
to the executive vice president and to the
president of Reston Land Corporation. She
has been with Reston's development
offices since the days of Bob Simon and
is the longest tenured employee at
Reston Land.
Courtesy of the Reston Times

An official tree planting ceremony was
held for Hunterlab's new building in
November 1979. Reston Land Corporation
presented the native oak tree to "a native
company." Participants were, left to right,
Fran Steinbauer, president of Reston Land
Corporation; and Philip Hunter, Richard
Hunter, and Elizabeth Hunter, all of
Hunterlab.
*Photograph by Warren Mattox.
Courtesy of Reston Land Corporation*

Harbor Point condominiums on Lake
Thoreau were under construction in 1980.
*Photograph by Abbie Edwards.
Courtesy of the photographer*

123

Survey building. CH2M Hill, consulting engineers, moved into a new building and the American Press Institute finished an addition to their existing building. Commerce Park I, at Reston Avenue and Sunrise Valley Drive, leased three of its four new office park buildings to Sky Courier, an international documents delivery system. In addition to these completed structures, seven more firms made plans to begin construction shortly on new buildings.

There were changes to come as the business forecasts for Reston were optimistic in the extreme. New executive staff appointments were announced by Mobil. Jim Todd was promoted to president of MLDC's eastern division in October 1980; Fran Steinbauer was appointed president of Reston Land in March 1981. Jim Cleveland became general manager and executive vice president of RLC. Michael Was, responsible for planning with Gulf Reston since 1973 and then vice president of planning with RLC, was made vice president of marketing for RLC. He was to inaugurate a successful cooperative program with Reston builders to market homes and encourage a wider selection of design and price.

The evolution of technology initiated by satellites and communication networks beyond the fixed wire has grown rapidly. Industry analysts called the evolution of high tech industries a complete third revolution of industrial uses. The rapid advancement of technology coupled with an almost simultaneous action of federal deregulation of the communications industry has allowed for the rapid growth of this new industry.

By spring of 1981, it was obvious that Reston was on the leading edge of the Washington area wave of the future—the establishment of a high technology center. With Washington's position as the fourth largest computer market in the United States, its function as seat of the national government, and Reston's location between Washington and Dulles Airport, it is not difficult to understand the frequent announcements of new companies leasing space or building facilities in the new town. Tandem Computers, at the time the fastest growing computer manufacturing company in the United States, built its eastern regional headquarters on a twenty-five acre site. At the special groundbreaking ceremony, on March 23, Tandem's chief operating officer, Robert Marshall, reminded many of those present of Simon's original goals for the Reston community. His firm had chosen to locate in Reston for its proximity to Dulles and Washington and also for a variety of housing, a

strong sense of community, fine quality of lifestyle, aesthetic environment, recreation and fitness facilities, and close accessibility of all amenities. GTE Business Communications Systems officials were to make a similar statement two years later at the opening of Tech Park Reston.

Other companies were building. Sperry Systems Management was in the process of expanding their quarters to accommodate more than double the number of employees. Advanced Technology, part of Cascades Center, had reasons similar to Tandem's for establishing themselves in Reston in order to attract high tech employees and keep them. Arthur Young began a six-story building to house the international training center for their worldwide accounting firm.

By way of providing a nice balance for the industrial development with new housing and amenities, clearing and dam construction for sixteen-acre Lake Newport and North Point Village began in early summer of 1981 in the fifteen-hundred-acre section of Reston north of Baron Cameron Avenue. This community included a lake, neighborhood schools, open space, pathways, and recreational facilities. The environment was protected and trees continued to be an important part of the ongoing conservation program. The North Point Village Visitors Center on Lake Newport opened in September 1982.

As one might expect, a number of issues of importance to the growing Reston community have emerged. All have required close cooperation between the developer, the community, and county officials and agencies. One such issue involved a Virginia Electric Power Company (VEPCO) high voltage overhead transmission line. As originally proposed by VEPCO in late 1980, the line would have bisected north Reston with a string of towers 110 feet high. A shock wave of reaction by Reston residents and developer alike surfaced. Efforts to relocate it farther east precipitated a controversy involving RLC, RCA, RHOA, the Town of Herndon, several subdivisions on Reston's periphery, Supervisor Nancy Falck from the Dranesville District, Supervisor Martha Pennino from the Centreville District, and the county's planning staff. After much debate, numerous "work sessions," public hearings, and appearances before the State Corporation Commission, a compromise was reached wherein the alignment of VEPCO's proposed overhead line would be parallel and basically contiguous to the east side of the proposed Springfield Bypass (later named Fairfax County Parkway) as it proceeded north along Stuart Road.

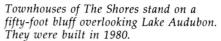

*Townhouses of The Shores stand on a
fifty-foot bluff overlooking Lake Audubon.
They were built in 1980.*
        Photograph by Warren Mattox.
    Courtesy of Reston Land Corporation

*This familiar logo originally graced the
Sperry Systems Management entrance.
Sperry and Burroughs have since 1986
joined forces and taken the name Unisys.*
        Photograph by Warren Mattox.
    Courtesy of Reston Land Corporation

*The Eastern Division Headquarters and
manufacturing facility for Tandem
Computers, Inc., had an official ground
breaking ceremony for their new building
on March 23, 1981. Present were, left to
right, Bob Marshall, Tandem; Chuck
Gulledge, Dynalectron; George Eckart,
Tandem; Fran Steinbauer, Reston
Land; Vic De Souza, Tandem; and Jim
Cleveland and Jim Todd, Reston Land.*
        Photograph by Warren Mattox.
    Courtesy of Reston Land Corporation

*An aerial view was taken in 1981 of the
United States Geological Survey headquarters, the Reston International Center,
and the Dulles Access Road.*
Photograph by Blue Ridge Aerial Surveys.
    Courtesy of Reston Land Corporation

In addition, the substation location which had been approximately a mile further north was relocated onto Reston Land Corporation property so that it would terminate in Reston and the Stuart Ridge subdivision would not have an overhead line immediately outside of their subdivision along Stuart Road. The key factor in the settlement of the controversy was the gift by RLC of valuable land to VEPCO for both the transmission line right-of-way and the new substation site.

Another issue involved a right-of-way which had been on the planning maps for many years. The Fairfax County Parkway has at various times been referred to as the Outer Beltway, Outer Circumferential Road, and the Springfield Bypass. The alignment of the Parkway has been on the Reston and Fairfax County master plan as it traverses Reston in largely the same alignment since before Bob Simon considered purchase of the property. In fact, one of the main reasons Simon purchased the property was the planned highway improvements represented by this Parkway and the commuter roads at that time designated within the Dulles Airport access road right-of-way. During 1982, the Fairfax County Board of Supervisors, after years of negotiation, finally agreed with the Virginia Department of Transportation on the entire alignment for future development. Actual construction of some segments began in 1986.

Intensive residential marketing and construction of commercial and industrial buildings during 1982 resulted in a remarkable turn of events during 1983. A prevalent and representative view was offered in a cover story of the Washington area's *New Home Guide* of May/June 1982. Residents interviewed spoke of the abundance of trees and natural beauty and the chance many residents had to work in an office nearby. Among those constructing industrial and office buildings in Reston was the Lee Sammis Company of Irvine, California. Sammis chose Reston as the site for their first East Coast development, a 400,000-square-foot office and technology park, to be called Campus Commons. Lee Sammis expressed the up-beat feeling of the high-tech community developing daily: "Reston is the best emerging office market on the East Coast. It not only has an outstanding total community concept and great environmental design, it also has a very strong pulse—and that is critical to the success of our project." It is also critical to the success of Reston.

In 1982, twenty years after the Residential Planned Community (RPC) ordinance was passed by Fairfax County enabling Simon to develop his New Town, Reston observed a landmark year. It was the best year to date for land sales, climaxed by the opening, with fireworks, of North Point Village and the Visitors Center on Lake Newport north of Route 606, Baron Cameron Avenue. All but one of Reston's former executive vice presidents attended the ceremony. It was also the year for the groundbreaking of the fourth village center, at South Lakes. Excitement ran high because Route 66 was opened east of the Beltway, Route 495, another major transportation improvement.

In January 1983, ground was broken at Reston for parallel toll lanes to the Dulles access road—Reston residents and employees would finally have a limited access highway all the way to Washington as well as to Dulles Airport. Virginia Governor Charles Robb, Virginia Senator John Warner, and many local government officials were present—they all knew the great significance of the occasion.

The Reston Homeowners Association had originally been incorporated to acquire, operate, and maintain, for the use and benefit of all inhabitants of Reston all lakes, parks, tennis courts, swimming pools, open spaces, and other facilities. After lengthy arguments and discussions regarding the adequacy of the designs of the dams by the Reston community and county officials, Lakes Anne, Audubon, and Thoreau were deeded by RLC to RHOA in March 1983 for operation and maintenance.

The toll road groundbreaking ceremony in the first month was only one of many significant events during a very full year for Reston's developers. A second groundbreaking took place in April when the North County Governmental Center was begun on fifty acres of land at the Town Center bounded by Reston and Baron Cameron Avenues. The Reston police station, county assessments, and Centreville District Supervisor Martha Pennino's offices were all moved into the new building in January 1985.

GTE's subsidiary, Business Communications Systems, Inc., located their national headquarters at Reston in May 1983 on the Tech Park Reston campus, bringing five hundred new jobs to Reston, providing a broad range of services for automated offices.

Governor Robb welcomed BCS to Reston. GTE Corporation president Thomas A. Vanderslice stated: "We chose to locate our headquarters here because Washington is truly the communications capital of the world; look at the other communica-

A large balloon on the shores of Lake Thoreau helped with the publicity for the Reston $50,000 Grand Tour, a successful marketing promotion featured in 1981.
Photography by Abbie Edwards

The Harden and Weaver WMAL Radio team participated in selection of the prize winner for the Grand Tour, Irene Paradowski. Shown left to right are Michael Was, marketing vice president for Reston Land, Jackson Weaver, drawing the winning ticket, Frank Harden, and Anne McCool, marketing services manager for Reston Land.
Photograph by Warren Mattox.
Courtesy of Peter McCandless

The new Reston Visitors Center opened on the shores of Lake Newport in September 1982.
Courtesy of Reston Land Corporation

tions firms here like COMSAT, MCI, Satellite Business Systems, and American Satellite."

Other changes made news in Reston during 1983. Lake Anne Village Center was enlivened in June by the opening of Leo Alonzo's Fresh Value grocery store in the space once occupied by the Safeway store. It immediately lived up to its name in several ways with good community response. The next month, a group of new owners purchased the Country Club of Reston, rehabilitated it, and gave it a fine new name, Hidden Creek Country Club. The membership doubled. The first stores opened in the new South Lakes Village Center in November.

December was full of beneficial happenings for the business and residential aspects of life in Reston. The Dulles connector road between Route 66 and the Dulles access road was opened, some access restrictions were lifted, and decals were issued to car pools for greater use of the highway by commuters until the new toll lanes opened. The connector cut the travel time between Dulles Airport and Washington by half.

It had been a banner year, 1983, the best for Reston land sales since 1973. In the year-end progress summary, the figures—$23.3 million in sales—bore out a whimsical statement from RLC that Reston was entering a "golden age." For the first time, residence and business development had begun to mesh and by the end of the year, there had been a rush of buyers for Reston land. The year had been the best yet for sales in both acreage and dollars, and in addition, the overall vacancy factor of existing space was less than 2 percent.

These were significant developments but the most amazing of all was that by the end of 1983, for the first time in Reston's twenty-two-year history, the number of jobs—15,195—was greater than the number of households—13,600.

The value of the new town development had appreciated over the years far beyond the inflationary rate experienced during the period. The Virginia Division of Industrial Development reported that Northern Virginia had fifty-two high-tech firms, 70 percent of the state's total, and of these, 25 percent were located in Reston. By the end of 1983, the total estimated value of investments in Reston on the developed land alone amounted to over $2 billion on just about half of the rolling, well-watered, forested land area of eleven square miles which Robert Simon had purchased for $13,150,000 in 1961.

Reston builders had led the way with contem-

porary designs in the 1960s and in the 1980s they were in the forefront with more traditional homes, especially in North Point Village. A nationwide wave of nostalgia was reinforced by Reston's lush forests and contour planning of streets to create wooded settings, dotted with Victorian-style homes.

The classic country cottage designed by architect Lester Walker of Woodstock, New York, won a 1983 countrywide contest sponsored by *House Beautiful*. This house, judged to have the most creative living space within an affordable fifteen hundred square feet, was built in Reston's model home village the following year.

With Reston's bright future virtually assured, James Todd resigned his position in June 1984 to accept new challenges elsewhere in Fairfax County. Fran Steinbauer was appointed to succeed him as president the following month. South Lakes, the fourth village center, officially opened in 1984. It was designed, built, and managed by the Western Development Corporation which also built Georgetown Park in Washington, D.C.

The Dulles Toll Road opened October 1, 1984, and by the end of the year, investments in Reston had come to an annual record of $250 million. This was largely due to the land rush triggered by the knowledge that the road, informally dubbed the Reston Expressway in Reston Land's advertising, would bring Reston closer to Washington and Georgetown in commuting time. With three interchanges available there was easy access along an attractive corridor with no used car lots, no strip retail outlets, and no clutter. The dream that Bob Simon had had in 1961 was actually coming true. In the four years since 1980, industrial and commercial land sales equaled what had previously taken sixteen years to accomplish. With the major transportation problems solved, accessibility was proving to be a major factor in the desirability of Reston for employers and employees.

By 1985, a wide range of residential options was available throughout Reston, from condominiums at $70,000 to single family homes at $500,000, with many choices in between. The urban space in a rural setting which was designed for living, working and playing now had over twenty thousand jobs in over nine hundred firms, with 14,500 households. And only part of the thousand-acre Reston business center was developed.

RLC bade farewell to Fran Steinbauer and Michael Was in 1985. Jim Cleveland was appointed president and Greg Friess, executive vice

Reston's developers' executive vice presidents paused at the Grand Opening of North Point Village and the Visitors Center on Lake Newport in September 1982. They are, left to right, John W. Guinee, Jr.; James C. Cleveland; Glenn W. Saunders, Jr.; Francis C. Steinbauer; and James W. Todd. Missing from the picture is James Selonick.
Photograph by Warren Mattox.
Courtesy of Reston Land Corporation

By September 1982, the aggressive marketing of Reston in all media had produced this delightful cartoon.
Courtesy of The Connection

Chadds Ford townhouses were here observed in the early morning mist along the shore of Lake Thoreau.
Courtesy of Reston Land Corporation

president, of Reston Land. Legions of people who worked for the developers have come and gone. Only two remain with Reston Land who worked with all three—Jean Balderson and Jim Cleveland. Others still with Reston Land who began during the Gulf Reston period are Don Frutchey, John Guilfoyle, Barbara Berke, Grace McGee, John Farrar, Arlene Ashton, Polly Erksa, Joy Caveney, Bill Steiner, and J. R. Davison.

February 18, 1986, was a day that will be remembered, for it marked the unveiling of development plans for Reston's Town Center. This amenity had been a key element in the original Reston master plan envisioned by Bob Simon, but it was a monumental undertaking and twenty-four years had passed before the economic practicality and the market demand reached maturity. Finally there was to be a "Downtown Reston." The role of Reston Land Corporation as solely a community developer, which had been assumed when Mobil purchased the thirty-seven hundred acres of undeveloped land from Gulf Reston in 1978, was experiencing a transition. Participation as an active partner in the planning, development, and operation of the urban core of Reston at Town Center turned out to be an exciting prospect when viewed as a joint venture with a major development partner. Two experienced teams came together when newly-formed Reston Town Center, Inc., a subsidiary of Reston Land Corporation, joined forces with the Himmel/Miller-Klutznick-Davis-Gray Company of Boston and Chicago to form Reston Town Center Associates. Himmel/MKDG had a string of successes to its credit nationwide including Boston's Copley Place, Chicago's Water Tower Place, and Denver's City Center. They were interested in developing the newest and most important element of the "urban place in a rural setting." The principals of the Himmel/MKDG team are Kenneth A. Himmel, managing partner; Kenneth P. Wong, senior development manager; and J. Hunter Richardson, development manager. The principals of Reston Town Center, Inc., are senior Reston Land Corporation officers James C. Cleveland, Gregory J. Friess, and Thomas J. D'Alesandro IV.

The ambitious project is part of the Reston Town Center District of 460 acres of which the urban core comprises 85 acres. On 20 acres of the urban core, Phase I will be built consisting of twin towers containing 530,000 square feet of office space, retail space of 240,000 square feet including seventy-five shops and restaurants at ground level, a 515-room Hyatt Regency Hotel, and an eleven-screen Cineplex Odeon theatre. The plan includes thirty-one hundred surface and structured parking spaces and an active pedestrian streetscape of urban parks, fountains, and extensive landscaping.

Kenneth Himmel looks upon the partnership as an opportunity to carry on the Reston tradition of design innovations, quality urban planning, and creation of a unique living environment. Jim Cleveland believes that the Town Center is one of the great real estate opportunities in America, and feels that the partnership has the talent and resources to transform the dream into a reality. The groundbreaking ceremony was held in June 1988 with Virginia Governor Gerald Baliles and Mobil Corporation's Chairman of the Board Allen Murray officiating.

Already in place or under construction just north of the urban core of Town Center were the North County Governmental Center, with Centreville District Supervisor Martha Pennino's offices, the Fairfax County Reston police substation and county assessments office; Cameron Glen elderly progressive care center; Reston Hospital Center; North County Community Shelter, and Reston Regional Library.

A long look into the twenty-first century was provided when the National Aeronautics and Space Administration chose Reston from more than sixty sites as the project headquarters for the space station program in November 1986. Thomas C. Moser, program director, listed the persuasive factors, including proximity to Washington, suitability and price of facilities, ability to work closely with and near the primary contractor, Grumman Corporation, and the presence of a highly skilled labor force in a high-tech community. He also called attention to an ironic fact of the modern age. His offices, which are at one end of Sunrise Valley Drive, can communicate with the staff at the United States Geological Survey at the opposite end of Sunrise Valley Drive in Reston—by satellite!

As a meaningful contribution toward solving a key problem of the present and future, Reston Land set aside five thousand square feet of day care space in Town Center for every one million square feet of commercial/office space to be built. Child care concerns were reflected in Reston's original master plan and Reston already had twenty-one private and nonprofit day care centers in 1988. But as more mothers enter the work force, there will be a greater need for good community day care. This perception led to the organization in February 1987 of the nonprofit Reston

This building is the eastern regional headquarters and manufacturing site for Tandem Computers, in Reston, Virginia.
Courtesy of Reston Land Corporation

Advanced Technology, a diversified firm specializing in systems management, engineering, design, personnel training, research and development, and computer software systems, moved its corporate offices to Reston's Cascades Center in June 1983.
Courtesy of Reston Land Corporation

Area Child Care Consortium, Inc., the outgrowth of a child care conference in November 1984. This initial meeting involved representatives from twenty-five Reston area businesses, state and federal government agencies, and childcare advocates.

The live, work, and play concept is alive and well. Management statistics for the Reston Association (RA, formerly called RHOA) in 1989, revealed that 1,030 acres of open space had been dedicated, including three lakes—Anne, Thoreau, and Audubon—with the expectation of receiving the fourth, Newport, from RLC in 1990. Ultimately, a total of 1,100 acres are anticipated when Reston Land completes their development. This amount of open space exceeds the hopes of Bob Simon when he first planned for this amenity in the new town. Other figures include forty-one miles of hard surface pathways, nine miles of natural surface trails, forty-two outdoor tennis courts, eighteen of which are lighted, and nineteen multipurpose courts. The Racquet Club is managed by RA under a long term lease arrangement. This facility offers six racquetball courts, four indoor tennis courts, a basketball court, and a fitness center. Other features managed by RA are sixteen swimming pools, two hot water spas, twenty-five athletic fields, fourteen play meadows, thirty tot lots, fifteen picnic areas, 194 garden plots, and four community buildings.

At the end of 1988, there were 18,200 homes in Reston with 53,000 residents. Places of business totalled 1,420, with 31,500 employees. Reston 1988 real estate taxes were over $41 million on $3 billion in assessed value, and one-third of that value was represented by the business community.

The expectations are that Town Center, Phase I will have a Grand Opening in September 1990. The plans are designed to make a bold urban statement as a community and regional focal point. The buildings will combine colorful materials and architectural elements which are at once reminiscent of Washington, D.C.'s classical architecture and yet have modern proportions and the attractive embellishments of an important place and space. The fountain square, parks and extensive plantings will promote the feeling of a pleasant "people place," a place for pleasurable strolling, shopping, dining and entertainment, with an eighteen-hour environment provided in part by the planned residential component. A multidiscipline cultural center of significance will be a part of Town Center's future, another of the many amenities for this "urban place in a rural setting," as it was called twenty-five years ago. The *New York Times* has speculated that the bold urban plan, designed by RTKL Associates of Baltimore, "may be setting a new national pattern for what would be called a new city."

131

With study after study being conducted about its adequacy in the early 1980s, the low, broad earthen dam holding back the waters of Lake Anne seemed to become a mountainous problem, as perceived by artist Michael Smith.
Courtesy of The Connection

Appealing to a national trend toward an interest in history and nostalgia, Fairfield Homes was the first builder to open model houses at North Point Village, in Bennington Woods, in 1983. Designs were reminiscent of turn-of-the-century houses.
Courtesy of Reston Land Corporation

Eurotherm, manufacturer of temperature control products for industrial use, was the first European-based firm to locate in Reston, in Isaac Newton Square, May 1970. This is their new plant on Sunset Hills Road, completed in 1982.
Photograph by Warren Mattox.
Courtesy of Reston Land Corporation

Virginia Governor Charles Robb addressed members of the Northern Virginia business, political, and educational community at the cornerstone laying ceremonies in May 1983 at GTE in Reston. Also included in the picture are Jim Todd, Reston Land; George Johnson, president of George Mason University; and Jack Herrity, chairman of the Fairfax County Board of Supervisors.
Courtesy of Peter McCandless

The South Lakes Village Center, Reston's fourth, is shown in an artist's rendering. The first shops opened in 1983.
Courtesy of Reston Land Corporation.

Karen and Bozy Bahary enjoyed the view of Lake Thoreau from the Blue Channel Inn at South Lakes Village in March 1989. Their waitress was Kathleen Drury.
Courtesy of the photographer,
Linda Rutledge

Telenet is located in this large three-building complex at 12490 Sunrise Valley Drive.
Courtesy of Telenet Communications Corporation, U.S. Sprint Data Communications Company

The efforts, largely donated, of over two thousand people went into the completion of the Builders' House '85 on Bennington Woods Road in Reston's North Point Village. This photograph was taken at the fifty-four-hour point in the seventy-two-hour construction goal. The successful project to raise over $1 million for three Northern Virginia charities was sponsored by the Outreach Committee of the Northern Virginia Builders Association. The winner of the raffle was William L. Oram.

Photograph by Warren Mattox.
Courtesy of Peter L. McCandless

This is the new parks building for the Vernon J. Walker Nature Education Center, a seventy-acre tract on Glade Drive, east of Soapstone Drive. The park was formally dedicated on October 17, 1987, and was established in honor of and named for the developer of the open space philosophy for Reston.

Various demonstrations represent a backyard habitat, a meadow, and a butterfly garden. Three study stations are designed for birdwatching, geology, and aquatic life. The entire nature center development plan reinforces the idea that "living in Reston is like living in a park."

Photography by Deborah Moss.
Courtesy of the Reston Association

Gary and Leslie Fox and baby Jessica were honored at a special ceremony in November 1987 as Reston's 50,000th-resident family. They purchased a Miller and Smith house in North Point Village. On hand to mark the occasion with the Foxes were Gregory Friess, executive vice president of Reston Land; Robert E. Simon, Jr., original developer of Reston; Leslie and Gary Fox; Dallas Peck, director of the USGS; and Thomas Moser, director of NASA's Space Station project in Reston.

In a congratulatory letter to the couple, Bob Simon expressed the hope that in 2064 Reston might still be a place where all sorts of people can grow up, mature and age gracefully, stretching their minds and bodies to the fullest.

Photograph by Warren Mattox.
Courtesy of Reston Land Corporation

The National Association of Letter
Carriers health benefit plan headquarters
is one of the major employers in Reston.
Courtesy of Reston Land Corporation

The GE Aerospace Data Center, located at
12300 Sunrise Valley Drive, was completed in 1987.
Courtesy of Mulligan/Griffin and
Associates, Inc.

The Reston Executive Center I was
completed in June 1988.
Photograph by Maxwell MacKenzie.
Courtesy of Centennial Development
Corporation

The Defense Mapping Agency Reston
Center at 12310 Sunrise Valley Drive was
completed in 1988.
Courtesy of Mulligan/Griffin and
Associates, Inc.

Executive IV, the fourth building in Centennial's Commerce Executive Park, was completed in June 1988. James Oesch Photography.
Courtesy of Centennial Development Corporation

Kenneth Himmel is senior project manager and a partner in Himmel/MKDG, a part of the development team of Reston Town Center Associates.
Courtesy of Reston Land Corporation

On a happy occasion in June 1988, Virginia Governor Gerald Baliles and Mobil Corporation's Chairman of the Board Allen Murray turned shovels of earth signifying the beginning of construction on Reston's ambitious new Town Center.
Photograph by Rhoda Baer.
Courtesy of Reston Land Corporation

136

Town Center, Phase I, will include the
Hyatt Regency Hotel, with 515 rooms,
and One Fountain Square, an eleven-
story, 260,000 square foot office building.
Courtesy Reston Town Center Associates

The office building at One Fountain
Square will overlook a colorful fountain
plaza in the heart of Reston's Town
Center.
*Courtesy of Reston Town Center
Associates*

137

Tapiola, Finland, was a New Town in the suburbs of Helsinki when Bob Simon visited it in the early days of Reston's development. Its high-rise buildings beside a small lake influenced the design of Lake Anne Village. Tapiola is governed by a special foundation with social and political backing. The administrative body has the flexibility and freedom of action of a private company and the power and influence of a public authority.

Courtesy of the Museum of Finnish Architecture, Helsinki

10

New Designs for Living

Town planning is a tradition rooted in antiquity. There were planned cities in ancient Greece over two thousand years ago. During the Middle Ages, hundreds of new towns were "planted" in the British Isles and in continental Europe. Leonardo da Vinci proposed ten satellite cities around Milan in 1484 to relieve overcrowding.

In the twentieth century many leading planners, architects, and philosophers in the western world contributed to the concept of self-contained communities. Beginning in 1902, Ebenezer Howard's *Garden Cities of Tomorrow* became the root from which England's New Town movement grew. Other important thinkers came along: Lewis Mumford, Sir Patrick Geddes, Frederick Osborn, Clarence Stein and Le Corbusier, to mention a few. British garden cities of the first half of the twentieth century were recognizable by their location beyond the urban fringes, mainly with row-house residences, and with commercial and industrial employment centers surrounded by open spaces.

America had seen many experiments with company towns and utopian communities in the nineteenth century, but the modern concept of New Towns first developed after World War I with the founding of Radburn, New Jersey, in 1929. Funded by private capital, it was never developed to its full plan because of the high cost of its ini-

tial capital investment requirements. Later, during the Depression, the federal government sponsored three "greenbelt" towns in Maryland, Ohio, and Wisconsin. None of these New Towns was able to attract industry. They remained residential in character and ultimately became suburbs with no economic self-sufficiency.

The post-World War II movement began in England in 1946 with a total effort involving twenty-eight new towns, all assisted by a government population dispersal policy and other economic stimulation. The Soviet Union reported over sixty-five New Towns within its borders by 1963. Dozens of other countries throughout the world built mostly government-aided or controlled New Towns with varying success. One of these New Towns which had especially interested Robert Simon when he visited it in the early period of Reston's development was Tapiola, near Helsinki, Finland.

The objectives and reasons for building the New Towns were varied. There were principally seven: to accommodate overpopulation of congested cities; to offer an alternative to urban sprawl with use of land, air, and watersheds (Reston has been included in this group); to isolate and protect special interest groups; to revive depressed areas where people and commerce had fled or the economic base had eroded; to provide support for a boom industry or project; to provide working and living space for new industry and research; and finally, to solve social problems and give low-income minority citizens a chance to own homes.

Urban patterns in America are changing from the factory city to the postindustrial society. Goods were once the principal product of the United States; we are becoming a society based on the creation and distribution of services and information. Along the nation's system of interregional and metropolitan expressways, urban corridors are being established consisting of new research organizations, modern light industry, regional schools, and housing. The automobile, telephone, airplane, television, and computers have replaced the need for close proximity, and the usefulness of the large city might seem to be waning. The United States is a predominately urban nation and our effort to solve urban problems is an important aspect of the current worldwide struggle for cultural, economic, and scientific leadership.

The post-World War II New Town movement got underway in the United States with a great burst of enthusiasm when Robert Simon began his ambitious plan for Reston as a concept of a better lifestyle than that offered by randomly-built proliferating suburbs. His emphasis on architectural design and innovative planning caught the fancy of the entire country and many of the countries abroad which were experimenting with their own government-sponsored and funded New Towns. Reston and, later, Columbia, Maryland, were the early principal ventures using private capital in the United States, followed later in the 1970s by the development of the Irvine Ranch in California. Encouraged by these initial successes, the federal government passed a Housing Act in 1970 with loan guarantees and grants to developers under Title VII of the act for New Towns throughout the United States. It was unfortunate that just five years later, for a variety of reasons related to mismanagement, government red tape, lack of funding due to revenue sharing, poor locations, and other factors, the federal government decided to withdraw from the program in 1975. Most of the properties purchased for the New Towns have since then been sold off for subdivision development. The federal government is unlikely to be interested in funding new towns again soon. In fact, the Reagan administration closed down the New Communities Division of HUD. Few large-scale planned communities will be begun in the near future because the private capital necessary to build these communities is too extensive for most investors.

Reston has been able to establish a firm foundation which assures its viability as a community. Job availability being a key to that success, the Reston developers were determined and able to persuade the United States Geological Survey to build its national headquarters in Reston, even to the extent of making a lease-purchase arrangement in order to accomplish the purpose. There was recognition of the need, from the earliest planning of the New Town to pursue aggressively commercial and industrial establishments. By maintaining high standards for both residential and business development, Reston became an attractive place in which to establish offices and light industry from the standpoint of high employee satisfaction and proximity to surface and air transportation, to Washington and to other interacting centers. That Reston was a fiscal asset to Fairfax County in FY 1972 because of its commercial and industrial components was an important revelation in a study published in 1973.

Reston is located within Fairfax County, which operates under the Urban County Executive form of government. If it were to become a separate incorporated area—a town or city—the state law would have to be changed. Most needed goods and services must be acquired from outside Reston's boundaries and include county schools, libraries, public safety, public works, land use regulation, public health, social services, and some recreational and leisure facilities and programs.

To enhance the structural and natural beauty as a necessity of the good life in the community, and to foster an appreciation for and involvement with nature, the Reston Association manages eleven hundred acres of open space, forests, wildlife habitat, and common land. It conducts educational programs for all ages through the Vernon J. Walker Education Center, maintains Reston's lakes and presents outdoor summer recreational programs for youngsters. The Reston Racquet Club provides indoor facilities and outdoor recreational amenities are provided by tot lots, tennis and other courts, swimming pools, picnic areas, garden plots, athletic fields, and pathways. There are four community buildings and a boat and trailer storage yard.

The Association assures design integrity in the community through the Design Review Board, which oversees exterior property changes to make sure they conform to the protective design covenants built into the Reston Deed, thus preserving property values on behalf of its membership. All

Reston is not a separate political jurisdiction but a part of Fairfax County, the most populous in the Commonwealth of Virginia. The Reston community is within the boundaries of the Centreville Magisterial District. Pictured in 1988 are the full Board, the sheriff, and the commonwealth's attorney. Seated in the front row, left to right, are Joseph Alexander, Lee District; Vice Chairperson Martha V. Pennino, Centreville District; Chairperson Audrey Moore; and Elaine McConnell, Springfield District. Standing in the back row, left to right, are Katherine K. Hanley, Providence District: Sharon Bulova, Annandale District; Gerry Hyland, Mount Vernon District; Lilla Richards, Dranesville District; Thomas M. Davis III, Mason District; Fairfax County Sheriff Wayne M. Huggins; and Commonwealth's Attorney Robert F. Horan.
Courtesy of the Office of Public Affairs

J. Hamilton Lambert, Fairfax County Executive, who serves at the pleasure of the Board, was born in Leesburg. He began working for Fairfax County in 1959, drafting maps in the assessments office. An exceptionally versatile person, he has by his own calculation held twenty-one different jobs including the county's top appointive position which he has held since 1980. He lives in Great Falls.
Courtesy of the Office of Public Affairs

Martha V. Pennino was elected Centreville District supervisor for the County Board in 1968, after having served for three terms on the Vienna Town Council. Vice chairperson of the Board of Supervisors since 1976, she has also been an officer or member of numerous other organizations. They include the Metropolitan Washington Council of Governments (COG), the Virginia Association of Counties, the Virginia Municipal League, the National Democratic County Officials, and the George Mason University Board of Visitors. Born in Roanoke, Virginia, she is a graduate of Emerson College in Boston and is married to Walter A. Pennino, Sr. She is the mother of four adult children.
Courtesy of Martha V. Pennino

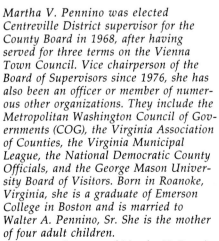

Reston resident Kenneth R. Plum was elected to represent the thirty-sixth Delegate District of Virginia from 1978 to 1980, and each term from 1982 on. The director of adult education for the Fairfax County Public Schools, he holds degrees from Old Dominion University and the University of Virginia.
Courtesy of Kenneth R. Plum

residents, homeowners and renters alike, are Reston Association members.

The Board of Directors determines Association policy. The Board is composed of nine members, three elected at-large, four representing geographic areas, and one each appointed by Reston Land Corporation and apartment owners. A professional staff carries out Board policies and programs, supported by members' assessments.

The administrative offices are located in the central building of Isaac Newton Square.

A proposition for municipal government for Reston failed in a 1980 referendum, apparently because Reston voters were generally satisfied with the level of services provided by the Reston Association (then called the Reston Home Owners Association) and the county, and because they were fearful of higher taxes and a new layer of government. But some longtime residents believe that if Reston is to survive and prosper, it needs some political autonomy. The examples of the towns of Vienna and Herndon are cited. As Reston grows, its increasing need for services, such as schools and police, and for a larger share of public works programs, must be faced by both Reston and Fairfax County.

Perhaps the most significant comment regarding possible future governance of Reston was made by E. A. Prichard, who has been retained by each developer as local legal counsel since the early days of the Simon period because of his knowledge and abilities. He is of the opinion that the problems of taxing, services, and other interrelationships between community/town/city/county are widely shared throughout the Commonwealth of Virginia and will become increasingly abrasive and difficult to resolve as the population and, therefore, local pressures, increase. A keen observer of the political scene, he believes that there will, in the 1990s, be a strong and probably successful movement to change the state constitution so that there can be a fair and equitable division of tax revenues among the various jurisdictions, thereby removing a principal cause of conflict and inequity under the present system. In the event the change does come about and the independent city/county structure that now exists is abolished, Reston might then be able to incorporate as a town or city with the full powers of a separate municipality and an electorate which would have a more direct influence on the decisions affecting their community's destiny.

Developer and residents alike are aware of the Town Center—Reston's downtown—in the original master plan. Town Center planning and development, with an integrated Fairfax County Governmental Center has moved forward under RLC. When the tall buildings—"exclamation points on the landscape"—are completed at Town Center, the beautiful views seen from them will be among the finest in Northern Virginia. Dulles Airport and the Bull Run Mountains will be visible to the west; the Blue Ridge Mountains will be seen to the north and the Potomac River to the east. The forested lands of Fairfax and Loudoun counties, carefully preserved by Reston's conservation-conscious development, as well as by other builders, will impress the observer on the ground, in high buildings, and in the air with views of the substantial remnants of a great forest.

Reston experienced an unprecedented growth from 1979 to 1989. Reston's mid-year 1989 employment force of 33,000 exceeded the number of households, which was 18,500. In 1989, more than 40 percent of the people who worked in Reston lived there. It has today the largest concentration of electronics and telecommunications firms in the county. Companies from all over the country are selecting the New Town for locations of their headquarters or regional offices. In remarks made at Tandem Computer's groundbreaking ceremony, George Eckert, eastern regional vice president for Tandem Computers, of Cupertino, California, in "Silicon Valley," reiterated typical reasons for having selected Reston for the company's East Coast regional headquarters:

The first thing we were looking for was a labor force with the appropriate skills. The second thing was that it should be a pleasant place to work, so we wouldn't lose our employees to the Sun Belt . . . .

The type of community we were looking for would be identifiable with Tandem's goals, a community that would identify with high technology companies in a rapid growth industry.

. . . One of the key things is the difference in housing styles. Californians are used to contemporary housing, and you can find that here. Plus, Reston has a rich architectural diversity which provides a style of home for every taste . . . .

We wanted a community with amenities close at hand. In California, we had a swimming pool next to our cafeteria, and we encourage our people to get out. A high-growth company requires high energy.

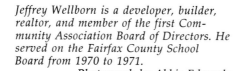

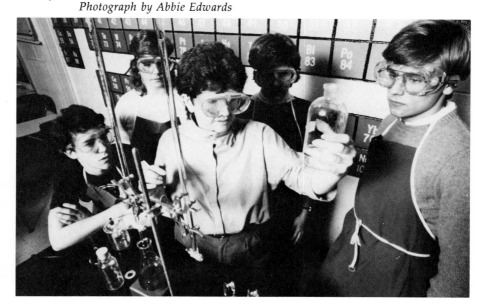

This meeting of the Inlet Cluster Association was photographed in 1978. The cluster consisted of sixty-three dwelling units and was completed in 1972.
Courtesy of the photographer, Chris Raphael

Jeffrey Wellborn is a developer, builder, realtor, and member of the first Community Association Board of Directors. He served on the Fairfax County School Board from 1970 to 1971.
Photograph by Abbie Edwards

Gene Bergoffen, an attorney, seen here in a 1978 photograph, headed an RCA study team in 1972 to prepare a paper on new town governance. He also served on the Fairfax County School Board 1971 to 1973.
Courtesy of Gene Bergoffen

Mona Blake of Reston, educator, served on the Fairfax County School Board from 1971 to 1975. Bradley Shipp, also of Reston, served on the Board as a student member from 1973 to 1974, during Mona Blake's term.
Courtesy of the Virginia Room, Fairfax County Public Library

Reston's first high school was in Herndon. South Lakes High opened in Reston in September 1978 and now about two-thirds of Reston's students attend there. The balance go to Herndon. Here students are photographed in a laboratory setting at South Lakes.
Courtesy of Reston Land Corporation

Reston's Growth

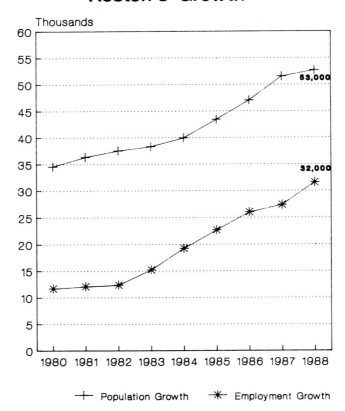

Thousands

Population Growth — ✳ Employment Growth

Gregory Friess, Reston Land's executive vice president, manages day-to-day operations for the developer. A resident of Reston, he understands the community life day-by-day as well. He evaluated progress in the past with a brief look into the future:

I feel that the two most important factors which have led to the many successes achieved in Reston over the past twenty-five years are the vision of Robert E. Simon as expressed in his original seven goals, and the commitment of the three developers which have guided Reston's development at various points in its history. As a result, today Reston truly is a community where its residents have the opportunity to enjoy a fulfilling lifestyle which is free of negatives such as long commutes to work, and is full of positives ranging from neighborhood tennis courts and swimming pools to fine shops and dining at the new Town Center as it evolves during the next decade.

It is very fitting that the silver anniversary of Reston's creation is being marked by the opening of the initial phase of Town Center. Robert E. Simon can rest assured that his endeavors to create a unique community have been fulfilled.

Reston has been cited by hundreds of planners, architects, and journalists as a fine example of modern urban design. In one way or another, new suburbs will be built in the coming decades designed to accommodate the growth of population which will occur in this country between now and the year 2000. This new town has proven probably better than any other that there are alternatives to the sprawling, monotonous and unattractive "cookie cutter" bedroom communities that so frequently mar the fringes of large cities. Journalist Marya Mannes has succinctly summed up dreams and reality concerning Reston. After describing the original master plan and its implementation, she wrote:

Reston's designers would be the first to decry the work or goal [of Utopia]. It is not a dream-state, an architect's whim or a sociologist's blueprint: It is an effort, born of long deliberation and the awareness of great need, to provide a fuller life for American Citizens.

Royce Hanson, project manager for the Commission on National Urban Policy and former chairman of the Maryland-National Capital Park and Planning Commission believes that "Reston has changed the course of suburban planning and design."

Restonian Rodney F. Page, an attorney, served on the Fairfax County School Board from 1974 to 1980 and was its chairman from 1976 to 1980.
Courtesy of Rodney F. Page

Kohann H. Whitney was appointed to the Fairfax County School Board to represent the Centreville District in 1985. Her term expires in 1989. A communications manager for TRW, she has served on numerous Northern Virginia boards and committees.
Courtesy of the Reston Times

Robert Frye of Hickory Cluster was an at-large member of the Fairfax County School Board from 1978 to 1985. He holds degrees from Howard University and the American University. He has since 1978 been director of the Hazard Analysis Division of the U.S. Consumer Product Safety Commission.
Courtesy of the photographer, Abbie Edwards

A Terraset Elementary School underground classroom is shown as it appeared in 1976.
Photograph by Abbie Edwards

Former South Lakes High School Principal George W. Felton is shown in this 1983 photo. His school had the largest number of National Merit Scholars in the State of Virginia—seventeen—in 1982.
Photograph by Bauer and Charles, Arlington. Courtesy of George W. Felton

South Lakes High School was photographed by Urban Photographics of Herndon.
  Courtesy of Reston Land Corporation

Langston Hughes Intermediate School, named after the black poet and novelist, was opened on Ridge Heights Road in September 1980.
  Courtesy of Reston Land Corporation

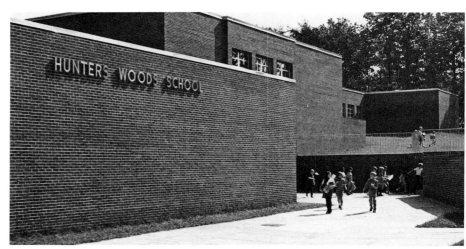

One of the Fairfax County's public schools, Hunters Woods Elementary opened in September 1969.
  Courtesy of Reston Land Corporation

*Audio-visual equipment is shown in use
at Hunters Woods Elementary in 1977.
Photograph by Abbie Edwards*

*Reston Regional, a branch of Fairfax
County's public library system at Hunters
Woods Village Center, was opened in
March 1974. When it was supplanted by
the new and larger Reston Regional Li-
brary at Town Center on Bowman Towne
Drive in 1985, this storefront facility was
reduced in size to a mini-library. It now
serves the local area including Hunters
Woods Fellowship House residents.
Courtesy of Reston Land Corporation*

*Police Captain Ronald C. Varner was
born in Washington, D.C., and raised in
Georgia. He is a graduate of American
University in law enforcement. He served
in the Navy for seven years, has been a
member of the Fairfax County Police
Department since 1969, and commander
of the Reston District since 1988. He is
married to Jane Terzick, a college profes-
sor in the computer field, and they have a
son. Captain Varner's hobby is raising
and showing domestic rabbits.*

*This photograph was taken in November
1988 with Centreville District Supervisor
Martha Pennino during a press conference
regarding a drug investigation at the
Stonegate apartments.
Photograph courtesy of Captain Varner*

147

Fox Mill low and moderate-income apartments (now called Stonegate) suffered for years from poor management, over-crowding, and a lack of proper supervision. It took a strong effort on the part of the community, the developer, and the federal government to turn the situation around and make the area a safe place in which to live. Picture taken in 1979.

Courtesy of the photographer, Abbie Edwards

^{SM} **RESTON ASSOCIATION**

When the Reston Home Owners Association name was changed to the Reston Association on January 22, 1987, the new logo featured two main elements.

The most prominent is the stylized tree, symbolizing the Association's role in caring for Reston's natural environment. A planning grid is superimposed over the tree symbolizing the planned community. The design expresses the commitment of the Association to maintain and enhance the quality of life that people come to Reston to find.

Courtesy of the Reston Association

Reston's first firehouse, Fairfax County Company No. 25, on Wiehle Avenue, became operational in April 1972.
Courtesy of Fairfax County Fire and Rescue Service

Newcomers Nights at the Reston Association, like the one pictured here in February 1989, are joint presentations by five of Reston's community organizations. The orientation program for newcomers is designed to introduce them to the community and to make them feel at home in it. Seated at the table, left to right, are Nancy Larson, Reston Community Association; David Haas, Reston Community Center; Mike Freeman, Reston Association; David Ross, Reston Board of Commerce; and Fran Milhouser, Reston Regional Library. Standing is Bryn Pavek, executive director of the Reston Community Center.
Photograph by Deborah Odell Moss.
Courtesy of the Reston Association

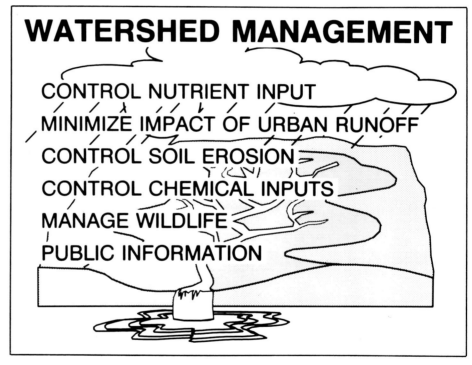

With four manmade lakes in Reston—Anne, Audubon, Newport, and Thoreau—constant maintenance is required to keep them as natural assets to the community. Major factors in watershed management are enumerated in this poster.
Courtesy of the Reston Association

Despite watershed management efforts, erosion does take place and soil slowly begins to build up on the lake beds. This photograph of dredging equipment was taken at Lake Audubon in 1987.
Courtesy of the Reston Association

The Reston lakes can be enjoyed in both active and passive ways as illustrated by these two photographs.
Courtesy of the Reston Association

Judi Ushio, president of the Board of RHOA from 1979 to 1983, posed here about 1983 with her family. Nathaniel is sitting in his mother's lap beside father David who is holding Cassandra. Jocelyn is standing, and Misti is seated on the right.

Courtesy of Judi Ushio

Susan Jones is an elementary school teacher with training in human development. She was elected RHOA president in the fall of 1983 and served for three-and-a-half years. Under her administration, the biggest change in the Association's history took place. In 1984, the Documents Review Committee, established in 1982, completed the task of rewriting the Deed, Articles of Incorporation, and the Bylaws which had originally been filed by Bob Simon. The new documents reflect the change from a developer-controlled to a resident-controlled administrative body. More open meetings and a more vigorous communications program with members were inaugurated along with other improvements.

Courtesy of Susan Jones

"While continuing to deliver a high level of services to the community, long range strategic planning characterized the third and final year of transition (1988) from developer to resident control for the Reston Association. Internally, a complete revision of Design Review policies and procedures was begun. Increased member participation in policy research and development was encouraged and fostered. A focus on finding alternative financial resources resulted in obtaining significant public funding of several community services which were either new or heretofore paid for by the Association. Externally, the Reston Association cosponsored and participated in three activities concerning the future of Reston: the Community Center Task Force, the Youth Task Force, and the Reston Forum."

Carolyn Lindberg is a computer consultant to small businesses in accounting applications. Previously, she worked for twelve years as a community planner. She was president of the Reston Association Board 1987-1988.

Courtesy of the Reston Association

Monroe E. "Mike" Freeman is an administrative judge on the Armed Services Board of Contract Appeals. He served as chairman of the Reston Association's Board of Directors from 1988 to 1989. The Reston Association has maintained the environmental, recreational and aesthetic amenities created by the developer over the past twenty-five years with a high degree of success, in his opinion.

Courtesy of the Reston Association

W. M. "Mac" Murray was elected to the Reston Association Board of Directors as North Point District respresentative and the president of the Board, in April 1989. He has served on several of RA's committees. Mac is program director for General Dynamics and chairman of the Board of Directors, Software Productivity Consortium.

Courtesy of the Reston Association

When the Brown's Chapel Concession
Building on Baron Cameron Avenue was
officially opened on August 26, 1985, a
representative group of people from sev-
eral diverse organizations joined in the
ceremony. They were, left to right, Ron
Morgan, assistant director of Open Space,
RHOA; Kurt Pronske, project engineer,
RHOA; Tom Burgess, executive vice pres-
ident, RHOA; Carl Hensler, Reston Youth
Association (football); Don McGuire and
Betsy Schultz, Board of Directors, RHOA;
Mike Freeman, Board president, RHOA;
Tom Wallace, Reston Soccer; Mike Wolf
and Chuck Novak, Reston Baseball; Susan
Grimm, secretary, Field Sports, RHOA;
Greg Friess, executive vice president,
Reston Land Corporation; Craig
Palmer, Fairfax County Sports Council;

Geoffrey M. Coon, architect, Hughes
Group; and Vicky Wingert, director,

Open Space, RHOA.
Courtesy of the Reston Association

With the cluster system of development in
Reston, there are many large and small
grassy areas which must be kept cut.
Some mowers are large enough to ride on,
and some, like this one, must be pushed.
A variety of functions is performed to
preserve the overall appearance of the
Reston community.
Courtesy of the Reston Association

The Reston Association has the responsibility of keeping pathways cleared of
snow in winter. Here "The Bombardier"
does an efficient job for the numerous
pedestrians who use the trails.
Courtesy of the Reston Association

Happily turning shovels of earth on January 20, 1987, for the foundation of the shelter building at the new Nature Center were Elfriede Walker, member of the RHOA Board and widow of Vernon Walker; Larry Craft, Open Space Committee project leader for the center; Jim Cleveland, president, Reston Land Corporation; and Susan Jones, president, Reston Home Owners Association. Nancy Davis was at the time chair of the Open Space Committee. The small pavilion building, designed by Reston architect Wayne Hughes, includes storage and exhibit space. It is surrounded by areas which provide places where people can study and appreciate nature. A backyard habitat attracts native wildlife; a butterfly garden contains plants and flowers attractive to these lovely creatures; and a sundial in the center, given by the Rotary Club of Reston, honors the memory of Vernon Walker. Study stations placed at various points highlight plants, unusual geological features, stream flora and fauna, and bird-watching.
Photograph by Warren Mattox. Courtesy of the Reston Association

The study of geology is one of the components in the Vernon J. Walker Nature Center educational programs. This interesting example of schist and other rock formations and outcroppings can be found along the Twin Branches Nature Trail.
Photograph by Deborah Odell Moss in 1988. Courtesy of the Reston Association

RHOA (known as the Reston Association since January 1987) has sponsored summer day camps since the early years of Reston. The healthy, happy youths in this photograph, taken in the 1970s, are now adults and other youngsters have taken their places, enjoying similar outdoor experiences annually.
Courtesy of the photographer, Abbie Edwards

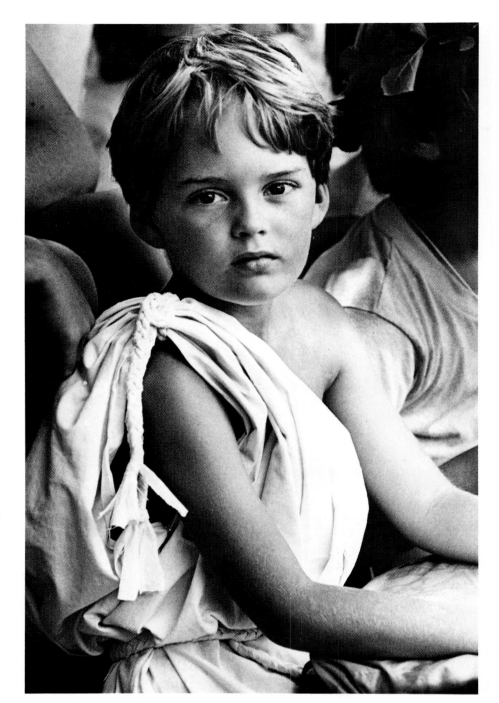

This young Restonian made his toga costume at a Summer Day Camp program sponsored by the Reston Association in 1983.
Courtesy of the Reston Association

Naturalist Roy Geiger, from the National Wildlife Federation, brought Lady, a trained red-tailed hawk, to the October 1988 Reston Fall Festival, which was attended by eight hundred people. The event, sponsored by the Reston Association, included nature games, craft displays and sales, storyteller Sharon Butler, the musical group Magpie, world-champion hula hooper David Williams, and naturalist Jim Pomeroy.
Courtesy of the Reston Association

154

One of the youth programs sponsored by the Reston Association is Hug-a-Tree, an effort to install within young residents a love for and understanding of the forests they see all around them. This learning group was photographed in 1985.
Courtesy of the Reston Association

Lake Fairfax is one of the five lakes in the Reston area, linked by the pathway system in 1988. It is used for boating only. The Lake was purchased by the Fairfax County Park Authority in 1966 from owner Jack Crippen.
Photograph in 1989 by Ken Frager.
Courtesy of Fairfax County Park Authority

The appointment of Vicky Wingert by the Fairfax County Board of Supervisors to the Fairfax County Trails Committee better enables her to coordinate Reston's pathway system and wildlife habitats with the county's. She has for the past six years been director of the Reston Association's Open Space Department which manages Reston's lakes, parks, and about fifty miles of paved and natural surface bridle paths, trails, and pathways. She holds degrees from Goshen College and the University of Illinois.
Courtesy of Reston Association

Nancy Held was one of the Reston children who grew up taking part in educational programs designed by Vernon Walker, such as this bulb-planting in 1969. In 1980, she began to work for RHOA as the staff naturalist. Living and growing up in Reston influenced Nancy's choice of career.
Photograph by Daniels. Courtesy of Reston Association

Nancy Held Herwig, "Nature Nancy" as she is fondly called, moved to Reston with her family in 1968 when she was nine. She remembers as an elementary school student taking nature walks led by Vernon Walker, Reston's first director of environmental management. After graduation from West Virginia University with a degree in Parks and Recreation, she worked at RHOA Day Camp and then as a naturalist. Here she shows a child how to turn the earth for planting a garden. Nancy and her staff design and put on programs of nature appreciation, preservation, and education that have grown as dramatically as Reston itself. She enjoys personal involvement with youth programs such as Nature Tots, Ranger Rick, and Junior Trailblazers.
Courtesy of Reston Association

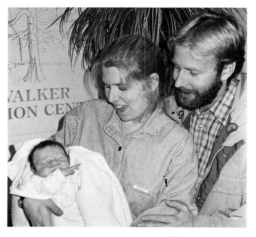

Even though Kyle Herwig is shown here as a newborn (birthdate January 19, 1989) it is clear that he will be given a good environmental education by his parents, Nancy and Craig Herwig. As he grows up, he will learn about Adopt-a-Path, Hug-a-Tree, and numerous other programs that the Reston Association sponsors to encourage individual responsibility for one's own corner of the world.
Photograph by Deborah Odell Moss. Courtesy of the Reston Association

The North County Human Services building opened on Cameron Glen Drive August 17, 1987. Within the building are offices of the County Health Department, Juvenile Court, Community Mental Health, Reston Herndon Senior Center, Human Services Office, Information and Referral, and Substance Abuse services.
Courtesy of the photographer, Linda Rutledge

Hikers from the RHOA summer program in 1976 watched the Great Falls of the Potomac River from an overlook. This is the cascade after which Thomas Fairfax's Great Falls Manor on which Reston is built, was named.
Photograph by Abbie Edwards

Families hiked on part of Reston's pathway system near Colts Neck Road and Hunters Woods Village Center in 1983.
Photograph by James Kirby.
Courtesy of the Reston Association

A group of students at Terraset gather under the solar collectors on the roof of this innovative earth sheltered elementary school in Reston.
   Courtesy of the Reston Land Corporation

11

A Sense of Community

From the first occupancy, Reston residents enjoyed the new adventure. There was a great deal of "pioneering spirit" among the early settlers of Reston. They knew they were conducting an unusual experiment and most of them enjoyed being a part of it. Robert Simon enjoyed knowing this about the people who shared his dream. When the fountain was turned on for the first time in Lake Anne in the spring of 1965, Simon announced that everyone who lived in Reston on that day belonged to the "FFRs"—the First Families of Reston.

Articulate members of the community—and there are many of them—are well represented by Tom Grubisich who has described some of the changes which have taken place. He is editor of the western Fairfax County/Reston newspaper, *The Connection*, a journalist with excellent credentials, and a long-time Reston resident and observer. He has summed up the feelings of many Reston residents beginning with the time when Gulf Reston took over from Simon:

There was fear that Reston would become a suburb. It is a well designed place, but some of the dreams and objectives some of us had at the time were incomplete. Communities grow and cannot be entirely planned by planners and designers. Reston went through a lot of ups and downs. What we have now is a town with a much more complex, diversified, and, I think, ultimately more interesting texture than the original Reston. We have discovered that the original Reston was as a matter of fact not as well designed and planned as we thought it was. Lake Anne Plaza is not a practical design. It does not have the critical mass that attracts customers. Offices and stores are too small—some get no sunlight . . . We will have to see how it can come up from the bottom and see how it can rise again—a renaissance. Lake Anne Center is stunning. It will come back.

There are some unintended consequences for the Simon plan. People are more ornery than we thought they were. They're not going to accept a plan laid out in great detail 20 years ago. I used to believe in the total plan, worked out in great detail. But now I realize there has to be a mix of ideas. No one person or group can satisfactorily determine the ultimate outcome.

Fred Flaxman, who had been on Simon's staff and was one of the most vocal residents opposing Gulf's takeover, admitted after Mobil's takeover that Gulf had developed the Reston community much better than anyone expected and that Reston was far superior to boring American suburbs. He thought Gulf Reston's development lacked the attention to detail that Simon gave it, and experimentation had been greatly reduced as emphasis changed from building the ideal community to building houses that would sell. But the good quality of overall development, he thought, still compared very favorably to the rest of the United States—it was still a model community under Gulf Reston and he felt confident that Mobil would continue the effort.

The Printed Word

There are many factors which affect everyday life in any community. One is the printed word. Reston is serviced by two local newspapers. *The Reston Times* weekly was in the beginning a monthly publication, started in November 1965 in their home by Restonians Mr. and Mrs. Ralph Segman with an 8 1/2 by 11 format, stapled. The paper was purchased a year later by Arthur W. Arundel, went to two issues per month and then to its present weekly publication.

The Connection, a newspaper with a free delivered circulation, was begun in September 1981, "to try to capture the spirit and passion of Reston." The editors, Restonians Paul Clancy, formerly of the *Washington Star*, and Tom Grubisich, formerly of *The Washington Post*, wanted to be the clearinghouse, the heart, lungs and mind of Reston, not necessarily the newspaper of record. The community response continues to be enthusiastic.

Carolyn Lindberg and Janet Hays began publishing the community directory called *A Place Called Reston* in 1967. The first edition had forty pages listing four hundred residents and thirty shops and services. Nancy Larson bought the directory from them in 1976. She has continued to expand it as Reston has grown. The 574-page 1989 directory listed between twelve and thirteen thousand residences, and 1,421 businesses. Her company, New Town Publications, produces two other annual directories and a Reston map.

The Reston Association publishes periodicals to keep the public informed including the *Pathways* newsletter which comes out six times a year. It is sent to every household in Reston. The Association also produces periodic informational brochures, pathways maps, fact sheets, the *User's Guides* and regularly updated literature on PLUS Services offerings including sports programs, summer youth programs, outreach activities for new members, and audio-visual presentations.

The monthly *Center Stage* newsletter with infor-mation on cultural and athletic programs and events is sent to each household by the Reston Community Center.

In the spring of 1984, a group of thirteen Reston women who owned their own businesses organized the Network of Entrepreneurial Women (NEW) and in December of that year began to publish a monthly newsletter called *NEW Trends*. Their membership has expanded greatly since to include entrepreneurial women in Maryland, the District of Columbia, and Northern Virginia.

Efforts to establish and continue the monthly *Restonian* magazine have been made by several hopeful publishers.

Books and Beyond

Libraries have long fostered a sense of place, not just because of the pleasant variety of reading materials, but also the opportunity to meet friends and neighbors and to do occasional volunteer assisting in the community. All of these experiences are available at Reston's three libraries.

The Carter Glass branch is the smallest in Fairfax County's public library system. It was named for a Virginian who served in elective and appointive positions in state and federal government for forty-seven years. Opened in a storefront on Washington Plaza on April 17, 1966, it was one of Bob Simon's prized amenities in the early development of Reston.

As Reston's population grew, a second library was opened at Hunters Woods Plaza in 1974. It became a regional library with increases in size in both 1978 and 1980. When the new Reston Regional Library opened on Bowman Towne Drive at Town Center, Hunters Woods became a mini-library mainly serving the area around the village center.

The Reston Regional Library opened on September 9, 1985, and serves as the community's reference source, keeping pace with today's technology. Among its 140,000 volumes are children's books, large print materials, books on tape, specialized encyclopedias and other reference works, video and audio cassettes, compact discs, records, and more than three hundred magazines and news services. Reston Regional Library offers complete information services, including access to hundreds of computer data bases. This information includes directories, abstracts, or, in some cases, even full texts of articles. A professionally-trained staff uses computer-assisted information retrieval to find in seconds what otherwise might take weeks. The multi-media center provides video and audio access, with cable access available within the next two years.

One of Fairfax County's six regional facilities, the library provides a beautiful setting which helps to fulfill its intended function. The thirty thousand square foot building contains clerestory windows to reinforce its passive solar heating system. Special features include meeting rooms, study carrels, a quiet study room, and lounge seating for two hundred people.

Numerous free programs take place throughout the year, among them special events and story times for children, workshops and lectures for adults, on-going book sales, and films for all ages. Programs are listed in the monthly *Calendar*, available at the information desk.

Public Schools

In a community like Reston, with a high achievement level in formal education, it is natural that the citizens should be deeply interested in schools at all levels, for both youths and adults.

Herndon High School served Reston's total secondary school population until 1978. Since then, students from northern Reston have continued to attend there. Herndon has had a good share of National Merit and National Achievement Scholars and a Presidential Scholar. Numerous other scholarships are awarded each year. The athletic teams have been competitive. Herndon first opened in 1908 and their exhibit case has athletic trophies dating from 1926. Their present building was completed in 1966. District, regional, and state championships have been theirs in past years in baseball and basketball, boys' gymnastics and track, girls' basketball, golf, and tennis. Herndon was the first Fairfax County school to have a soccer program.

After South Lakes High School opened in September 1978, it became the principal secondary school for Reston. Students also excelled at the new school, earning academic and athletic honors every year. There have been National Merit and National Achievement Scholars and a Presidential Scholar at South Lakes. Numerous other scholarships have been awarded. Athletic honors have included a number of local, district, and regional championships for both girls and boys in gymnastics, cross country, track, basketball, and soccer.

One of the reasons for high achievement in both schools is the high standards of Fairfax County's School Board and administration policies for the tenth largest public school system in the United States. This fact was well expressed by former South Lakes Principal, George Felton: "In Reston schools, computer literacy is as important as conventional literacy. Students today need both."

Herndon and Langston Hughes in Reston, named after the famous black poet and novelist, are the intermediate schools. Dogwood, Forest Edge, Hunters Woods, Lake Anne, Sunrise Valley, Terraset, and Neil Armstrong, named for the famous astronaut, serve as Reston's elementary schools. A seventh, Aldrin, (named for Edwin Eugene (Buzz Aldrin, Jr., also an astronaut) is proposed in North Point Village.

Civic Affairs
Reston Community Association

Since fall 1967, volunteers have built the Reston Community Association into a powerhouse that defies conventional wisdom about what is needed to succeed: RCA has no permanent "home," no staff, no current dues structure, and no official status.

RCA makes Reston a better place. Formidability without financing is perhaps its most unusual aspect.

RCA's highly-regarded Planning and Zoning Committee (P & Z) is a watchdog which sometimes rejects, sometimes amends, sometimes fully approves Reston-area development plans—major success follows most recommendations.

The Transportation Committee has hastened solutions to area traffic and road problems. It often initiates ideas, many times working in concert with other groups.

RCA leadership helped bring to Reston comprehensive health care, at least four public schools ahead of original county scheduling, and a variety of other services. It initially sponsored the Reston commuter bus, which Metro later absorbed (in its earliest days RCA volunteers worked the telephones each morning to tabulate the day's ridership, reported by volunteer busmeisters).

RCA has collaborated with other organizations in pursuit of affordable housing, exploration of local governance as an option, a nursing home for the elderly, expanded childcare, and many other programs.

RCA's revenues come chiefly from sponsoring the annual Reston Festival, when the president is elected to a one-year term and seven of fourteen two-year Board seats are filled. Any resident sixteen or older can run for office and vote.

Knowing their efforts make a difference is an exhilarating reward for participants. The depth of RCA's concerns and quality of its contributions have earned respect far beyond Reston's borders.

One of the jointly planned activities that RCA has been involved in was the Reston Issues Forum, first held in November 1987 as part of the celebration on the occasion of Reston's fifty thousandth resident. The cosponsors were the Reston Association, the Reston Board of Commerce and the Reston Community Association. For eight hours, nearly two hundred Reston citizens worked to identify the community's strengths and weaknesses, its opportunities and challenges. Topics included the need to balance master plan goals such as preservation of trees, beauty, amenities, and a sense of community, with the rapid urbanization taking place with attention needed for roads, increasing traffic, affordable housing, and childcare. The question was raised as to whether the residents would have a stronger voice with more direct government under town or city status, rather than being a part of a much larger county, Fairfax.

Live, Work, Play

Many families in Reston have fulfilled Bob Simon's dream for life in an ideal new town. The Don Baldersons are good examples of the live-work-play concept. Don and Jean met and married when both were employees of Reston. Each had children by previous marriages, so they bought a large house for all in Reston. Gradually, as the seven children grew, they all participated actively in outdoor sports as well as having part-time jobs. Many days when baseball games were being played by different youthful members of the family, the busy parents would finish work and share responsibilities, transporting the different age groups to different playing fields and a couple of kids to their places of employment. They all loved Reston and felt in the early days that they knew everyone and that Reston was really home.

The people who live, work and play in Reston are all individuals with their own unique combinations of backgrounds, education, experiences, likes and dislikes. It would be impossible to explore in detail the lives of all in order to illustrate the variety represented there. Many have found that Reston is a place to live, to leave, and to return to, a place that is home for all ages, as anthropologist Margaret Mead stated it would be when she visited the community in 1973.

Examples of two elected community leaders,

Harry Mustakos, 1982-1983 president of RCA and Judi Ushio, 1979-1983 president of the RHOA Board of Directors are good illustrations.

Harry and Diana Mustakos became interested in Reston in 1962 when they came out to see the Fairfax Hunt at Sunset Hills. By 1966 they had moved into an area within Lake Anne Village. Later, he was in Vietnam for two years, in Thailand and in Laos, but Reston was always home. Wherever the family was stationed, they always received the *Reston Times* and kept up with happenings in the community. They returned in 1973, moved to the Dogwood area, then later settled in the South Lakes area. There are three children and the Mustakos family members think Reston is a great place to live both because of neighborhood schools and also because it is like being in a resort year 'round—you don't need to leave home for a vacation. There is housing for every individual need throughout the entire life cycle—apartment, townhouse, detached home, luxury condo, and Fellowship Houses. Harry recalls a resident complaining during the early days about the developer taking meadows and "virgin forest." "As I look around at the more maturing developed areas, I remember then the beautiful trees were little bushes and now they form a large forest themselves."

He feels the RCA is a channel for the residents of Reston to manifest a continuing concern for informed, responsible participation in the growth of the New Town. A sense of trust and mutual respect have developed between the community and developer, who has continued with the basic Reston concept. Continuity in the planning and zoning issues is most important to insure that individual developers are held to the common goals. RCA has a responsible voice to speak to county officials regarding issues involving the greatest good for the community as a whole. He thinks Supervisor Pennino is doing well representing Reston and working well with the competing approaches to solutions to problems which inevitably arise. He believes there are many talented volunteers out in the community who have particular interests which could involve them in RCA activities. If they can just be approached on a personal basis, there would be more involvement in accomplishment of shared goals.

Unlike the typical reactionary citizens association, RCA's involvement in the development process, from the developer's viewpoint, has been a positive force in recent years, discussing issues

Arthur W. Arundel purchased the Reston Times from Mr. and Mrs. Ralph Segman of Hunters Woods in November 1966, and he has published it as a weekly newspaper since October 1969. A graduate of Harvard with a major in government, he is also a Marine Corps veteran of Korea and Vietnam. "Nick" Arundel was founder of ArCom, Inc., which publishes ten Northern Virginia community and county weekly newspapers and is himself a journalist. He was a cofounder and first chairman of the Board of George Mason University. Photograph in 1984 by Chase Studios.

Courtesy of Arundel Communications

Thomas Grubisich is a long-time Reston resident, former Washington Post *feature writer, and a cofounder and editor of* The Connection *newspapers.*

Courtesy of The Connection

Nancy Larson bought the community directory, A Place Called Reston in 1976 from Carolyn Lindberg and Janet Hays. It has been published annually since 1977. Her New Town Publications company publishes two other annual directories and a Reston map.

Courtesy of Nancy Larson

Long-time Reston resident Carlos C. Campbell is the author of New Towns: Another Way to Live, *published by the Reston Publishing Company.*

Courtesy of Carlos C. Campbell

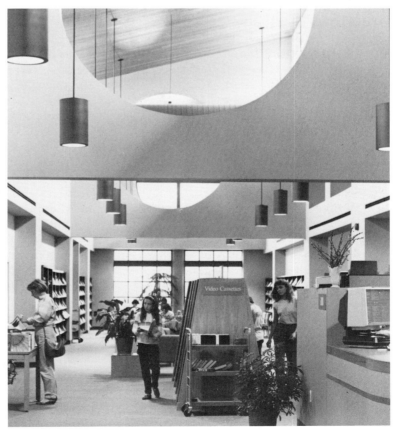

Reston Regional Library, designed by architect Mark Baughman of LBC&W was opened on Bowman Towne Drive at Town Center September 9, 1985. The Friends of the Library group had strongly supported the construction of this new facility, and the circulation figures have confirmed their statement of need.

Photograph by Georgette Blanchfield.
Courtesy of the Fairfax County
Public Library

with the developer in advance of hearings, providing input, and often supporting zoning actions at the appropriate times. Community and developer alike have matured and cooperation has replaced confrontation to benefit both sides.

Judi and David Ushio came from Utah in 1971, rented a unit at Fairway Apartments in Reston, and worked in Washington. They left in 1972 for jobs in San Francisco, where they lived for nearly five years. When a job opportunity opened up again in Washington, they moved back to the area, looked at other places, but decided Reston was where they really wanted to be, and bought a townhouse in Bentana Woods. By this time they had three daughters who would be attending Reston schools. Judi was interested in finding out what was going on in the community and her neighbors encouraged her to attend the Tall Oaks Village Council, which she did. She was president of the RHOA Board of Directors from 1979 to 1983. She was involved in issues like the referendum for limited town status, which was defeated at the polls, the takeover by RHOA of the lake dams, the VEPCO transmission lines, the Fairfax County Parkway and rehabilitation of the Stonegate complex. Another important issue was the building of a RHOA maintenance facility for offices and proper storage and service of equipment and materials to support operations which are represented today by a 1989 RHOA operating budget of over $6 million. She ran a strong public education campaign in order to obtain the residents' approval for the Association's first indebtedness which the construction of the new structure required.

In these days of space exploration, one family is particularly interesting. T. Keith Glennan and his wife Ruth have lived in Reston since 1965, when they purchased a Waterview Cluster townhouse. They and their four children and their families have enjoyed the experience of growth with a "new town" spirit. The Glennans now live in Heron House.

Before moving to Reston, Keith had held many key positions in the country's scientific community, one of the most significant being the first administrator of the National Aeronautics and Space Administration (NASA) from 1958 to 1961. With the selection of Reston as the location for NASA's Space Station program in 1987, New Town Publications named their 1988 Reston directory, *A Place Called Reston*, the T. Keith Glennan Edition.

From its inception, Reston was a place where people could rent or buy a home regardless of their race, creed, color, or ethnic origin. Open housing was a policy of Bob Simon's. As was the case with the white residents, the economic cross section of black residents ranged from those who lived in federally assisted housing to those who lived in luxury homes; the majority were successful professionals in many fields including highly placed government executives, doctors, dentists, attorneys, corporation managers, professional athletes, airline ticket agents, real estate salesmen, school teachers, principals, engineers, technicians, and construction workers. The black population comprised about 9 percent of Reston's total number of inhabitants. Restonian Carlos Campbell wrote in his book *New Towns: Another Way to Live:* "Reston is a rare instance where the racial mix is close to the national average and one that allows blacks to enjoy some real visibility in a predominantly white environment. For many blacks, the experience of living among whites is entirely new and one that may cause some psychological discomfort." The residents' attitudes were to a great extent shaped by the knowledge that Reston has been an open community from the beginning and most people had moved there with a willingness to take full part in the experiment of living together amicably and cooperatively.

Black Focus was an educational and cultural organization of black Restonians which was activated during the late 1960s. The group sponsored the Reston Black Arts Festival annually from 1969 to 1976. The event was briefly revived in 1982, and programs were presented at Lake Anne Village Center and at the Reston Community Center.

In 1983, the organization initiated an informal sister city relationship between Reston and Nyeri, Kenya, as a means of fostering cultural and technical exchanges, and through them, world peace.

As part of their Black History Month observance in February 1988, the Reston Community Center held a public forum whose topic was "Blacks and Class: What Separates Us?" The moderator was Maria Harris, executive director of Rising Star Productions and a professional broadcaster. Prominent Reston and area residents served on the panel and shared their viewpoints. The forum's stimulating presentation built hopes for more of such opportunities in the future.

There is a sense of humor 'round about Reston. For example, perhaps it is the common experience of the residents' associations with federal government jobs which provides a daily serving of "alphabet soup." In addition to FHOA, SHOA, and RHOA, there have been or are now FISH,

'Remind me never to be a principal.'

Terraset has been an ongoing attraction to visitors both domestic and foreign, since its first construction phase. After the school opened, a steady stream of guests of all nationalities continued to tour the innovative structure designed by Doug Carter. It was a winner of architectural awards.
Cartoon, 1978, courtesy of the
Reston Times

LANK, the Lake Anne Nursery and Kindergarten, moved from Lake Anne to its own building. An architectural award was given to its designers, KDA Architects in 1973.
Courtesy of Reston Land Corporation

A holly tree was planted near Reston's Lake Anne Elementary School in March 1970 by the Honorable Branko Pesic, Mayor of Belgrade, Yugoslavia, in a special symbolic ceremony of international friendship.
Photograph by Daniels.
Courtesy of Peter McCandless

A LANK student shares in a demonstration of law and order put on for his class by a friendly Fairfax County police officer in 1976.
Photograph by Abbie Edwards

165

RIBS, RATS, COLTS, RUMP, LANK, USE, RAFT, GRACE, and PALS. At a time in 1979 when a lot of houses were for sale all at once, and signs announcing the fact were seen everywhere on rights-of-way, cluster entrances, and street corners, a resident wrote the *Reston Times* that the RES in Reston stood for *Real Estate Sign!* And then there was the funny remark made by a resident when the developer changed in 1978: "It's not enough to have been enGulfed; now we'll be imMobilized!"

Reston Community Center

After two fruitless attempts to build a community center in Reston, a Community Center Task Force was formed in April 1972 to investigate the need for and the feasibility of such a project. A volunteer group of residents, with a much larger group who served on several working committees, the Task Force received financial assistance from RHOA to retain an architect to prepare a preliminary plan.

Constructive suggestions were submitted by individuals and organizations, and the Task Force and architects Jansons, Roberts, Taylor and Associates produced a detailed proposal in the fall of 1974. It included a site, a proposed program, an architectural concept, and the means for financing the center through creation of a Special Service District (Small District No. 5) which was formed on March 24, 1975, by the Fairfax County Board of Supervisors. It was established in order that bonds might be sold to pay for the Community Center if voters within the district approved a bond referendum, which they did. The boundaries of the district, generally the Reston area, were established after public advertisement and hearings.

The grand opening of the Reston Community Center on May 20, 1979, was a great success. Bob Simon was a special guest speaker who endorsed the idea as a great unifying opportunity to pull North and South Reston together. Centreville Supervisor Martha Pennino urged her constituents to enjoy using the building and to "breathe into it a heart and soul . . . keep the spirit alive." It was a real community celebration. Music was provided by the Reston Chorale. A tapestry designed and executed by artist Hildegarde Klene had been commissioned by the Reston Rotary Club and was hung in the theater lobby, dedicated by them to the memory of the late George Jansons, architect of the Community Center building and a member of RHOA's Architectural Board of Review since its inception.

Bringing people together and developing a sense of community guide the mission of the Reston Community Center. Programs and facilities are designed to meet the community's cultural, economic, educational, recreational and social needs.

The Center facility features a fully-equipped, 266-seat theater, twenty-five meter indoor pool and diving well, photography darkroom, woodshop, community social hall, snack bar, art studio, dance studio, and seven meeting and classrooms, available for rental to the community. People of all ages can participate in the myriad classes, special events, holiday activities, aquatics, performances, dances, potlucks, films, concerts, and receptions offered at the Community Center and throughout Reston.

The Center maintains a registry of community information and referral resources. It is "home" to a variety of clubs and organizations and offers volunteer opportunities through the Friends of the Reston Community Center.

Housed at the east end of Hunters Woods Plaza, the Center facility was built in 1979 with locally-raised funds. The residents and businesses of Small Tax District No. 5 believed so strongly in the Center's purposes they voted to tax themselves to pay for the Center's operations. The Center remains close to the community through its eleven-member Board of Governors, nine adults and two teens who must reside in the District and are elected to staggered terms each October. The volunteer Board establishes policies and represents the interests of the community in fulfilling the Center's mission. A professional staff supports the daily operations and programs.

The Reston Community Center has had three executive directors: Dan Weimer, 1978 to 1985; Peter Gray, 1985 to 1987; and Bryn Carpenter Pavek, 1987 to the present. The extensive use of the Center averages 1,866 people per week.

Reston Board Of Commerce

The Reston Board of Commerce encourages the growth of the business community, provides stimulating activities for its members, and creates a dynamic forum for the exchange of ideas among Reston business and professional people for the enlightenment and the betterment of the entire business community.

For the past quarter century, Reston has been a wonderful place to start a business and watch it

A meeting of the Reston Community Association's Board of Director's is here being televised as are all such meetings. Discussing housing needs in Reston are, from left going clockwise, Connie Pettinger, executive director of Reston Interfaith; Janet Howell, RCA president; Kevin Burke, RCA vice president; Katherine Danish; Glenda Amick; Avis Burtis; Peggy Axelrod (almost totally obscured); Betty Fingerette; and Baba Freeman, second vice president (back to camera). The hand belongs to Gary Braithwaite.
Courtesy of Janet Howell

Lee Libman, who has been a resident since Reston's beginning, is still involved in the local activities of the Lake Anne Village Council and the Planning and Zoning Committee of the Reston Community Association.
Courtesy of the Photographer, Arvil Daniels

Harry and Diana Mustakos are shown here in 1983. Harry was elected president of the Reston Community Association for 1982-1983 and 1983-1984.
Courtesy of Harry Mustakos

The Francis Steinbauer family, residents of Reston since 1967, are left to right, Linda Slingluff (financé of Kenneth), Kenneth, Francis, Michele, Jane, Jennifer, and James.
Courtesy of Francis Steinbauer

flourish. Reston today has more than fifteen hundred places of employment providing more than thirty-three thousand jobs. With nearly twelve million square feet of office space, Reston now is the second largest "downtown" in the Commonwealth.

In 1982, residents involved in Reston's business life knew the time had come to complete the business contribution to the Reston concept. They hammered out by-laws and forged a fledging RBC. The organization has grown by emphasizing the integration of large and small businesses' interests and promoting members' active role in community life. RBC's business activities include educational seminars, lectures, youth job fairs, local networking opportunities, and the School Partnership Program, and their annual, highly successful trade expo. RBC's commitment to human services is expressed through its involvement and investment in programs including the creation of the Child Care Consortium, cooperative benefits options for small businesses, a scholarship program, the Benevolent Fund, and encouragement of member's community participation.

With more than five hundred members today, RBC promotes the economic, industrial, professional, retail, cultural, and civic welfare of the greater Reston area and enjoys the largest membership of any comparable area organization. Application for membership is open to firms doing business in Reston.

The Arts

The arts have always been important in Reston. Two organizations, the Reston Community Players and the Reston Chorale, were both founded in 1966. Many of the early residents recall the first production of the Reston Players, shortly after the town was officially dedicated in May 1966. It was an original musical, *The Greatest Game in Town*, performed at the Hunters Woods stable, which is now gone. About four hundred people participated in the production, cleaning out the stalls, set-building, acting, selling tickets, and offering Reston home-cooked meals to ticket purchasers before curtain time. It was Reston's first largescale citizen effort and it was a roaring success. In October and November, the thespians gave their first play, *Dracula*. It, too, was well received and had an unusual professional touch. George Zacko, Reston's dentist, fabricated fangs for the ferocious Count. The first three presentations of the Reston Players were produced by Frank Matthews, who

was also the Players' first president. With Bob Simon's encouragement, he decided to develop a commercial venture and his Hayloft Dinner Theater in Manassas was the result.

The Reston Players brought honor to the community when they walked off with top honors in the D. C. Annual One-Act Play Tournament in the spring of 1968. They received three prizes: Best Play—*Waiting for Godot*, Best Director—Frank Johns, and Best Performer—Robert Perce.

Before the Reston Community Center was opened in 1979, the Players gave productions in various places: Brown's Chapel, Lake Anne Hall, and once, a large circus tent where *The Threepenny Opera* was given in 1968. When the tent was destroyed in a storm, the cast performed under the stars. Their performances are now given in the theater at the Reston Community Center. Playbills from past years included many familiar works such as *Sleep of Prisoners* (1969), *Private Lives* (1977), *Death of a Salesman* (1982), *The Mousetrap* (1985), and Gilbert and Sullivan's *Pirates of Penzance* (1988).

The Reston Chorale began giving programs at Christmas in 1966 under the direction of James Christian Pfohl, founder of the Brevard Music School in North Carolina. Simon had brought Dr. Pfohl to Reston with the idea of establishing a professional school for the performing arts but necessary funding was never available to get it started. When Dr. Pfohl left in 1973, he was replaced by Wilbert A. King, followed by Mary Gay Craig, who died in 1982 in an automobile accident. The current director of the Chorale is Fred Wygal. The group is composed of one hundred amateur and semi-professional singers and performs both traditional and contemporary music at the Reston Community Center and at many other places giving four concerts during the year.

Reston has been known for award-winning architecture through the years and special appreciation for livability once took the form of a celebration for an architect. One of Simon's personal selections for Reston had been the architect Louis Sauer, who designed the Golf Course Island townhouses. The response of the residents after they had enjoyed living there for a few years was noteworthy. In 1971, the Golf Course Island Association Board decided to invite the architect back to Reston to witness the livability of the prize-winning houses he had designed. He, his wife and baby came down from New York for a day, and were shown through some of the houses, decorated in both traditional and contemporary styles.

Immediately after the United States astronauts returned to earth with Apollo II and the first moon rocks in July 1969, these Reston children set up their own commerical enterprise.
Photograph by William A. Graham.
Courtesy of Peter McCandless

T. Keith Glennan and his wife Ruth have lived in Reston since 1965, when they purchased a Waterview Cluster town-house. They and their four children and their families have enjoyed the experience of growth with a "new town" spirit. The Glennans now live in Heron House. Before moving to Reston, Keith had held many key positions in the country's scientific community, one of the most significant being the first administrator of the National Aeronautics and Space Administration (NASA) from 1958 to 1961. With the selection of Reston as the location for NASA's Space Station program in 1987, New Town Publications named their 1988 Reston directory, A Place Called Reston, the T. Keith Glennan Edition.
Courtesy of Ruth and Keith Glennan

Yellow ribbons, American flags, and a community parade welcomed home Reston's John Graves in February 1981 after he and other hostages had been released from Iranian captivity.
Photograph by Linda Rutledge.
Courtesy of Reston Land Corporation

Jean Balderson (seated left) and family members are seen here at the wedding of her daughter, Robin, in 1983. They are, left to right, Carol Gustavson McGinnis, Melissa Balderson, Laurence McGinnis, Alexander Matjan, Donald Balderson, Jean Balderson, Sharon Melcher, Robin Walesiewicz, John Walesiewicz, Jeffrey Balderson, Laura McGinnis, and Robert Melcher.
Courtesy of Jean Balderson

The Board then gave the Sauers a dinner at the Lake Anne Hall. It was truly an "appreciation day." Sauer told his hosts how much he had enjoyed the experience, especially since no one had ever before invited him back to see houses he had designed.

The arts have an important place in Reston community life. The Greater Reston Arts Center (GRACE) was incorporated as a nonprofit organization in the Commonwealth of Virginia in December 1973. It was the realization of goals central to concepts underlying the founding of the New Town of Reston. GRACE occupied The Gallery on the ground floor of Heron House. In this location, it was very accessible and a vital part of Washington Plaza on Lake Anne. Ten or more exhibits were held each year. An Art in the Schools program begun in 1977 has been a major focus for both the staff and Board of Directors and has received attention and commendation. In 1979, a Gallery Shop was opened which expanded the opportunities for local and area artists and craftsmen to show and sell their work. Anne Thomas became executive director of GRACE in January 1981. Her art book *Colors from the Earth*, had just been published by Van Nostrand Reinhold in 1980.

A special children's art exchange was held cooperatively with the Peoples' Republic of China in May 1986. Fifty art works by students ages five to fourteen on the theme of celebrations were selected from Reston's elementary and intermediate schools and sent to Beijing. An equal number of art works were sent from China for exhibition in Reston.

The Sunset Hills Land Company made a gift of a brick warehouse (the old Wiehle Town Hall) in 1985 and some funding to help GRACE with renovation for use as a headquarters. In February 1988, the organization moved to temporary quarters in the Town Center Office Building. The membership of five hundred hopes that GRACE will be in its new home by the summer of 1990. The Reston Art Gallery now occupies the former GRACE facilities at Heron House.

Two other arts groups are active in Reston. The focus for the Reston Institute for the Arts (RIA) is to offer older students a well-rounded theater experience. Dance, music, and drama are offered at the Reston Community Center and the Reston Community Players workshop. Several productions are given during the school year and RIA has received excellent notices for imaginative, well-performed presentations.

League of Reston Artists membership covers arts and crafts as well as fine arts, exhibited by members in the USGS building and doctor's offices. Meetings are held monthly, except during the summer. All artisans are welcome, no matter what the discipline.

Not all artistic events occur within the organizations devoted to the arts in Reston. In February 1988, a delegation of Russians including artists and writers from the Soviet Peace Committee visited Washington. Four of them came to see the New Town of Reston about which they had read in their native country. Sculptor Zurab Tzereteli was among them and so impressed was he with what he saw that he presented a large book devoted to his work to the Reston Regional Library. He also offered to donate a thirty-foot sculpture of a man "breaking through the wall of misunderstanding" to be placed in front of the library as a gesture of international friendship. This aroused a great deal of interest and controversy within the community which ultimately resulted in a group trip to Russia in July to visit the artist at his estate overlooking the city of Tbilisi. Centreville Supervisor Martha Pennino led the visitors who included, among others, artist Tom Hutchins; Michael LeMay, chairman of the Design Review Board; and Elfriede Walker. Mrs. Pennino, believing the proposed work to be overwhelming in size and obvious in its political statement, selected a piece of sculpture from his book which the group did like. However, the artist's proposal was withdrawn, to the disappointment of the visiting delegation from Reston.

Realizing that questions like this might arise in the future, the Reston Association later appointed a permanent Outdoor Arts Committee to act if and when needed.

Sports and Recreation

Orientation to water and water-related recreation is very strong in Reston. With four man-made lakes in place—Anne, Audubon, Thoreau, and Newport—there has been great visual enhancement of the community. Lake Anne and its plaza have been photogenic from the beginning of Reston and have often been seen as a design symbol for the community. There are some large fish in the lakes, grown from the original stock placed there and many a fisherman, young and old, has tried to catch them. In addition to the occasional sailing regatta, the old booze barges—the party boats—there are pleasant experiences of the Sun-

The Common Ground Bus shown here in 1976, later became the Reston Internal Bus System (RIBS). Tommy Rosamond leased Reston's first gasoline station from Gulf Oil Corporation in 1968 and by providing gas and service, kept the internal bus running during its most difficult years.

Photograph by Al Whitley.
Courtesy of Reston Land Corporation

Open Air Market entertainment at Lake Anne in 1978.
Courtesy of the photographer, Abbie Edwards

This view from the Common Ground Coffee House in 1977 looks toward the fountain designed by James Rossant.
Courtesy of the photographer, Abbie Edwards

An artist at the Open Air Market at Lake Anne in 1975.
Photograph by Abbie Edwards

day Afternoon Lake Anne Rubber Rafting Association whose members anchor out in the middle with their coolers and while away pleasant afternoons. Swimming in the lakes is not permitted—numerous swimming pools with lifeguards are provided for this purpose. Lakes are open to all residents for boating.

The Fairfax County Park Authority owns Baron Cameron and Lake Fairfax parks. The Fairfax County Recreation Department supervises active recreation programs for Reston and other county residents in these parks and at the Reston public schools. Privately sponsored team organizations for baseball, soccer, and other sports also share facilities of the Reston Association, the schools, and the county park and recreation systems.

In addition to operating practically all kinds of water craft on the lakes, except for the gasoline-powered types, Restonians participate in or watch numerous other sports. A number of Washington Redskins players live in Reston and this heightens an already lively interest in watching professional football. Tennis, soccer, Little League baseball, softball, youth football, basketball, volleyball, racquetball, hockey, sledding, skiing, ice-skating, swimming, bicycling, fishing, running, and walking all have their devotees. The annual triathalon, which has been held since 1984, is a race in which all of the contestants have to swim, bike, and run.

Health and Human Services

Embry Rucker, an Episcopal minister, established the Common Ground Foundation in the early 1970s. With its corps of dedicated volunteers, the Foundation for years provided many of Reston's community services including the Coffee House, a day care center, bus service, information service, baby sitting, rooms for rent, part-time jobs, and help with runaways. It mobilized Reston's human resources and coordinated efforts with appropriate county agencies.

The Reston Interfaith Housing Corporation was organized in January 1970 to address housing needs and services for low and moderate income families and families displaced from urban renewal areas. Other purposes stated were to provide housing and services including nonprofit hospital and health care for the elderly and handicapped. The six organizations who originally sponsored the program were the Episcopal Congregation of Reston, Fairfax Unitarian Church, Northern Virginia Hebrew Congregation, Redeemer United

Methodist Church, St. Thomas à Becket of the Reston Catholic Community, and Washington Plaza Baptist Church. Douglas Reans was the first executive director; Constance L. Pettinger succeeded him in 1982.

Reston Interfaith, Inc., was formed in 1984 as a successor organization with a broader mission. Community services now include operation, under contract with Fairfax County, of the Embry Rucker Shelter for the Homeless, and the Laurel Learning Center, a developmental day care center for ninety children ages 2 1/2 to 10. The facility is located in part of the old library space at the Hunters Woods Village Center. Other community services include food and nutrition programs with an emergency food pantry and weekly surplus food; job counseling and placement; youth programs; clothing resource center (new clothes for children); support and development of affordable housing; social services information and referral; and community outreach programs. The office is located in Hunters Woods Plaza.

The fifteen religious organizations who currently sponsor Interfaith efforts are: All Dulles Area Muslim Society (ADAMS), Christ the Servant Lutheran Church, Good Shepherd Lutheran Church, Heritage Fellowship United Church of Christ, Martin Luther King, Jr. Church, Northern Virginia Hebrew Congregation, Reston Friends Meeting, St. Anne's Episcopal Church, St. John Neumann Catholic Church, St. Thomas à Becket Catholic Church, Shoreshim, Southview Baptist Church, Unitarian Universalist Church in Reston, United Christian Parish, and Washington Plaza Baptist Church.

Major advances in health care for the community were culmination of years of work by the developer, the Reston citizens and the county. Health care was upgraded when "ACCESS" opened in May 1977. The Ambulatory Care Center-Emergency Service System, which is an emergency care extension of Fairfax Hospital, had been a compromise agreed upon by numerous civic and political groups and Reston citizens who had studied the delivery of health services and decided that the population in the northwestern part of Fairfax County was not yet large enough to justify the complete hospital facility which Bill Magness had wanted to build. The Facilities Review Committee of the Comprehensive Health Planning Council of Northern Virginia rejected a proposal urged by Magness for an out-of-state firm's 120-bed Beverly hospital plan for Reston and instead approved ACCESS.

The post office in the Lakeside Pharmacy still has that "down home" feeling after all these years of operation. It is a great place to buy stamps and mail packages when there are long lines everywhere else. In this picture taken in 1989, postmistress Lynn Baker handles a package for patron Delia Gaughan.
Courtesy of the photographer, Linda Rutledge

This headquarters of the National Center for Aeromodeling and its museum of the Academy of Model Aeronautics on Samuel Morse Drive are yet another example of Reston's involvement with aerospace programs. The academy was founded in 1936 and now has a membership of over 139,000 model airplane enthusiasts worldwide. The facility was built in Reston in 1981.
Courtesy of Geoffrey Styles, Academy of Model Aeronautics

Leo Alonzo is proprietor of the Fresh Value grocery store which opened at Lake Anne Village Center in June 1983.
Courtesy of Reston Land Corporation

The original Reston Community Association-sponsored Reston Community Center Task Force is pictured here in the early 1970s with the developer's representative and the Centreville District Supervisor. Shown are, left to right; Elinor Perez, David Edwards, Sarah Glennon,

Dave Beecy, Margaret Boyd, James Allred, Elfriede Walker, Baba Freeman, Supervisor Martha Pennino, Gulf Reston's Fran Steinbauer, and the Reverend Douglas Ibach.
Photograph by Abbie Edwards

Later the Fairfax Hospital Association and the Hospital Corporation of America both had applications turned down for a facility in the Fair Oaks vicinity because of a perceived over-supply of hospital beds in the Washington metropolitan area.

However, in December of 1983, the Virginia Health Commission did approve an application by the Fairfax Hospital Association for a 125-bed nursing home, Cameron Glen, on the county-owned site next to ACCESS in Reston's Town Center.

Then the Hospital Corporation of America, based in Nashville, Tennessee, was successful in getting approval for their plan. They built, in Town Center, a 127-bed full service medical-surgical community hospital, with a 24-hour emergency room. There was strong community support for the project from Reston residents and from Reston Land Corporation. The doors opened for patients on November 10, 1986. An obstetrical unit, the Reston Hospital Maternity Center, was later approved and opened on February 14 (Valentine's Day) 1989.

The operation of the Reston Hospital Center is overseen by a local Board of Trustees chosen from among community leaders. Karl Ingebritsen is the current chairman.

The Reston/North County Community Shelter opened with provisions for individual men and women, and for families, in December 1987. The Fairfax County Board of Supervisors renamed the facility the Embry Rucker Shelter for the Homeless on May 3, 1989, because of his long-standing dedication to the welfare of Restonians and others in need of help. The human services available in Reston by this time meant a potential for the improvement in the quality of life for all residents, whatever their needs might be. Reston Interfaith, Inc., operates the shelter under a contract with Fairfax County. Jana Graves is the administrator.

The very youngest segment of the population has not been forgotten As early as 1965, the Lake Anne Nursery and Kindergarten (LANK) was begun because there was no public school kindergarten in Fairfax County at the time. Bob Simon believed that the preschooling of children was a necessary beginning for their life of learning. In 1975, Simon's daughter, Lynn Lilienthal, and her codirector Peggy Jansons, received the first county license for infant care in their PALS Early Learning Center. This was an age group for which there was a scarcity of provisions made.

The community rallied 'round in the mid 1980s

to form a childcare consortium to help solve problems for working parents.

In January of 1988 the Nyscare Center opened in the Centennial Company's Sunrise Technology Park, the first local center to rent space in an office building under newly-amended zoning regulations that automatically permit childcare activities in an office complex. Carole Nysmith is the administrator. In all, there are now twenty-one providers of various types of pre-school and day care in Reston.

Planned Community Archives

In 1984, aware of the interest in New Towns and similar projects, a group of Restonians who had realized that there were no official Reston archives, organized Planned Community Archives, Inc. Their plans are to collect Reston and other planned community archives and to encourage George Mason University and other institutions to consider curriculum planning for graduate programs in urban and suburban studies. The George Mason University Library has agreed to be the repository for the collection and an information resource, through satellite dish technology, for interested individuals and organizations worldwide. William Nicoson, who worked on federal government New Town programs in the 1970s, is chairman of the Board of Directors.

James Allred holds his 1980 Outstanding Community Service Award from the National Recreation and Parks Association for his significant contribution to the planning and building of Reston's Community Center. Pictured are, left to right, John Davis, president of the National Recreation and Parks Association; Nancy Davis, chairperson, Reston Community Center's governing board; Allred; Daniel Weimer, executive director of the center; and Larry Fones, director, Fairfax County Recreation Department.
Courtesy of Reston Community Center

Daniel Weimer was the first executive director of the Reston Community Center, which opened in 1979. He worked in Robert Simon's community in Riverton, New York, and watched and admired Reston's development. He applied for and got the job when it was first offered in October 1978 and served in the position until 1985.

Courtesy of Reston Community Center

Peter Gray was appointed executive director of the Community Center in 1985. He was a native of Indianapolis, Indiana. An ordained Episcopal priest, he specialized in social action programs and shelter for homeless people.

Courtesy of Reston Community Center

Bryn Carpenter Pavek has a degree in fine arts from Arizona State University. She came to the Reston Community Center as director in August 1987. She had previously been associated with the McLean Community Center and with the Arlington County Recreation Department's visual and performing arts. She and her husband, C. Christopher Pavek, have been Reston residents since 1985.

Courtesy of the Reston Community Center

Dancers enjoy an old-fashioned social at Reston Community Center in 1982.

Photograph by Linda Rutledge. Courtesy of Reston Community Center

175

A pie-eating contest was held at the old-fashioned social in June 1982.
Photograph by Linda Rutledge.
Courtesy of Reston Community Center

Conservation and Preservation

The primary importance of the open space, trees and design of the community overall in influencing the selection of Reston as a place to live and work is borne out by two independent opinion surveys. They were conducted in 1979 and in 1982 by Robert Charles Lesser and Company and the Dominion Research Corporation.

After Vernon Walker, director of open space management and development for RHOA, died of cancer in July 1982, Restonians read a reprint in *The Connection* of a charming article he had written some years before regarding the pleasure of discovery of natural beauty enjoyed by community members of all ages. He had been hired by Simon in March 1966 and had operated a program to foster protection of Reston's natural resources and public awareness, through dynamic educational experiences, of the need and desirability to understand and continue that protection. He summed up the program's success by writing: "Reston, then, is celebrating rather than entombing its natural resources . . . adults and children of the New Town of Reston are both discovering their natural environment, often in similar ways. Having done so, the odds must be hopeful that they will want to, that they will work to conserve it."

There is an impressive amount of evidence that individuals working together in common cause can still make a difference—can improve a community and the lifestyles of its inhabitants in their business life or leisure time activities.

Even though Reston is just this year observing its twenty-fifth anniversary of residential and commercial occupations, it has already received significant recognition as an historical site in the Commonwealth of Virginia. On November 3, 1988, Governor Gerald L. Baliles' Commission to Study Historic Preservation presented him with its final report, entitled *A Future for Virginia's Past.* The concluding paragraph of the Introduction reads, in part:

Virginia is unique among the states in that we so strongly identify ourselves through our historic resources, from our colonial heritage at Yorktown and Civil War sites in Petersburg, to our turn-of-the-century residential neighborhoods in Roanoke and the twentieth century planned community of Reston. As we look toward 2007, * we must begin to set goals and establish programs that will ensure that the visible reminders of our past remain for the benefit, enjoyment and education of future generations.
* 2007 will be the 400th anniversary of the settlement of Jamestown in the Virginia colony.

The residents of Reston often give it high marks. After more than two decades of living and working in Reston, Embry Rucker had this to say:

I think it's probably the greatest place in the world to live. Of course the beauty, the amenities, and the friendliness, and the "Reston-ness" of it. There's just nothing like Reston. It's just a remarkable place to live.

It takes commitment—a great deal of time, effort, attention to detail, and many right-minded people—to keep a dream like the New Town of Reston going until the eventual buildout projected for the 1990s. It is to the lasting credit of thousands of Reston citizens as well as to the successive developers that a statement made by designer Vladimir Kagan in 1966 continues to be true: "Somebody cared all the way."

This group of dancers was part of the Black Focus organization in Reston. They were performing at a festival in the early 1970s at the Hunters Woods Village Center.

Courtesy of the photographer, Arvil Daniels

This South Lakes/Herndon High School swim meet was held at Reston Community Center in 1982.

Photograph by Linda Rutledge. Courtesy of the Reston Community Center

Members of this group presented their views at a public forum held in February 1988 at the Reston Community Center as part of the observance of Black History Month. The topic was "Blacks and Class: What Separates Us?" Seated are, left to right, David Toatley, Maria Harris (the moderator), Lawrence Bussey, Jr., and Haywood Hopson. Standing, same order, are George Felton, Doris Briggs, Edward Sechrest, and Vincent Rice.

Photograph by Linda Rutledge. Courtesy of Reston Community Center

Patrick Kane was one of the founders of the Reston Board of Commerce and served as its president for the first two terms, 1982 to 1984. He was chosen RCA's Restonian of the Year in 1984. He is a consultant on community planning for KRS Associates, and is a faculty member at the University of Virginia.

Active in many facets of community life since 1966, he was a member of the original Board of Directors of the Reston Community Association and serves on Herndon's Affordable Housing Committee.

Courtesy of the Reston Board of Commerce

Harry May was president of the Reston Board of Commerce in 1986 and has also served as Board secretary. He is a charter member of the Rotary Club of Herndon and served as its second president in 1972-1973. He had thirty years of experience in printing before he opened his own business, Printing and Graphics, Inc., in Herndon in 1980, and he was named Printing Broker of the Year in 1986.
Courtesy of Reston Board of Commerce

Patricia Noboa Stanton was president of the Reston Board of Commerce in 1985 and has also served as its vice president and secretary. Chosen as Reston Citizen of the Year in 1985, she was selected as Small Business Person of the Year in 1986. She is president of Reston Copy Center and Renaissance Reprographics.
Courtesy of Reston Board of Commerce

Charles R. Smith was one of the founders of the Reston Board of Commerce and served as its president in 1987. He is president of CRS Associates, a chain of dry cleaning and laundry outlets, and of Photo-Tec, Inc., a photo finishing service.
Courtesy of Reston Board of Commerce

Catherine Cleveland was secretary of the Board of Commerce in 1986 and 1987 and its president in 1988. She is currently chairman of the Business Arts Partnership.
Photograph by Abbie Edwards. Courtesy of Reston Board of Commerce

Andrea M. Field was elected president of the Reston Board of Commerce in 1989, after having served on the Board for two years and as executive vice president in 1988. She is president of Andrea Field Commercial Interiors, an interior design firm specializing in service for small and medium-sized companies.
Photograph by Abbie Edwards. Courtesy of Reston Board of Commerce

The late Frank Matthews was founder and chairman of the board of the Hayloft Dinner Theater in Manassas and also its master of ceremonies. He first became interested in the dinner theater concept as a Reston resident after he and others founded the Reston Community Players. He was producer of the first three productions. Photograph in 1982.
Courtesy of the Hayloft Dinner Theater

All of the developers of Reston have contributed to arts groups and the Reston Chorale, organized in 1966, has consistently been one of the recipients. They have given several concerts each year, singing great works both traditional and modern. Here the group of about eighty musicians is shown at a concert in 1987 at the Reston Community Center, with conductor Fred Wygal.
Courtesy of the photographer, Linda Rutledge

Warner Cable, in operation in the early 1970s, serves Reston. It was the first cable system in Fairfax County. Community and local origination programs are part of its overall presentation to subscribers. This crew is video taping the Annual Reston Festival in May 1984, at Lake Anne.
Courtesy of the photographer, Linda Rutledge

A Youth Art Month celebration in March 1981 included costumes and the release of colorful balloons at GRACE, the Greater Reston Arts Center in Heron House.
Courtesy of the photographer, Don Byrum

Restonians line up periodically at the Reston Community Center to register for classes, as seen here in 1982. A great variety of cultural and recreational activities has always been available to residents.

Courtesy of the photographer, Linda Rutledge

A bit of silliness every once in a while is good for the soul. This pet provided a generous portion of it at the dog show held at the Reston Community Center in 1985.

Courtesy of the photographer, Linda Rutledge

Part of the cast from the Conservatory Ballet's production of The Nutcracker, directed by Julia Redick. The production is given at the Reston Community Center to sell-out crowds each Christmas season. Left to right are Greta von Kirchmann, Jared Redick, and Seanna Tully.

Courtesy of Julia C. Redick

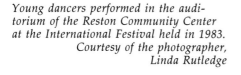

Two promising young gymnasts demonstrated their skills at the Reston Community Center in 1979.

Courtesy of the photographer, Abbie Edwards

Young dancers performed in the auditorium of the Reston Community Center at the International Festival held in 1983.

Courtesy of the photographer, Linda Rutledge

Cartoonist Don Edwing has worked for Mad *magazine since 1961. He lived in Reston from 1974 to 1988 and continues to be a regular contributer to the Connection *newspapers, among others. So prolific and able is he that in 1987 he received the award for being the top suburban cartoonist in the United States and Canada, winning first place out of eleven hundred entries. He is shown here in caricature through the eyes and pen of his colleague, cartoonist Jack Davis.*

Courtesy of Don Edwing

Cartoonist Don Edwing has dealt with numerous topics in his career of sketching the social and political oddities of life. Here he addresses the problems of stickers and permits galore; funding needed to improve West Ox Road; and the grass-eating carp "planted" in Reston's lakes.*

Courtesy of the artist and Media Consultants, Reston

A family takes a leisurely sail on Lake Anne.
Courtesy of the photographer, Abbie Edwards

Most types of watercraft, except for those powered by gasoline engines, can be seen on the lakes on a fine day. This photograph was taken by James Kirby for RHOA in 1982. Scenes like this have prompted some observers to call Reston the "Golden Ghetto."
Courtesy of the Reston Association

Little League baseball teams were already in full swing in the Reston community when this picture was taken in the summer of 1967.
Photograph by William A. Graham. Courtesy of Reston Land Corporation

Young fishermen try their luck on Lake Thoreau.
Photograph by Abbie Edwards

A lone cyclist pedals past the sun boat sculpture near Heron House on a misty, rainy day in 1978.
Courtesy of the photographer, Arvil Daniels

An impromptu basketball game occupies the court at Wainright Cluster.
Courtesy of the photographer, Arvil Daniels

Annette and Erin Dobbs were finalists in their respective divisions in the 1986 Simon Cup Tennis Tournament, women's singles. They played each other and mother Annette beat daughter Erin in three hard-fought sets.
Courtesy of the photographer, Linda Rutledge

Reston's Road Runners pound the pavement in this 1977 race.
Courtesy of the photographer, Abbie Edwards

Ice hockey enthusiasts get in a game on
Lake Thoreau in 1980.
Photograph by Abbie Edwards

Sledding on Mount Reston is an enjoyable
sport in the wintertime as depicted by
Matt Monroe, fifth grader at Lake Anne
Elementary School. His art works have
been exhibited and published.
Courtesy of the artist

Kids and pets enjoy the out-of-doors at
Lake Thoreau in 1979.
Photograph by Abbie Edwards

Dudley the cat enjoyed watching from his
balcony as the Canada geese swam on
Lake Thoreau in 1980. Even animals
enjoy the amenities in Reston.
Courtesy of the photographer,
Abbie Edwards

The annual triathlon, which has been held since 1984, is a race in which all contestants have to swim, bike and run. Here the contestants begin the course at Lake Audubon in September 1988. The event is sponsored by the Reston Triathlon Association.

Courtesy of the photographer, Abbie Edwards

The Rev. John A. Scherzer, D.D., recently retired as president of Fellowship Square Foundation. The Fellowship Houses at Lake Anne, Hunters Woods, and Tall Oaks village centers have all been built by the Foundation. Sponsored by the Lutheran Church, the corporation builds senior citizens housing for men and women of all faiths.

Courtesy of Fellowship Square Foundation

The Reston Hospital Center opened its doors in November 1986. Two other corporations had failed in their attempts to establish a hospital at Town Center, but the Hospital Corporation of America was successful in getting approval for a 127-bed medical-surgical facility with 24-hour emergency service. In February 1989, a maternity unit was added.

Courtesy of the photographer, Linda Rutledge

The Reston/North County Community Shelter opened its doors in December 1987, on Bowman Towne Drive next to the Reston Regional Library. On May 3, 1989, because of his deep concerns and demonstrated desire to improve the lot of the needy, the Fairfax County Board of Supervisors renamed the facility the Embry Rucker Shelter for the Homeless. Shown in this 1989 picture are Priscilla Ames, community activist; Embry Rucker; and the Shelter's administrator, Jana Graves.

Courtesy of the photographer, Linda Rutledge

The Planned Community Archives (PCA), a collection housed in George Mason University's Fenwick Library, is dedicated to improving the quality of community development—the built environment—in the United States. Through analysis of historical records and dissemination of information to scholars, teachers, developers, and members of the public, the board of directors hopes eventually to encourage interdisciplinary courses at all educational levels.

The corporation was organized in 1984, there having been no previous effort to preserve Reston's archival materials. Other planned community materials are being considered for inclusion in the Planned Community Archives. Shown in this 1989 photograph taken in front of the main George Mason University satellite dish for transmitting documents worldwide are: Peter L. McCandless, PCA secretary-treasurer; Mark Flynn, chief archivist at GMU: Dr. Charlene Hurt, director of GMU libraries; Gregory J. Friess, executive vice president of Reston Land Corporation; Charles A. Veatch, president of Environmental Concepts, Inc.; Thomas Grubisich, editor, Connection newspapers; Dr. Joseph Fisher, special assistant to GMU president George Johnson; and William Nicoson, attorney, PCA chairman.

Courtesy of Planned Community Archives

This article about Reston, published in the Look magazine issue of November 30, 1965, was the first major national coverage of the development of the New Town in Northern Virginia's hunt country outside of Washington, D.C. The journalist, John Peter, and photographer, Fred Maroon, said of the community: "Hopeful planners, developers, architects and investors throughout the U.S., where an estimated 75 new towns are in the planning or construction stage, are watching closely to see how Simon's gigantic gamble pays off."

Courtesy of Reston Land Corporation

The game of soccer was organized in teams in Reston in 1972 and rapidly grew in popularity. Presently about eighteen hundred children are involved in competitive games.

Courtesy of Reston Land Corporation

Off in the distance is the water spout, or fountain, in Lake Anne. Close to the viewer is one of the many party boats operated on Reston lakes, using electric motors. Gasoline engines are prohibited. All kinds of watercraft are put in the water on nice days.
Courtesy of Reston Land Corporation

Meadows and forests are part of the overall environmental protection and open space planning by the developer, Reston Land Corporation. Once property is deeded to the community for public use, the Reston Association (formerly called RHOA) assumes ownership and the responsibility for its management. The Association owns over a thousand acres at the present time with the expectation of receiving approximately a hundred more by the time the development is completed in the 1990s.
Courtesy of Reston Land Corporation

Reston's first hotel was the Sheraton Inn, built next to the Reston International Center in 1973 on Sunrise Valley Drive. The plaza was named in honor of Dag Hammerskjold for his world contribution to peace through his work with the United Nations.
Photograph by the William C. Pflaum Company.
Courtesy of Reston Land Corporation

Day care for children of working parents has been a matter of concern for many years in Reston. A consortium of business organizations demonstrates a continuing interest in the availability of high quality care. There are already twenty-one licensed providers in the community and the number continues to grow as the number of available jobs increases.
Photograph by Henley and Savage.
Courtesy of Reston Land Corporation

187

Marketing Reston has through the years included advertising in national magazines. In this display, which appeared in 1981, the opportunity to enjoy a variety of outdoor recreation experiences right at home is emphasized.
Courtesy of Reston Land Corporation

This week, visit the neighborhood that makes the most of every weekend.

With over a dozen pools, four dozen tennis courts, two championship golf courses, lakes, ball fields, bridle trails, bike paths and more, moving to Reston can obviously keep you moving.
You could take a woodworking course, learn ballet or play a role in a stage production. Dining out means anything from a picnic by a lake to dinner by candlelight. There are festivals, block parties and concerts.
And a terrific variety of houses promises you'll find the perfect place to go home and rest up. Don't let another week pass without learning how Reston makes the most of the weekend. Take Capital Beltway to Exit 10W or 11S. Go west on Rt. 7 and follow signs to the new Reston Visitors Center. Or simply call (703)471-7030.

Reston

Inlet Cluster was built off Wiehle Avenue on the shores of Lake Anne in 1971. It consists of sixty-three units, and like the other clusters in Reston, has its own association to manage services and maintenance in the complex.
Courtesy of Reston Land Corporation

Mallards Landing was designed by architects Cohen and Haft. Built by Castro-Holdsworth beside Lake Audubon in 1978, the forty-eight-unit townhouse complex received numerous design awards.
Courtesy of Reston Land Corporation

The Classic Country Cottage, designed by New York architect Lester Walker, was the winning design in a countrywide competition for the most livable, innovative, 1,500-square-foot wood home. The contest was co-sponsored by the American Wood Council and House Beautiful magazine. The house was built in Reston's North Point Village on Bennington Woods Road in 1984, and reflects an architectural style popular in the mid-1920s.
Courtesy of Reston Land Corporation

Lantern Way is a thirty-two-unit townhouse cluster by Fairfield Homes with "Hilton Head" character design, completed in 1987.
Courtesy of Reston Land Corporation

The commerical boom of the mid-1980s spurred the evolution of higher quality materials in new office buildings, as seen in this view of the lobby of Building 2 in Commerce Executive Park, developed by Centennial Contractors, Inc. Photograph in 1985 by Anthony Sylvestro, Jr.
Courtesy of Reston Land Corporation

The U.S. Headquarters of Spot Image is a thirty-two thousand square foot office building in the Branches office park, completed in 1984. It was designed by Davis and Carter, PA.
Courtesy of Reston Land Corporation

Intergraph's sixty-seven thousand square foot office building was completed in 1985. It was designed by SHWC Architects.
Courtesy of Reston Land Corporation

Fairfield compact, single-family, detached cluster homes with New England style architecture were offered by Fairfield Homes in the mid-1980s.
Courtesy of Reston Land Corporation

The Reston Regional Library opened in Town Center on Bowman Towne Drive in September 1985. Designed by architects LBC&W Associates, it offers many services beyond books alone, including information searches in a variety of computerized data banks. The circulation figures show consistently high usage by Reston area residents.
Courtesy of the Fairfax County Public Library

The Reston Visitors Center building was designed by architect Doug Corkern of Hilton Head, South Carolina. It opened beside Lake Newport in North Point Village in 1982.
Courtesy of the photographer, Kathy Steiner

The urban core of Reston's Town Center, part of the original master plan, will eventually consist of the Hyatt Regency Hotel, now under construction, twin office buildings, commercial and residential components, and a cultural center. The grand opening is scheduled for fall 1990. The architects are RTKL Associates.

Courtesy of Reston Land Corporation

In cooperation with Canada, Europe, and Japan, the United States is developing a permanently manned space station. A research laboratory in space—with crews on board from the participating countries—the space station will increase scientific knowledge, stimulate the development of new technologies, and help realize the commercial potential of space. Shown here is an artist's conception of the future station floating in space.

Courtesy of the National Aeronautics and Space Administration

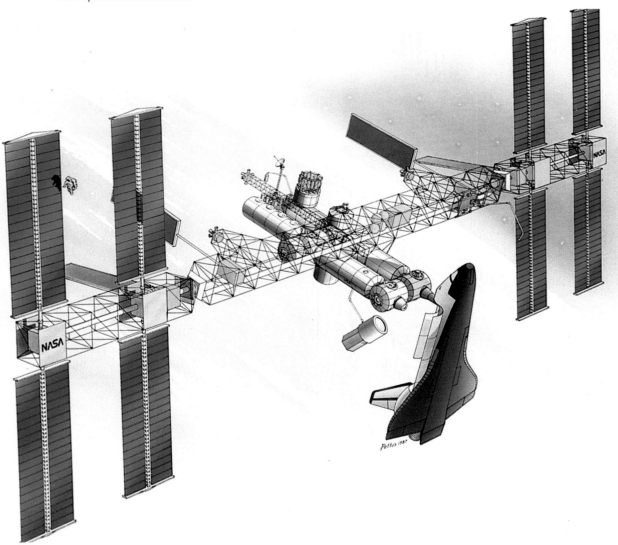

Bibliography

Bailey, James, ed. *New Towns in America: The Design and Development Process.* New York: John Wiley and Sons, 1971.

Bain, Henry. *The Reston Express Bus.* Washington, D.C.: Washington Center for Metropolitan Studies, 1969.

Brown, Stuart E., Jr. *Virginia Baron: The Story of Thomas 6th Lord Fairfax.* Berryville, Va.: Chesapeake Book Company 1965.

Burby, Raymond J., III, and Weiss, Shirley F. *New Communities U.S.A.* Lexington, Mass.: Lexington Books, D.C. Heath and Company, 1976.

Campbell, Carlos C. *New Towns: Another Way to Live.* Reston, Virginia: Reston Publishing Company, 1976.

Corden, Carol. *Planned Cities: New Towns in Britain and America.* Beverly Hills, Calif.: Sage Publications, 1977.

Dawson, Grace. *No Little Plans; Fairfax County's PLUS Program for Managing Growth.* Washington, D.C.: Urban Land Institute, 1977.

Eichler, Edward P., and Kaplan, Marshall. *The Community Builders.* Berkeley and Los Angeles: University of California, 1967.

Eichler, Edward P., and Norwitch, Bernard. "New Town," in *Towards a National Urban Policy,* Daniel P. Moynihan, ed. New York: Basic Books, Inc. 1970.

Fairfax County Office of Comprehensive Planning. *Reston's Legislation: Residential Planned Community Zoning.* October 1967.

Fishman, Robert. *Urban Utopias in the Twentieth Century.* Cambridge: MIT Press, 1982.

Fraser, Jack B. *New Towns: What Architects Should Know About Them.* Washington, D.C.: The American Institute of Architects, 1969.

A Future for Virginia's Past: The Final Report of the Governor's Commission to Study Historic Preservation. Richmond, Va., 1988.

Golany, Dr. Gideon. *New Towns Planning and Development: Worldwide Bibliography.* Washington, D. C.: Urban Land Institute, 1973.

Gottmann, Jean. *Virginia in Our Century.* Charlottesville: University Press of Virginia, 1969.

Grubisich, Tom, and McCandless, Peter. *Reston: The First Twenty Years.* Reston, Va.: The Reston Publishing Company, 1985.

Harrison, Fairfax. *Landmarks of Old Prince William.* Berryville, Va., Chesapeake Book Company. Reprint, 1964.

Harwood, H. H., Jr. *Rails to the Blue Ridge.* Falls Church, Va.: Econoprint. Reprint, 1969.

Hays, Allison Feiss. "Reston, Virginia, 1964-1984: An Evaluation of the New Town in Terms of Robert E. Simon's Original Goals." Master of Urban and Regional Planning thesis, George Washington University, Washington, D.C., 1985.

Historic Northern Virginia: Understanding and Protecting Our Shared Heritage. Falls Church, Va.: Northern Virginia History Officials Advisory Committee, 1981.

Howard, Ebenezer. *Garden Cities of Tomorrow.* Cambridge: MIT Press, 1965.

Ingebritsen, Karl S. *Reston Home Owners Association: A Case Study In Community Management.* Chicago: The Institute of Real Estate Management, 1977.

Johnston, Angus James, III. *Virginia Railroads in the Civil War.* Chapel Hill: University of North Carolina Press, 1961.

Kilmer, Kenton, and Sweig, Donald. *The Fairfax Family in Fairfax County: A Brief History.* Fairfax, Va.: Office of Comprehensive Planning 1975

Klauber, Martin, et al. *Reston, Virginia.* Washington, D.C.: George Washington University, 1967.

Klaus, Susan L. *Links in the Chain: Greenbelt, Maryland and the New Town Movement in America. An Annotated Bibliography on the Occasion of the Fiftieth Anniversary of Greenbelt, Maryland.* Washington, D.C.: Center for Washington Area Studies, George Washington University, 1987.

Kulski, Julian E. *Reston, Virginia: Analysis of a New Community.* Graduate Program in Urban and Regional Planning, George Washington University, Washington, D.C., 1967.

Larson, Nancy. *A History of Reston, Virginia's Unique Community.* Reston: New Town Publications, 1981.

Mandelker, Daniel. *Green Belts and Urban Growth.* Madison, Wis.: University of Wisconsin Press, 1962.

[McCandless, Peter.] *A Brief History of Reston, Virginia.* Reston, Va.: Gulf Reston, Inc., 1973.

Mitchell, Beth. *Beginning at a White Oak . . . Patents and Northern Neck Grants of Fairfax County, Virginia.* Fairfax, Va. Office of Comprehensive Planning, 1977.

Muse, Benjamin. *Virginia's Massive Resistance.* Bloomington, Ind.: Variety Press, 1961.

Neill, Edward D. *The Fairfaxes of England and America . . .* Albany, N.Y.: Joel Munsell, 1868.

Netherton, Nan; Sweig, Donald; Artemel, Janice; Hickin, Patricia; and Reed, Patrick. *Fairfax County, Virginia: A History.* Fairfax, Va.: Fairfax County Board of Supervisors, 1978.

Netherton, Ross, and Netherton, Nan. *Fairfax County in Virginia: A Pictorial History.* Norfolk, Va.: The Donning Company, 1986.

Norcross, Carl. *Open Space Communities in the Market Place . . . A Survey of Public Acceptance.* Washington, D.C.: Urban Land Institute, 1960. 97 pp. (Technical Bulletin No. 57.)

Northern Virginia Regional Park Authority. *Trail Guide: W & OD Railroad Regional Park.* Fairfax, Va.; 1981.

O'Neal, William B. *Architecture in Virginia.* New York: Walker and Company, Inc., for the Virginia Museum, 1968.

Opstad, Donald O. *The History of the Fairfax Hunt, 1929-1972.* Fairfax County, Va.: The Fairfax Hunt, 1972.

Owen, Wilfred. *Cities in the Motor Age.* New York: Viking Press, 1958.

A Place Called Reston: Reston Directory, 1989. Reston, Va.: New Town Publications, 1989.

Reps, John. *The Making of Urban America: A History of City Planning in the U.S.* Princeton: Princeton University Press, 1965.

Rowland, Norman, and Drury, Margaret. *Reston Low Income Housing Demonstration.* Reston, Va.: Foundation for Community Programs, Inc., April 1969.

Schaffer, Daniel. *Garden Cities for America: The Radburn Experience.* Philadelphia: Temple University Press, 1982.

Simon, Robert E., Jr. *The Reston Story.* Fairfax, Va.: Victor Weingarten Company, 1962.

Stetson, Charles W. *Washington and His Neighbors.* Richmond, Va.: Garrett and Massie, Inc. 1956.

Strong, Ann Louise. *Planned Urban Environments.* Baltimore: The John Hopkins Press, 1971.

Sundquist, James L. *Dispersing Population.* Washington, D.C.: The Brookings Institution, 1975.

Sunset Hills Farms: The 4000 Acre Estate of the late Hugh B. Hutchison, n.p., n.d., c. 1927 Archives of A. Smith Bowman Distillery.

Templeman, Eleanor Lee, and Netherton, Nan. *Northern Virginia Heritage.* Arlington, Va.: Privately published, 1966.

A Trip through . . . Sunset Hills Farm, Fairfax County, Virginia. Pamphlet published by Bowman Brothers, c. 1956.

Urban Land Institute Bulletin No. 42, *Zoning Provisions for Planned Residential Developments.* Washington, D.C.: Urban Land Institute, 1961.

War of the Rebellion: A Compilation of the Official Records of the Union and Confederate Armies. Series I. Washington, D.C.: Government Printing Office 1880-1901.

Washington Center for Metropolitan Studies. *Reston: A Study in Beginning, A History of Reston from the Purchase of the Land in 1961 to the Period of First Occupancy in 1964.* 2 vols., 1968.

Wayland, John. *The Bowmans: A Pioneering Family.* Staunton, Va.: The McClure Company, 1943.

Who Was Who In America, 1607-1896. Chicago: Marquis, 1963. (William McKee Dunn).

Williams, Ames W. *The Washington and Old Dominion Railroad.* Alexandria: Meridian Sun Press, 1977.

Wolfe, Tom. *The Electric Kool-Aid Acid Test.* New York: Farrar, Straus and Giroux, 1968.

An additional listing of a select group of articles about Reston which have appeared in newspapers and periodicals through the years may be seen at the Reston Regional Library, Reference Section, at the Fairfax city Regional Library's Virginia Room, and in the George Mason University Library's Planned Community Archives.

Reston Chronology

Prehistory Indians belonging to northern tribes used Northern Virginia for traditional hunting grounds for centuries. (Hulbert, *Historic Highways*, Vol. II, "Indian Thoroughfares," p. 45; Harrison, *Landmarks*, p. 28.)

1649 The Northern Neck Proprietary was granted to seven loyal followers including two Culpepers, by Charles II of England, in exile in France. (Brown, *Virginia Baron*, pp. 26-32.)

1689 Catherine Culpeper inherited five-sixths of the Proprietary upon the death of her father, Thomas, Second Lord Culpeper, who was the son of John, First Lord Culpeper, one of the seven original grantees. (Kilmer and Sweig, *Fairfax Family*, pp. 5-7.)

1690 Thomas, Fifth Lord Fairfax, married Catherine Culpeper and thereby acquired all of her property including five-sixths of the Proprietary. The remaining one-sixth was owned by Alexander Culpeper, Catherine's cousin. (Brown, *Virginia Baron*, pp. 32, 35.)

1710 On the death of her husband, Thomas, Fifth Lord Fairfax, Lady Catherine Fairfax, as a widow, again became owner of five-sixths of the Proprietary. (Brown, *Virginia Baron*, p. 4.)

1719 Lady Catherine Fairfax died leaving her oldest son and heir, Thomas, a life interest in five-sixths of the Proprietary. Her cousin Alexander had left his one-sixth to her mother, Margaret, Lady Culpeper, who in turn left it to her grandson, Thomas, Sixth Lord Fairfax, on her death in 1710. (Brown, *Virginia Baron*, pp. 9, 20.)

1735 Thomas, Sixth Lord Fairfax, visited the Virginia colony to inspect his holdings and arrange for an official survey of his lands to the headsprings of the Rappahannock and Potomac rivers. (Brown, *Virginia Baron*, pp. 49, 61-63.)

1736 Bryan Fairfax was born to William and Deborah Clarke Fairfax, in Westmoreland County, Virginia. (Harrison, *Virginia Land Grants*, p. 172.)

1737 John Warner, William Mayo, and others surveyed the boundaries of the 5,280,000 acres of the Proprietary. (Brown, *Virginia Baron*, pp. 80-91.)

1739 Great Falls Manor was surveyed for Lord Fairfax by John Warner. (Kilmer and Sweig, *Fairfax Family*, p. 63; Northern Neck Grant Book E, pp. 38-39, Virginia State Library.)

1745 The Privy Council entered an order confirming the Fairfax title to the Proprietary. (Brown, *Virginia Baron*, p. 98.)

1747 Thomas, Sixth Lord Fairfax, emigrated from England and lived for a while with his cousin William at Belvoir on the Potomac before moving to his own residence, Greenway Court, in the Manor of Leeds, near Winchester in the Shenandoah Valley. (Kilmer and Sweig, *Fairfax Family*, p. 26.)

1765 Thomas, Sixth Lord Fairfax, gave the 12,588-acre Great Falls Manor to his cousin Bryan Fairfax. (Kilmer and Sweig, *Fairfax Family*, p. 36.)

1802 Bryan, Eighth Lord Fairfax, died, leaving to his eldest son Thomas, Ninth Lord Fairfax, among other properties, Great Falls Manor. (Fairfax County Will Book; Kilmer and Sweig, *Fairfax Family*, p. 65.)

1843 Thomas, Ninth Lord Fairfax, and his wife, Margaret, deeded over eight thousand acres of the Great Falls Manor to their son Reginald Fairfax. (Fairfax County Deed Book.)

1849 The Republican Mills post office was established. (National Archives, Fairfax County, Virginia, postal records.)

1852 Reginald Fairfax sold over eight thousand acres to Benjamin Thornton, late of York, England, and Orange County, Virginia. (Fairfax County Deed Books; Orange County Deed Books.)

c. 1852 Benjamin Thornton built a Gothic-Revival-style house. (Bowman, "Sunset Hills," p. 37.)

c. 1857 The Alexandria, Loudoun and Hampshire Railroad builders came through laying track on their way to the first terminus at Leesburg. (Harwood, *Rails to the Blue Ridge*, p. 3.)

1860 The Republican Mills post office name was changed to "Thornton's Depot." (National Archives, Fairfax County, Virginia postal records.)

1861-1865 Civil War activities took place along the railroad and in the Thornton's Mill area. This was the southeast corner of a territory called "Mosby's Confederacy." (Wayland, *Historic Homes . . .*, p. 414, map.)

1865 Joseph Thornton was appointed an agent of the Alexandria, Loudoun and Hampshire Railroad. (Virginia State Library Archives, Loose papers, Board of Public Works.)

1886 Commissioners in a circuit court suit in Alexandria city conveyed to Dr. Carl Adolph Max Wiehle and Gen. William McKee Dunn a tract of land, part of that conveyed to Benjamin Thornton by Reginald Fairfax, containing 6,449 acres, surveyed in 1878 by R. R. Farr. (Fairfax County Deed Books; Chancery Causes, *Thorps Administrators vs. Hine and Kent*.)

1886 The land was divided: Dunn received 3,221 acres south of the Washington, Ohio and Western Railroad; Wiehle received 3,228 acres north of the railroad. (Fairfax County Deed Books.)

1887 Thornton's Depot became the "Wiehle" post office. (National Archives postal records.)

1888 Dr. Wiehle built a wooden summer house. (Bowman, "Sunset Hills," *Yearbook*, p. 40.)

1892 A plat of the Town of Wiehle was prepared for Dr. Wiehle by Joseph Berry, surveyor, of Ash Grove. (Fairfax County Plat Book.)

1892-1893 Corporations were set up to quarry stone, cut and market timber and sell real estate. (Fairfax County Charter Books.)

1894 A one-room schoolhouse was built by Dr. Wiehle and turned over to the Fairfax County schools. (Bertie Poston interview by James Polzin, April 1980.)

1892-1900 A brick kiln, sawmill, soapstone mill, private residences, a Town Hall, the Aesculapian Hotel, lakes, a bridge, icehouse, and tennis courts were built. Bridle paths were cut through the woods for riding and hunting. (Bowman, "Sunset Hills"; Poston interview, 1980.)

1898 The town of Wiehle was incorporated. (Virginia Acts of Assembly, 1898.)

1899 Plans for a brick mansion for the Wiehles were completed. (Bowman, "Sunset Hills.")

1901 Dr. Wiehle died. (*Washington Star* obituary, February 28, 1901.)

1902 Wiehle's brick mansion was completed. (Bowman, "Sunset Hills".)

1907 The Wiehle Methodist Episcopal Church was built. (Poston interview, 1980.)

1908 Dr. Hugh Barbour Hutchison and William Crighton of Herndon purchased from the Wiehle heirs approximately thirty-five hundred acres, then deeded them to the Cuthbert Land and Development Company established by the two. (Fairfax County Charter Books and Deed Books.)

1908-1919 Land was cleared, dairy and horse barns were built, as were poultry houses and residences for tenants. (Poston interview; Cuba Curtice interview; Sunset Hills brochure.)

1919 Dr. Hutchison bought out his partner Crighton and dissolved Cuthbert Land and Development Company. (Fairfax County Deed Books and Charter Books.)

1923 The Wiehle post office name was changed to "Sunset Hills." (National Archives postal records.)

1924 Dr. Hutchison died. (*Washington Star* obituary July 16, 1924.)

1927 The Hutchison heirs sold almost four thousand acres to A. Smith Bowman, Sr., of Indianapolis, Indiana, for dairy and beef cattle farming. (Bowman, "Sunset Hills.")

1928 The Fairfax Hunt was established by A. Smith Bowman, Sr. (Opstad, *History of the Fairfax Hunt.*)

1934 The Fairfax Hunt was sanctioned by the Master of the Fox Hounds Association of America. (Opstad, *Fairfax Hunt.*)

1934 Repeal of Prohibition in Virginia; the old soapstone mill at Sunset Hills was converted into the main bourbon distillery building; grain was grown on the farm; mash byproduct was fed to a thousand dairy and beef cattle. (Bowman, "Sunset Hills.")

1942 The E. DeLong Bowman house was built. (E. DeLong Bowman interview, September 28, 1981.)

1944 White oak trees were cut from the "Wiehle Woods" to make staves and hogsheads for whiskey barrels. (*Spirits*, May, 1948.)

1941-1945 The Bowmans distilled alcohol for the U.S. government war effort. (The *Fairfax Journal*, December 24, 1942; Aubrey Graves in the *Washington Post*, December 13, 1953.)

1947 Bowman purchased the former Dunn tract on the south side of the Washington and Old Dominion Railroad. (Fairfax County Deed Books; Bowman, "Sunset Hills.")

1951 Passenger service was officially ended on the W&OD Railroad in May. (Harwood, *Rails*, p. 65.)

1952 A. Smith Bowman, Sr., died on June 27. (*Washington Star*, June 28, 1952.)

1955 The old Thornton house burned down. (Bowman, "Sunset Hills.")

1956 The Aesculapian Hotel was torn down. (Bowman, "Sunset Hills.")

1957 A satellite city of thirty thousand population was proposed for the seven thousand acres owned by the Bowman brothers. It was designed by Seward H. Mott and Associates to be a "self-contained" community. (Paul Hope in the *Washington Star*, June 19, 1957.)

1957 The Bowman brothers offered 250 acres to the University for a branch. (Frances Lanahan in the *Northern Virginia Sun*, October 7, 1957.)

1958 The Chantilly area was selected for a second metropolitan Washington airport by General E. R. Quesada, chairman of a national airport study committee. (Netherton in *Fairfax County, Virginia*, p. 643.)

1960 Lefcourt Realty Company purchased seven thousand acres from the Bowmans for land development and home building. (*Wall Street Journal*, May 5, 1960.)

1960 Federal government plans were revealed for a twenty-five-mile sewer line from the Chantilly airport site to Great Falls and beyond. (McLean *Providence Journal*, May 6, 1960.)

1960 Herndon Elementary moved into a new school building in September. (School Administration.)

1960 Chantilly Airport was under construction, building materials moved through Sunset Hills on the W&OD Railroad. (Harwood, *Rails*, p. 77.)

1961 Palindrome Corporation, formed by Robert E. Simon, Jr., purchased the former Bowman tract from Lefcourt Realty in March. (Fairfax County Deed Books.)

1961 James B. Selonick was appointed executive vice president of Simon Enterprises of New York in May. (*Reston Letter*, February 1965.)

1961 Glenn W. Saunders, Jr., joined the staff of Palindrome as vice president for planning, engineering, and construction of Reston. (Glenn Saunders' resume.)

1962 The Fairfax County Board of Supervisors adopted the "Residential Planned Community" (RPC) zoning ordinance, July 18. (Board of Supervisors' Minute Books.)

1962 The (Chantilly) Dulles Airport Access Road was completed (Washington Center for Metropolitan Studies, (Reston, p. 189.)

1962 Construction began simultaneously in October on Lake Anne and the seven-thousand-yard championship golf course in Lake Anne Village. (WCMS, Reston, p. 245.)

1963 An Information Center with a little branch post office was opened in May. (WCMS, Reston, p. 348.)

1964 Reston Deed of Dedication was drawn up for open and community-owned lands. (WCMS, Reston, p. 160.)

1964 The Gulf Oil Corporation, for certain considerations, loaned Robert E. Simon, Jr., $15 million in March. (*Reston Letter,* 2 [May 1964]1.)

1964 Jane Gilmer Wilhelm was hired as an educational advisor consultant in January; she became a full-time staff director of community relations in July. (WCMS, Reston, p. 178.)

1964 Whittlesey and Conklin, Charles Goodman, and Chloethiel Woodard Smith designed Fairfax County's first townhouses, for Reston. (McCandless, *Brief History*, p. 15.)

1964 The Reston north golf course opened for public play in the summer. (McCandless, *Brief History*, p. 16.)

1964 Francis Steinbauer, formerly resident engineer for the Dulles Airport project, joined the Reston staff. (Steinbauer interview, October 2, 1981.)

1964 Models were ready and first purchases were made in the fall. (McCandless, *Brief History*, p. 17.)

1964 The first industrial firm, Air Survey Corporation, moved into Isaac Newton Square in November. (McCandless, *Brief History*, p.17.)

1964 The first couple, Mr. and Mrs. Samuel Furcron, moved into a Smith townhouse in Waterview Cluster on Lake Anne, December 9. (*Reston Letter*, February 1965.)

1965 The first single person, Miss Bessie Burton, moved into her Charles Goodman-designed Hickory Cluster house in January. (*Reston Letter*, February 1965.)

1965 The first wedding ceremony in Reston was performed at Lake Anne Community Center in June. It was the marriage of Edward L. Keenan III to Eleanor Ochs of Annapolis. (Keenan interview.)

1965 The first baby was born to Reston residents, July 30; Jennifer Leigh Regan of Waterview Cluster, daughter of the Rev. and Mrs. J. Robert Regan, of Redeemer Methodist Church. (Edith Keenan interview, September 10, 1981.)

1965 The *Reston Times*, a monthly newsletter, was started in their basement by Mr. and Mrs. Ralph Segman of Hunters Woods in November. (*Reston Times*, December 2, 1966.)

1965 The Lake Anne Village Center officially opened in December. (*Reston Letter*, December 1965.)

1965 The Redeemer Methodist Church building opened for Christmas services. (Rev. Mr. Robert Regan, August 1981.)

1965 The John Hancock Mutual Life Insurance Company provided money for long-term development in December. (Robert Bidwell, How Reston is Governed, p. 83. Ph.D. dissertation.)

1965 The Lakeside Pharmacy and Mooring Restaurant opened in Lake Anne Center. (*Reston Letter* May 21, 1966.)

1966 Thursday Night Movies, four separate feature film series, began in January at Lake Anne Center, to run weekly through August. (*Reston Letter* May 21, 1966.)

1966 First Lecture Series opened in January with a talk by Robert E. Simon, Jr., and concluded in March with one by architectural critic Wolf Von Eckardt. (*Reston Letter* May 21, 1966.)

1966 The Safeway opened, after 250 families had settled in Reston, on January 26. (*Reston Times*, January 26, 1966.)

1966 Heron House Gallery opened February 12. (*Reston Letter*, May 21, 1966.)

1966 Miss Brenda J. Carmer became Reston's first Community Center Director, February 14. (*Reston Letter*, May 21, 1966.)

1966 A "rural post office" was established at Lake Anne Community Center, Evelyn Doolin, postmistress. (*Reston Times*, February 15, 1966.)

1966 Vernon Walker was hired in March to organize an environmental education program. (Walker interview, August 25, 1981.)

1966 *Deeds of Dedication, Reston Sections One and Two* were recorded in the Clerk's Office of Fairfax County, Virginia, March 25, 1966, Deed Book 2431, p. 319.

1966 Meenehan's Hardware, already in operation, opened Reston's first garden center at Lake Anne in March. (*Reston Letter*, May 21, 1966.)

1966 The Carter Glass Branch, Fairfax County Public Library, opened at Lake Anne, April 17. (Library Administration.)

1966 Reston's official dedication was held at Lake Anne Plaza on May 21. Thirty-seven countries with New Towns programs participated. Secretary of Interior Stewart Udall announced that USGS would build a $30 million headquarters building at Reston on an eighty-five-acre tract. (*Reston Letter*, May 21, 1966, January 1967; Official Invitation.)

1966 Golf Course Island, designed by architect Louis Sauer, fifth cluster of townhouses, opened May 28. (*Reston Letter*, May 21, 1966.)

1966 A special joint meeting of Reston First and Second Homeowners Associations was called by Glenn W. Saunders, Jr., president of both associations, for June 30, 1966. (Bidwell, How Reston is Governed, p. 77.

1966 The Reston Players gave their first public performance, an original musical, *The Greatest Game in Town*, in July. (*Reston Letter*, January 1967.)

1966 The Reston Players gave their second performance, *Dracula*, in October and November. (*Reston Letter*, January 1967.)

1966 Dr. James Christian Pfohl, founder and director, announced the Reston Chorale's two forthcoming Christmas concerts at Lake Anne Center and Plaza. (*Reston Times*, November 1, 1966.)

1966 Arthur W. Arundel bought out the Segman interest in November and began to publish the *Reston Times*. (*Reston Times*, December 2, 1966.)

1967 Lake Anne Elementary School opened with three hundred students in January. (School Administration.)

1967 Janet Hays and Carolyn Lindberg distributed Reston's first community telephone directory, *A Place Called Reston*. (*Reston Times*, January 19, 1967.)

1967 The Fairfax County Board of Supervisors hired a fox trapper to get rid of numerous rabid foxes running wild in the county, in March. This meant the end of the Fairfax Hunt in the county. (Fairfax County *Weekly Agenda*, January 31, 1967.)

1967 An announcement was made that Reston Music Center's Summer Camp would begin June 26 under the direction of James Christian Pfohl. (*Reston Times*, February 2, 1967.)

1967 Alexander Schneider, former member of the Budapest String Quartet, gave a violin demonstration to students at LANK. (*Reston Times*, March 1967.)

1967 Reston Children's Center opened for full day care for children of working mothers, and for part-time care. (*Reston Times*, April 7, 1967.)

1967 The Reston Nature Center opened in April, with Vernon Walker as director, for the purposes of study and control of the environment. (Walker interview, August 25, 1981.)

1967 First set of twins were born in Reston to Mr. and Mrs. Robert Abrash, Nicholas Pyle and Daniel Lawrence, on April 28. (Interview with Robert Abrash, September 14, 1981.)

1967 The Lions Club was formed, first service club in Reston. David Conlon was elected president. (*Reston Times*, May 19, 1967.)

1967 The Fairfax County Board of Supervisors approved condemnation of the Alexandria Water Company by the Fairfax County Water Authority. (*Reston Times*, June 2, 1967.)

1967 James Cleveland joined the Reston staff in Marketing, real estate sales, in July. (Reston Land Corporation office.)

1967 Mrs. Lyndon Johnson made a surprise visit to Reston and the Reston Music Center accompanied by Supreme Court Justice Abe Fortas on July 13. (*Reston Times*, July 21, 1967.)

1967 A six-week music camp directed by James Christian Pfohl came to an end for 160 music students from all over the United States. (*Reston Times*, August 4, 1967.)

1967 Widening of Route 7 from the Dulles Access Road west to Route 606, Baron Cameron Avenue, was begun. It was scheduled to be completed by July 1968. (*Reston Times*, September 8, 1967.)

1967 Reston's first voting registrar, Mrs. Frank J. Sherlock, was appointed for the Sugarland Precinct. (*Reston Times*, September 22, 1967.)

1967 The Artmobile III was scheduled for Reston from the Virginia Museum of Arts on September 30. The exhibit was titled, "The Human Figure in Art." (*Reston Times*, September 22, 1967.)

1967 Gulf Oil, with a substantial financial stake in the faltering project, decided to take over management of the new town of Reston. Gulf Reston, Inc., was formed and the assumption of operation took place September 28. (McCandless, *Brief History*, p. 21.)

1967 Robert Ryan, real estate consultant, became chief operations officer and chairman of Gulf Reston in October. (*Reston Times*, May 22, 1969.)

1967 Herndon High School moved into a new building. (School Administration.)

1967 The Fairfax County Police made arrests, at Lake Anne, of Mrs. Margo C. Kronenberg, daughter of Robert E. Simon, Jr., and eighteen-year-old Robert "Rocky" Gregg Dixon for possession and use of marijuana. (*Reston Times*, October 20, 1967.)

1967 Robert E. Simon, Jr., was fired by Gulf Reston October 26. (Frank Lalli in *House and Home*, December 1967.)

1967 First Reston Fall Festival was held in conjunction with a farewell party given by the residents for Robert Simon, November 4, Dr. George Zacko, Master of Ceremonies. (Bidwell, How Reston Is Governed, p. 90.)

1967 Martha Pennino of Vienna was elected to represent the Centreville District (including Reston) on the Fairfax County Board of Supervisors in November. (*Fairfax County, Virginia*, p. 647.)

1967 The Reston Community Association was formed as a reaction to the change in developers and fear of future lack of planning. (Bidwell, How Reston Is Governed, p. 90.

1968 The Reston Commuter Bus System was inaugurated under sponsorship of the Reston Community Association on March 4.) (Bain, *The Reston Express Bus*, p. 14.

1968 The Reston Players took top honors in their first venture into the D.C. Annual One-Act Play Tournament. They received three prizes: Best Play—*Waiting for Godot*; Best Director—Frank Johns; Best Performer—Robert Perce. (*Reston Times*, April 5, 1968.)

1968 The Reston Music Center was renamed the Northern Virginia Music Center, Pfohl, director. (*Reston Times*, May 17, 1968.)

1968 Glenn W. Saunders, Jr., was appointed executive vice president of Gulf Reston, Inc. (Resume, Glenn Saunders.)

1968 Reston's second church, the Washington Plaza Baptist, was dedicated on July 14. (Church office.)

1968 The Virginia Polytechnic Institute opened for classes in graduate degree programs with 250 students. (VPI & SU.)

1968 Gulf Reston's community relations division published the first edition of *The Residents Handbook*. (Karl J. Ingebritsen, *Reston Home Owners Association*, p. 8.)

1968 Brown's Chapel was moved from its original location on Route 7 to a lot on Route 606 opposite Lake Anne Village. Dedication in December. (*Reston Times*, December 6, 1968.)

1969 Karl Ingebritsen was appointed the first executive director of both First and Second Home Owners Associations in February by Glenn Saunders, executive vice president of Gulf Reston. (Ingebritsen, *RHOA*, p. 9.)

1969 An Advisory Committee was appointed to assist Nature Center director Vernon Walker in a two-year study of the ecology and physical characteristics of Lake Anne. (*Reston Times*, February 20, 1969.)

1969 Consultant Robert Ryan left in April. William Magness, a Gulf Oil executive, became chief operations officer of Gulf Reston. (*Reston Times*, May 22, 1969.)

1969 CBS Morning News, August 29, televised the Reston Commuter Bus story (*Reston Times*, September 4, 1969.)

1969 The Black Focus organization sponsored a successful three-day "Black Festival" at Lake Anne Plaza. Dances, exhibits, church services, poetry, art, and culture were scheduled for thousands of visitors. (*Reston Times*, September 4, 1969.)

1969 Hunters Woods Elementary opened in September. (School Administration.)

1969 The *Reston Times* became a weekly newspaper on October 21. (*Reston Times*, October 21, 1976.)

1969 A Booz-Allen and Hamilton study of FHOA and SHOA recommended combining the two into one organization for future effectiveness. (Booz-Allen and Hamilton, Study, October 27, 1969.)

1969 Metropolitan Life Insurance Company signed a $10.5 million long-term mortgage agreement for existing income-producing properties with Gulf-Reston. (McCandless, *Brief History*, p. 23.)

1969 Count Basie performed before two hundred people at the Newton Cafeteria at Isaac Newton Square. (*Reston Times*, November 20, 1969.)

1969 John Anderson found a centuries-old Indian stone axe on the shores of Lake Anne. (*Reston-Times*, November 27, 1969.)

1969 Builder Jeffrey Wellborn was appointed to serve on the Fairfax County School Board replacing William Hoofnagle who had been appointed to serve as chairman of the Fairfax County Board of Supervisors. (*Reston Times*, December 18, 1969.)

1970 Reston Interfaith Housing Corporation was established in January (Interfaith files.)

1970 The Cedar Ridge Garden Apartment complex was completed with 198 low and moderate-income units. (Von Eckardt, *Washington Post*, April 6, 1970.)

1970 Reston Home Owners Association (RHOA) was created by consolidating the First Home Owners Association (FHOA) and the Second Home Owners Association (SHOA) on April 22. Robert Perce was its first president, Karl Ingebritsen its first executive director. (Ingebritsen, *RHOA*, pp.12-13.)

1970 Ground was broken for Fellowship House at Lake Anne for senior citizens in February. It was the first project of its kind in an American New Town. (McCandless, *Brief History*, p. 26.)

1970 The Fairfax Hunt huntsman and hounds were moved to the Goose Creek area in Loudoun County due to the Dulles Access Road, Reston and other developments encroaching on the forest lands. (Opstad, *Fairfax Hunt*.)

1970 Eurotherm, a manufacturer of temperature control products for industrial use, was the first European-based firm to locate in Reston, at Newton Square in May. (*The Reston Industrial Landsales Newsletter*, October 1979.)

1970 Earth Day in May ended in disaster as a sewer line backed up at Lake Anne Plaza. (*Reston Times*, May 7, 1970.)

1970 The National Education Association purchased fifty-six acres of land for the campus-like Reston Center for Associations and Educational Institutions. (McCandless, *Brief History*, p. 26; *Reston Industrial Landsales Newsletter*, January 1978.)

1970 The Reston North Golf Course was converted to a private enterprise and renamed the Reston Golf and Country Club, June 1. On the same day, Reston South Golf Course was opened to the public. (McCandless, *Brief History*, p. 28.)

1970 Cable TV came to Reston with 1500 subscribers in July. (Tom Grubisich in the *Washington Post*, June 18, 1970.)

1970 Gulf Reston deeded to RHOA more than $600,000 worth of debt-free recreational facilities, walkways, bridges, parks, lakes and open space. (McCandless, *Brief History*, p. 28.)

1970 A $90,000 pedestrian overpass at North Shore Drive and Wiehle Avenue was deeded to RHOA in August. (McCandless, *Brief History*, p. 28.)

1970 James W. Todd joined Reston's staff as director of residential marketing in October. (Press release from Gulf Reston June 10, 1974 on his promotion at that time.)

1970 Northgate Square, Reston's first cluster of townhouses with FHA-VA financing, were for sale. (McCandless, *Brief History*, p. 24.)

1970 Gulf Reston, Inc., as part of the agreement for construction of the new USGS headquarters in Reston, agreed to build subsidized housing near the facility. (*Reston Times*, January 3, 1980.)

1970 A study for the U.S. Department of Transportation released by the Institute of Social Research, University of Michigan, showed a high level of satisfaction among residents of Reston. (McCandless, *Brief History*, p. 30.)

1971 Westbound Dulles Access Road ramps were opened by Senator William Spong, Supervisor Martha Pennino, and Board of Supervisors Chairman William Hoofnagle. (*Reston Times*, February 11, 1971.)

1971 The Virginia Department of Highways approved widening of Baron Cameron Avenue from two lanes to four. (*Reston Times*, March 14, 1971.)

1971 Cable television transmission began in April. (*Reston Times*, January 3, 1980.)

1971 First residents moved into Fellowship House for the elderly in May, 140 units near Lake Anne Village Center. (Dr. John Scherzer interview, July 29, 1982.)

1971 Official ground breaking was held July 29 for USGS $54 million national center. (McCandless, *Brief History*, p. 33.)

1971 Karl Ingebritsen was fired as executive director of RHOA and left as of August 1. (Ingebritsen, *RHOA*, p.27; interview.)

1971 Joyce Pfeffer, a Hunters Woods resident and RHOA treasurer, was appointed acting executive director. (Ingebritsen, *RHOA*, pp. 27-28.)

1971 Forest Edge Elementary opened in September. (School Administration.)

1971 The Glenvale garden apartments were begun, the first FHA condominiums in the Washington area. (McCandless, *Brief History*, p. 31.)

1971 In the fall, work was begun on Reston's first FHA (236) moderate income garden apartments at Fox Mill. (McCandless, *Brief History*, p. 32.)

1971 Reston's first townhouses built on the south side of the Dulles Expressway were begun at Southgate Square. (McCandless, *Brief History*, p. 32.)

1971 Reston's first modular townhouses were begun at Golf Course Village at the end of the year. (McCandless, *Brief History*, p. 31.)

1971 Construction was begun on the first townhouses on the South Golf Course, Hunters Green. (McCandless, *Brief History*, p. 32.)

1971 Glenn Saunders was appointed executive vice president Gulf Oil Real Estate Company (GOREDCO) in September and to the Board of Directors of Gulf Reston. (Glenn W. Saunders, Jr., resume; (McCandless, *Brief History*, p. 35.)

1971 Gene Bergoffen was appointed the Centreville District's member on the Fairfax County School Board. (*Fairfax Globe*, November 18, 1971.)

1972 Reston/Herndon/Sterling Soccer League organized. (Larry

Fones, director, Fairfax County Department of Recreation.)

1972 Mona Blake was appointed minority representative on the Fairfax County School Board on January 12, 1972. (*Reston Times*, January 20, 1972.)

1972 Thomas Burgess was appointed executive director ofRHOA in March. (Ingebritsen, *RHOA*, p. 28.)

1972 The Reston Commuter Bus was given permission by FAA to use the Dulles Access Road into Washington in March. (McCandless, *Brief History*, p. 39.)

1972 Common Ground established an intra-Reston, mini-bus service with one route in Lake Anne and one in Hunters Woods. (McCandless, *Brief History*, p. 39.)

1972 A Community Center Task Force was organized in April to begin with plans for a facility. (Fact Sheet, undated.)

1972 Fairfax County Fire Company No. 25 became operational April 13. (Fire and Rescue archives, Stephanie Strass, September 20, 1981.)

1972 Fairfax County Board of Supervisors imposed a county-wide sewer moratorium May 19. (Board of Supervisors Minute Book.)

1972 Francis C. Steinbauer was appointed vice president of planning, engineering, and design for Gulf Reston in June. (*Restonian*, August 1974.)

1972 Shadowood condominiums opened in June. (*Restonian*, August 1974.)

1972 The Hunters Woods church of the United Christian Parish of Reston on Colts Neck Road held their first religious service in September. (Church office.)

1972 Hunters Woods Village Center was dedicated with a sixteenth century Renaissance theme in November. (*Reston Times*, November 23, 1972; McCandless, *Brief History*, p. 38.)

1973 Gulf Reston filed suit against Fairfax County on January 10 to get sewer taps for new construction. (*Reston Times*, January 25, February 8, 1973.)

1973 The RCA and Gulf Reston appeared at the Fairfax County Planning Commission in support of a 624-acre rezoning of the southeastern portion of Reston, low density. (*Reston Times*, January 25, 1973.)

1973 James Christian Pfohl resigned his music post held seven years. He had been brought to Reston by Robert E. Simon, Jr., to establish a performing arts school which did not materialize. (*Reston Times*, January 25, 1973.)

1973 Groundbreaking ceremonies were held for the Laurel Glade Apartments, a two-hundred-unit complex for low and moderate income families. (*Reston Times*, January 3, 1980.)

1973 RCA Housing Committee Chairman Pat Garfinkel resigned. Low and moderate-income housing funds were unavailable due to recent impoundment of certain appropriations by the Nixon Administration. (*Reston Times*, February 15, 1973.)

1973 The Fairfax Hospital Association made an informal offer to provide emergency health care to Reston. (*Reston Times*, February 22, 1973.)

1973 Vernon Walker was named director of RHOA's Department of Open Space Management and Development by Tom Burgess, executive director. (*Reston Times*, March 15, 1973.)

1973 The RCA expressed opposition to the Beverly hospital plan backed by Gulf Reston. The County Planning staff also opposed it. (*Reston Times*, March 22, March 29, April 5, 1973.)

1973 The Georgetown University Medical School opened a health care center at Hunters Woods Village Center. (*Reston Times*, April 12, 1973.)

1973 James Todd was named executive vice president of Gulf Reston (*Reston Times*, June 14, 1973.)

1973 Reston Home Owners Association hired John W. Frece to be their ombudsman. (*Reston Times*, July 19, 1973.)

1973 The Sheraton Inn and International Conference Center opened in July, dedication September 29. (The *Orange Disc*, November-December 1973.)

1973 The Dulles Express Bus lanes were opened to traffic on July 31. (*Reston Times*, July 26, 1973.)

1973 St. Thomas à Becket Catholic Church on Wiehle Avenue was formally dedicated on September 9. (Church office.)

1973 The USGS staff began moving into their new headquarters building in September. (*Reston Times*, October 4, 1973.)

1973 Dag Hammerskjold Plaza in the International Conference Center was dedicated in September. (*Reston Times*, October 4, 1973.)

1973 Michael Was joined the GRI staff as design planner. (Reston

1973 An International Film Festival was held at the Sheraton. (*Reston Times*, October 4, 1973.)

1973 Anthropologist Margaret Mead visited and commented on Reston in November. (*Reston Times*, November 15, 1973.)

1973 Robert E. Simon, Jr. wrote an open letter to Martha Pennino praising her for guiding the recent Reston rezoning to adoption by the Board of Supervisors. (*Reston Times*, November 22, 1973.)

1973 Fairfax County School Administration. Fairfax County Teacher of the Year (among six thousand): "Kiki" Tamashiro, Lake Anne Elementary. (*Reston Times*, November 29, 1973.)

1973 The Watergate Scandal and Arab Oil Embargo caused a national economic downturn particularly affecting housing and transportation.

1973 Rodney Page was appointed Centreville District's member on the Fairfax County School Board (later elected chairman). (*Fairfax Journal*, December 27, 1973.)

1974 Reston Youth Soccer was organized, playing on local school fields. (Larry Fones, Director, Fairfax County Department of Recreation.)

1974 Reston's first movie house, the Biograph Twin Cinema, opened on Hammerskjold Plaza, March 21, with Charlie Chaplin's *Limelight*, and the modern film *A Touch of Class*.

1974 The Greater Reston Arts Center (GRACE) was established as a nonprofit organization to promote and support arts in the greater Reston area. (Fact sheet, GRACE.)

1974 The Reston Regional Library was opened at Hunters Woods on March 10. (Library Administration.)

1974 Jim Todd was appointed president and chief operating officer of Gulf Reston by Bill Magness. (Gulf Reston press release.)

1974 John W. Guinee was appointed executive vice president of Gulf Oil RE Co. (*Reston Times*, September 12, 1974.)

1974 Gulf Reston Chairman of the Board Bill Magness told the annual meeting of the Fairfax County Chamber of Commerce that the Board of Supervisors' "slow-growth" and "no-growth" policies had virtually spelled doom for the new town of Reston. (*Reston Times*, June 27, 1974.)

1974 Gulf Reston won a law suit against the County's sewer hookup moratorium, in June. (*Fairfax County Newsletter*, July 11, 1974.)

1974 Confrontations between blacks and whites at Herndon High escalated from verbal to physical fights, forcing the closing of the school for one day. (*Reston Times*, January 3, 1980.)

1974 Dogwood Elementary School opened in September. (School administration.)

1974 *Gulf Reston vs. Fairfax County Board of Supervisors* suit was settled for plaintiff, October 22. (Fairfax County court records.)

1974 The financial crisis brought on in part by the Arab oil embargo depressed the building industry and reduced mortgage money available. (*Reston Times*, January 3, 1980.)

1974 County voters turned down a school bond issue that would have financed construction of a Reston high school and an elementary school. (*Reston Times*, January 3, 1980.)

1974 Tall Oaks, the third village center, was dedicated on November 18. Designers were Collins and Kronstadt, architects. (*Restonian*, August 1974.)

1975 The United States Department of Housing and Urban Development announced the end of their new town development program in the United States in January. (*Washington Post*, January 11, 1975.)

1975 Special Service District (Small District No. 5) was formed by the Board of Supervisors on March 24 and a local bond issue was approved for construction of a community center at Hunters Woods Village Center. (*Reston Times*, January 3, 1980.)

1975 Lynn Lilienthal and Peggy Jansons received Fairfax County's first license for infant care at PALS Learning Center (Reston Regional Library files.)

1975 The Lake Anne Office Building was completed and opened. (*Reston Times*, January 3, 1980.)

1975 The *Ladies Home Journal* selected Reston as one of the fifteen best suburbs for living in the United States. (*Ladies Home Journal*, August 1975.)

1975 Floris Elementary moved into a new school building in April. (School Administration.)

1975 Mona Blake was commended for four years of service on the Fairfax County School Board as the minority representative. (*Reston Times*, September 18, 1975.)

1975 *A Place Called Reston* community phone directory business was purchased by Restonians Nancy Larson and Ann Page. (Nancy Larson, October 6, 1981.)

1976 Reston obtained its first post office building in Isaac Newton Square.

1976 Reston Community Church (Unitarian-Universalist) on Wiehle Avenue was formally dedicated May 16. (Church office.)

1976 Fox Mill Apartments residents complained about mismanagement of their low and moderate-income complex. (*Reston Times*, January 3, 1980.)

1976 Reston District Police Station opened in Isaac Newton Square May 26 with an authorized strength of forty-four sworn personnel. (Capt. Ronald P. Miner, Reston Station.)

1976 The controversial British and French supersonic transport Concordes began landing at Dulles Airport in May. (*Fairfax County, Virginia*, pp. 603-604.)

1976 Rodney Page was elected Chairman of the Fairfax County School Board. (He served until June 1980.) (School Board Clerk Shirley Brooks.)

1976 Reston Racquet Club opened (indoor tennis) September 25. (RLC office.)

1976 Work began on widening Reston Avenue from a two-lane roadway to a major four-lane highway from Baron Cameron Avenue to South Lakes Drive. (*Reston Times*, January 3, 1980.)

1977 A promotion in cooperation with Bloomingdales in March was a great success. (Reston Land Corporation files.)

1977 Terraset School opened in September. It was the first underground solar heated/cooled elementary school in the United States (*Fairfax County, Virginia*, p. 585.)

1977 Water shortage in Northern Virginia was critical due to lack of rain in the Potomac River basin resulting in abnormally low water levels. Fairfax County placed rigid restrictions on water use. (*Reston Times*, January 3, 1980.)

1977 Common Ground, due to financial losses, discontinued intra-Reston jitney bus system. (*Reston Times*, January 3, 1980.)

1977 ACCESS opened; Reston's first emergency hospital facility, May 3. (Fairfax County Government *Weekly Agenda*, May 12, 1977.)

1977 Reston Avenue was widened and a new bridge built over the Dulles Access Road in August. (RLC, Richard Bonar.)

1977 DeLong Bowman house was closed in June. (*Reston Times*, June 16, 1977.)

1977 The Reston Community bus system was reestablished as Reston Internal Bus System (RIBS) in September under joint sponsorship of RHOA, Fairfax County and Northern Virginia Transportation Commission. (RLC office.)

1977 Kenneth Plum of Reston was elected to the Virginia House of Delegates in November. (*Reston Times*, January 3, 1980.)

1977 Good Shepherd Lutheran Church, Moorings Drive, was dedicated November 20. (Church office.)

1977 Gulf Oil Corporation, deciding to concentrate on its "basic business"—energy—put its income-producing property on the market, planning to divest itself of all real estate holdings including Reston. (*Reston Times*, January 3, 1980.)

1978 Widened Reston Avenue bridge was opened in January (Reston Land Corporation files.)

1978 The Design House, by architect Hugh Newell Jacobsen, was a successful promotion (Reston Land Corporation files.)

1978 Planners met in Reston to discuss "lessons learned." (*Reston Times*, May 25, 1978.)

1978 The Sperry Division of Sperry Rand Corporation purchased 36.5 acres of land at Reston Avenue and Sunrise Valley Drive. (*Reston Industrial Landsales Newsletter*, April 1979, August 1980.)

1978 Reston Bowling Center opened in September. (Reston Recreation Center Office.)

1978 Forest Edge Elementary School children, "looking back," wrote "The Ballad of Reston." (*Reston Times*, June 8, 1978.)

1978 RPC ordinance was changed to Planned Residential Community (PRC) with the adoption of a new zoning ordinance by the Fairfax County Board of Supervisors on June 12, 1978, Article 6, Part 3.

1978 The Mobil Oil Corporation purchased thirty-seven hundred acres of undeveloped land in July. A subsidiary company, Reston Land Corporation, was formed and Jim Todd was appointed president. (Fairfax County Deed Books; *Reston Times*, July 27, 1978; May 24, 1979.)

1978 Lake naming—upper south lake was first called Wyeth, then Thoreau. The lower lake was called Snakeden by the Bowmans, then Lake Elsa after Simon's mother, then Audubon. (*Reston Times*, August 31, 1978.)

1978 South Lakes High opened in September. (School administration.)

1978 Wiehle Avenue bridge was dedicated September 20. (Reston Land Corporation office.)

1979 Reston Community Charter bill passed General Assembly in February. (Kenneth Plum.)

1979 Fellowship House opened in Hunters Woods in March. (*Reston Times*, December 27, 1979.)

1979 Reston Community Center opened at Hunters Woods on May 20. Robert E. Simon, Jr., was the guest speaker. (*Reston Times*, May 24, 1979.)

1979 Dulles Access Road parallel toll lanes were approved by the Virginia General Assembly. The road was opened to four-person carpools during rush hours with the approval of F.A.A., owner of Dulles Airport. (*Reston Times*, January 3, 1980.)

1979 Island Walk, Reston's first apartment cooperative, opened. (Larson, *History*, p. 10.)

1979 Fairfax County Fire Company No. 31 became operational July 27. (Stephanie Strass, Fire and Rescue Service, September 20, 1981.)

1979 Clearview and Sunrise Valley elementary schools opened in September. (School administration.)

1980 Hunters Woods South Riding stables collapsed January 25. (RHOA records.)

1980 Gulf Reston, Inc., sold its income-producing properties on February 5 to Donatelli and Klein, Inc., Mark Winkler Management, Inc., and Stephen Yeonas. (*Reston Times*, February 14, 1980.)

1980 The Community Charter for Reston which was passed by the Virginia General Assembly in February 1979 was rejected at the polls by Reston residents in November. (Interview with Kenneth Plum, delegate, October 6, 1981.)

1980 The prepaid health plan management was taken over by Kaiser health systems in cooperation with Georgetown University. (Larson, *History*, p. 11.)

1980 National Recreation and Parks Association. Outstanding Community Service Award to James Allred.

1980 Langston Hughes Intermediate School opened in November. (School Administration.)

1981 John Graves, U.S. Embassy staff Iranian hostage, to return home to Reston in February. (*Reston Times*, January 22, 1981.)

1981 Tandem Computers broke ground on March 23 for eastern regional headquarters in Reston.

1981 North Point Village and sixteen-acre Lake Newport construction began. (*Reston* letter, Spring/Summer 1981.)

1981 Jim Todd was appointed chairman of the board of Reston Land Corporation; Fran Steinbauer, president; and Jim Cleveland, executive vice president in March 1981. (Reston Land Corporation files.)

1981 Northern Virginia Hebrew Congregation Temple on Wiehle Avenue was formally dedicated in March. (Temple office.)

1981 Reston Recreation Association Skateway was opened on May 3. (Reston Recreation Center office.)

1981 A. Smith Bowman, Jr., died of cancer in his McLean home. (S. Y. Smith in the *Washington Post*, May 8, 1981.)

1981 Ribbi Rosaline Gold became the first woman to head a synagogue in the Washington area when she took over the pulpit in September at the Northern Virginia Hebrew Congregation in Reston. (*Fairfax Journal*, August 19, 1981.)

1981 The Fairfax County Parkway (outer beltway) issue was being discussed in the fall in an effort to come to an acceptable plan for a new cross-county arterial road which would intersect or abut Reston land. (Fairfax County BOS minute books.)

1981 *The Reston Fairfax West Connection* began publication as a bi-weekly newspaper on October 14, Paul Clancy, publisher and Tom Grubisich, editor. (prototype edition September 30, 1981.)

1981 Kenneth Plum was elected for a second term in the Virginia House of Delegates in November.

1981 *The Connection* began publication as a weekly edition. (December 9.)

1982 St. John Newman Catholic Church on Lawyers Road held the formal dedication of their church on June 28. (Church office.)

1982 Vernon Walker died of cancer, after a long illness, on July 13. (RHOA office staff.)

1982 North Point Village Visitors Center opened on September 28.

(*Reston Times*, September 30, 1982.)

1982 Ground was broken for Reston's fourth village center, South Lakes, in size second only to Hunters Woods, on October 7. (*Reston Times*, October 14, 1982.)

1982 Final approval of the Dulles Toll Road was given by the Virginia State Highway Commission, December 16. (Fairfax *Journal*, December 17, 1982.)

1982 I-66 opened between I-495 and Washington, D.C., by way of Theodore Roosevelt Bridge, December 22. (Reston Land Corporation office.)

1983 Ground was broken for the Dulles Toll Road, January 29. (Reston Land Corporation office.)

1983 First election was held for officers, Reston Board of Commerce, with 120 member firms, Patrick Kane, president, March 16. (Karl Ingebritsen, Membership Committee chairman.)

1983 Ground was broken for North County Government Center, April 23. (Reston Land Corporation office.)

1983 Fresh Value grocery store and Il Cigno restaurant opened in Lake Anne Village Center. (*The Connection*, August 1, 1984.)

1983 Country Club of Reston was purchased by a group of new owners, rehabilitated, and renamed Hidden Creek Country Club, July 19. (Hidden Creek office.)

1983 GTE, a major communications company, announced plans to bring two of their divisions to Reston. (*The Connection*, September 7, 1983.)

1983 RLC transferred dams for Lakes Thoreau and Audubon to RHOA on November 18. (RLC memo from J. W. Todd, November 28, 1983.)

1983 AT&T leased space for three new marketing groups in Linpro Park. (*Reston* newsletter, Fall/Winter, 1983.)

1983 Kenneth Plum was elected for a third term in the Virginia House of Delegates, November. (Fairfax County Library.)

1983 First group of stores opened in new South Lakes Village Center in November. (Reston Land Corporation office.)

1983 Dulles connector highway opened between Route 66 and the Dulles Access Road, December 5. (Reston Land Corporation office.)

1983 Location of 125-bed nursing home was approved for Fairfax Hospital next to ACCESS in Town Center, December. (Reston Land Corporation office.)

1983 General Electric announced plans for eventual location in Reston Town Center of a work force of eight to nine hundred people. (*Reston Times*, December 22, 1983.)

1983 Black Focus initiated an informal sister city relationship with Nyeri, Kenya. (Reston Regional Library.)

1983 By the end of the year, for the first time in Reston's history, the number of jobs exceeded the number of households (Reston Land Corporation files.)

1983 Classic country cottage design by Lester Walker won a *House Beautiful* contest. Later a model was built in Reston. (Reston Land Corporation files.)

1984 Lake Anne Village Center was declared a historic district by the Fairfax County Board of Supervisors. (*Reston Times*, February 16, 1984.)

1984 South Lakes Village Center officially opened. (*Reston Times*, May 16, 1984.)

1984 James Todd resigned from Reston Land. (RLC files, June.)

1984 James Cleveland was appointed president in July. (RLC files.)

1984 Reston's first Triathlon was held. The three events were a 1-mile swim, a 23-mile bike ride, and a 6.2 mile run. 164 participated. (Reston Regional Library files.)

1984 The Dulles Toll Road (thirteen miles) opened. By 1985— 25,956,344 motorists had used it; in 1987, the number was 35,321,687. (Reston Regional Library files.)

1984 RHOA opened its new central services facility. (*Reston Times*, October 11, 1984.)

1984 Reston's first Volksmarch was held. (*Reston Times*, November 1, 1984.)

1984 Reston Interfaith, Inc., was formed to broaden the scope of services. (Interfaith, Inc., files.)

1984 Planned Community Archives was formed to collect Reston's New Town development records and those of other planned communities.

1984 A Reston childcare conference was held in November. (Reston Regional Library files.)

1985 North County Government Center opened in Town Center in

January. (Supervisor Pennino's office.

1985 Francis Steinbauer, MLDC president, resigned in February. (RLC files.)

1985 Michael Was, executive vice president of RLC resigned in May. (RLC files.)

1985 Gregory Friess was appointed executive vice president of RLC in May. (RLC files.)

1985 Reston's twentieth anniversary was celebrated in May. (Reston Regional Library files.)

1985 Fairfax Hospital changed from a rotating system to a permanent nursing and technical staff at ACCESS. (*Reston Times*, June 18, 1985.)

1985 Restonian John David Bartoe was due to blast off in the Challenger space shuttle in July. (*Reston Times*, June 27, 1985.)

1985 Browns Chapel concession building was opened. (Reston Association files.)

1985 Black Focus Festival was held at Lake Anne. (*Reston Times*, September 5, 1985.)

1985 Reston Regional Library was opened at Town Center. (Reston Regional Library files.)

1985 Kenneth Plum was elected to his fourth term as delegate in November. (Reston Regional Library files.)

1985 GRACE received the gift of an old warehouse from the Bowman Distillery in November. (*Reston Times*, November 23, 1985.)

1986 Plans were unveiled on February 18 for development of Reston Town Center core. (RLC files.)

1986 A special GRACE student art exchange program exhibited children's art from the Peoples Republic of China. (GRACE files.)

1986 Dr. Raymond G. Wilkins, South Lakes High, was named Fairfax County Teacher of the Year. (*Reston Times*, May 10, 1986.)

1986 Metrorail opened new stations on the Orange Line at East Falls Church, West Falls Church, Dunn Loring, and Vienna. (*Reston Times*, June 11, 1986.)

1986 New elementary school in North Point Village was named after astronaut Neil Armstrong. (*Reston Times*, June 14, 1986.)

1986 Lord Nicholas John Albert Fairfax of Great Britain visited Washington Plaza. (*Reston Times*, June 14, 1986.)

1986 Black Focus Festival was held at Washington Plaza. (*Reston Times*, September 3, 1986.)

1986 Neil Armstrong Elementary School opened in September. (*Reston Times*, June 14, 1986.)

1986 Reston Hospital Center was opened on November 10. (Public Relations Office.)

1987 Ground breaking was held for the Vernon J. Walker Nature Education Center on January 19. (*Reston Times*, January 21, 1987.)

1987 RHOA's name was changed to the Reston Association (RA) on January 22. (*Reston Times*, February 4, 1987.)

1987 Lake Newport swimming pool opened in May. (*Reston Times*, May 13, 1987.)

1987 The *Reston Times* was named the best weekly newspaper in North America by Suburban Newspapers of America. (*Reston Times*, July 1, 1987.)

1987 Grumman Corporation won a contract from NASA for support of the development of the space station. (*Reston Times*, July 5, 1987.)

1987 Susan Norwitch was inducted as the first woman member of the Reston Lions Club; Patricia Zylka was approved as the first woman member of the Reston Optimist Club. (*Reston Times*, July 22, 1987.)

1987 RCC opened a snack bar as a meeting place. (*Reston Times*, July 29, 1987.)

1987 North County Human Services Building opened August 17. (North County Human Services.)

1987 An Exposition was sponsored by the Reston Board of Commerce. (*Reston Times*, September 1987.)

1987 The old charter oak blew down. (*Reston Times*, October 14, 1987.)

1987 NASA announced plans to base space station project in Reston. (RLC files.)

1987 Kenneth Plum was elected to his fifth term as delegate. (Reston Regional Library files.)

1987 Reston welcomed its fifty-thousandth resident in November. (RLC files.)

1987 First day-long town forum was held at RCC. It identified twelve principal issues (November 14). (*Reston Times*, November 18, 1987.)

1987 Reston/North County Community Shelter opened in December. (Shelter office.)

1988 First childcare facility opened in a Reston office complex in January. (Reston Regional Library files.

1988 Cameron Glen Care Center opened in February (Cameron Glen office.)

1988 GRACE moved from Heron House to temporary quarters in the Town Center Office Building in February. (*Reston Times*, January 27, 1988.)

1988 Russian delegation including sculptor Zurab Tzereteli visited Reston. He offered to give the community a thirty-foot statue. (Reston Regional Library files.)

1988 Dr. John Scherzer retired in April at age eighty-six. (*Reston Times*, June 22, 1988.)

1988 The *Reston Times* was named best suburban newspaper in U.S. and Canada for second straight year by Chicago-based Suburban Newspapers of America. (*Reston Times*, May 25, 1988.)

1988 The last barrel of aged whiskey left the Sunset Hills Distillery site. (Bowman Distillery office.)

1988 The Town Center complex ground breaking was held June 22. (*Reston Times*, June 29, 1988.)

1988 A delegation of Restonians went to Russia to visit Zurab Tzereteli. The sculpture offer was discussed and withdrawn in July. (*Reston Times*, August 3, 1988.)

1988 Tall Oaks Fellowship House was dedicated in September. (*Reston Times*, September 14, 1988.)

1988 In November, the governor's commission of historic preservation released a report, *A Future for Virginia's Past* in which Reston was prominently mentioned as being historically important. (Gov. Baliles' office.)

1989 Reston Hospital's Maternity Center opened on February 14. (Public Relations office.)

1989 Ground was broken for the Hyatt Regency hotel at Town Center. (*Reston Times*, March 6, 1989.)

1989 Plan was announced in March by the Board of Supervisors to purchase the Stonegate apartments in July. (*Reston Times*, March 8, 1989.)

1989 Charter for the town of Wiehle was repealed in March. (Delegate Kenneth Plum's office.)

1989 Reston/North County Shelter was renamed the Embry Rucker Shelter for the Homeless. (office of Martha Pennino.)

1989 Memorial sundial at the Nature Center given by the Rotarians in memory of Vernon Walker was formally dedicated in June. (Reston Association files.)

Reston Architectural, Construction, Environmental and Marketing Awards

1966 American Institute of Architects. Honor Awards Jury. Special Tribute: Robert E. Simon, Jr.

1966 American Association of Newspapers. Industrial Landscaping Award. Certificate of Merit: Reston for Beautification of America (presented by Mrs. Lyndon Johnson).

1966 American Institute of Architects. Homes for Better Living Awards. Award of Merit: Reston.

1966 *House and Home.* Top Performer of 1966: Robert E. Simon, Jr.

1967 Metropolitan Washington Board of Trade Design Awards: Conklin and Rossant Architects for the Gulf Service Station at Lake Anne; Juris Jansons Architect for Scope, Inc.; Chloethiel Woodard Smith for Waterview Cluster; Conklin and Rossant Architects for Lake Anne Village Center.

1968 *Architectural Record. Record* House of the Year: Louis Sauer for Golf Course Island.

1969 Metropolitan Washington Board of Trade. Excellence in Architecture Award: Ward and Hall Architects for Washington Plaza Baptist Church.

1969 Metropolitan Washington Builders Association. Finest for Family Living Awards. Awards of Excellence: Gulf Reston, Inc., for Bridges Cluster; and Wellborn for Mediterranean Villa.

1970 Fairfax County. First Annual Fairfax County Beautification Awards: William Magness for Reston; Conklin and Rossant Architects for Lake Anne Village Center; Vlastimil Koubeck Architect for the Newton Center Building; Ronald L. Taylor Architect for the Lake Anne Professional Building.

1970 Metropolitan Washington Builders Association. Finest for Family Living Awards. Award of Excellence; Gulf Reston, Inc., for Bridges Townhouses; J. Wellborn for the Wellborn House and the Wellborn Speculative House.

1970 American Institute of Architects. Honor Award: Ward and Hall Architects for the Washington Plaza Baptist Church.

1970 Guild for Religious Architecture. Honor Award: Ward and Hall Architects for the Washington Plaza Baptist Church.

1971 American Institute of Architects. Northern Virginia Section Honor Awards: Kamstra, Abrash and Dickerson Architects for South Golf Course Clubhouse.

1971 Metropolitan Washington Builders Association. Finest for Family Living Awards. Awards of Excellence: Gulf Reston, Inc., for Woodside Homes and Hillcrest Townhouses; Berlage/Bernstein Builders for Chatham Colony; and Wellborn Company for Country Courts.

1971 *Environmental Monthly* Magazine. Environmental and Educational Excellence Award: William Magness for Reston; Vernon Walker/RHOA for the Reston Nature Center.

1972 Metropolitan Washington Builders Association. Finest for Family Living Awards. Awards of Excellence; Gulf Reston, Inc., for Southgate Square Townhouses and Hillcrest Cluster, and Bennett Company for Bentana Woods.

1972 Northern Virginia Builders Association. Awards for Excellence in Construction and Craftsmanship: Gulf Reston, Inc., for Moorings Cluster, Inlet Cluster, and Southgate Square Cluster; and Wellborn Company for Country Courts.

1972 *Environmental Monthly* Magazine. Citation for Environmental Excellence in Lande Use: Gulf Reston, Inc.

1972 American Forestry Association. Certificate of Merit "for his outstanding contribution to American conservation through tree planting in Reston, Virginia": William Magness.

1973 American Institute of Architects. Northern Virginia Section Honor Awards: Kamstra, Dickerson, Abrash Architects for Lake Anne Nursery Kindergarten and Golf Course Island Swim Club; Jansons Roberts Taylor Associates Architects for 11480 Isaac Newton Square and the St. Thomas à Becket Catholic Church; and Jansons and Roberts Architects for Scope, Inc.

1973 Metropolitan Washington Builders Association. Finest for Family Living Awards. Awards of Excellence; Gulf Reston, Inc., for Sanibel Cluster, Hillcrest Townhouses, Hunters Green, and Golf Course Square Cluster.

1973 Northern Virginia Builders Association. Awards for Excellence in Construction and Craftsmanship; Bonner, Inc., for Colts Neck Cluster; Gulf Reston, Inc., for Southgate Square Cluster, Hunters Green Cluster, Golf Course Square Cluster, Glenvale Condominium, and Hunters Woods Village Center.

1974 American Institute of Architects. Virginia Chapter Honor Awards: Kamstra, Dickerson, Abrash Architects for Lake Anne Nursery Kindergarten; Jasons Roberts Taylor Associates Architects for the St. Thomas à Becket Catholic Church.

1974 Metropolitan Washington Builders Association. Finest for Family Living Awards. Award of Excellence: Gulf Reston, Inc., for Hunters Green Townhouses, and Newbridge Cluster. Award of Merit: Gulf Reston, Inc., for Golf Course Square Townhouses.

1974 Northern Virginia Builders Association. Awards for Excellence in Construction and Craftsmanship: Gulf Reston, Inc., for United States Geological Survey National Headquarters.

1975 Owens-Corning Glass. National Energy Design Awards: Davis, Smith, Carter and Rider Architects for Terraset Elementary School.

1975 *Ladies Home Journal* Magazine. Fifteen Best Communities in the U.S. Award for Best Community in Washington Metropolitan Area: Reston.

1975 National Home Builders Association and *Better Homes and Gardens* Magazine. Sensible Growth Awards: Collins and Kronstadt for Tall Oaks Village Center.

1975 Northern Virginia Builders Association. Awards for Excellence in Construction and Craftsmanship: Gulf Reston, Inc., for Tall Oaks Village Center.

1975 American Institute of Architects. Northern Virginia Section Honor Award: Abrash, Eddy and Eckhardt Architects for Mattas Residence.

1975 Realtors National Marketing Institute Annual Awards, Honorable Mention: Davis, Smith, Carter and Rider for Chimney House Real Estate Interiors.

1976 American Association of School Administrators and the AIA AASA Annual Conference: Walter Taylor Award for School Architecture: Davis, Smith, Carter and Rider for Terraset Elementary School.

1976 American Institute of Architects. Northern Virginia Section Honor Award. Special Citation for Energy Design: Davis, Smith, Carter and Rider for Terraset Elementary School.

1977 Washington Metropolitan Builders Association. Finest for Family Living Awards. Award of Excellence: Gulf Reston, Inc., for Wethersfield Townhouses.

1978 Northern Virginia Builders Association. MAME (Major Achievement in Marketing Excellence) Awards. Award of Excellence: Reston Land Corporation for Best TV Commercial.

1978 Association of School Business Officials of the United States and Canada. Award of Excellence: Davis, Smith, Carter and Rider for Terraset Elementary School.

1978 The One Club for Art and Copy. The One Show Awards. Certificate of Merit: Reston Land Corporation for Best Newspaper Advertisement.

1979 American Advertising Federation. National ADDY Awards. Certificate of Merit: Reston Land Corporation for Best Direct Mail Advertisement.

1979 The Advertising Club of New York. ANDY Awards. Award of Excellence: Reston Land Corporation for Best Small space Magazine Campaign. Certificates of Merit: Reston Land Corporation for Best Direct Mail Campaign, Best Magazine Advertisement, Best Small Space Newspaper Campaign, and Best Poster.

1979 The CLIOS. CLIO Award. Certificates of Excellence: Reston Land Corporation for Best Regional Trade Promotion and Best Special Packaging Promotion. Award of Recognition: Reston Land Corporation for Best Packaging Design.

1979 *Communication Arts* Magazine. Communication Arts Awards. Awards of Excellence: Reston Land Corporation for Best Newspaper Advertisement and Best Direct Mail.

1979 The One Club for Art and Copy. The One Show Awards. Gold Medal: Reston Land Corporation for Best Direct Mail. Certificates of Merit: Reston Land Corporation for Best Newspaper Trade Campaign, Best Poster, and five for Best Single Direct Mail.

1979 Northern Virginia Builders Association. MAME (Major Achievements in Marketing Excellence) Awards. Awards of Excellence: Reston Land Corporation for Overall Creative Excellence and Best Overall Advertising Campaign.

1980 American Advertising Federation. National ADDY Awards. Gold Medal: Reston Land Corporation for Best Magazine Campaign.

1980 Metropolitan Washington Builders Association. Finest for Family Living Awards. Award of Excellence: Castro-Holdsworth, Inc., for Mallards Landing.

1980 Northern Virginia Builders Association. MAME (Major Achievement in Marketing Excellence) Awards. Award of Excellence: Reston Land Corporation for Best TV Commercial.

1980 The One Club for Art and Copy. The One Show Awards. Certificate of Merit: Reston Land Corporation for Best Consumer Magazine Campaign.

1980 Northern Virginia Builders Association. MAME (Major Achievement in Marketing Excellence) Awards. Award of Excellence: Reston Land Corporation for Special Achievement in Overall Campaign and Best Continuing Advertising Campaign for a Developer.

1980 American Marketing Association/New York. EFFIE Awards. Silver Award: Reston Land Corporation for Best Overall Campaign.

1981 Metropolitan Washington Builders Association. Finest for Family Living Awards. Award of Excellence: Christopher Companies for Hunters Square. Award of Merit: The Yeonas Company for Glencourse.

1981 Fairfax County. Conservation Awards: Reston Land Corporation for Excellence in Land Conservation.

1982 National Association of Home Builders Institute of Residential Marketing and *Builder* Magazine. MIRM (Member Institute of Residential Marketing) Awards. Gold Medal: Reston Land Corporation for Best Sales Office (Reston Visitors Center). Silver Medal: Reston Land Corporation for Best Advertising and Promotional Campaign.

1982 Metropolitan Washington Builders Association. Finest for Family Living Awards. Grand Award for Energy Efficiency; Clubhouse Court, Ltd., Partnership for Clubhouse Court. Award of Merit: Chestnut Grove Associates for Chestnut Grove.

1982 Northern Virginia Builders Association. MAME (Major Achievement in Marketing Excellence) Awards. Award of Excellence: Reston Land Corporation for Best Continuing Campaign and Best Color Ad.

1982 Fairfax County. Conservation Awards: Reston Land Corporation for Excellence in Land Conservation (two awards) and Outstanding Commitment to Tree Preservation.

1983 National Association of Home Builders Institute of Residential Marketing and *Builder* Magazine. MIRM (Member Institute of Residential Marketing) Awards. Silver Awards: Reston Land Corporation for Best Special Promotion and Best Overall Marketing and Merchandising.

1983 American Institute of Architects. South Carolina Chapter Design Award. Doug Corkern Architects, Inc., for the Reston Visitors Center.

1983 Northern Virginia Builders Association. MAME (Major Achievement in Marketing Excellence) Awards. Awards of Excellence: Reston Land Corporation for Best Creative Marketing Promotion and Best Continuing Campaign.

1983 The Advertising Club of New York. ANDY Awards. Certificates of Merit: Reston Land Corporation for Best Consumer Newspaper Advertisement, Best Consumer Magazine Campaign, and Best Radio Advertisement.

1983 American Marketing Association/New York. EFFIE Awards. Silver Award: Reston Land Corporation for Best Real Estate Advertising Campaign.

1983 Fairfax County. Conservation Awards: Reston Land Corporation for Outstanding Commitment to Tree Preservation (two awards.)

1983/84 Metropolitan Washington Builders Association. Finest for Family Living Awards. Awards of Excellence: Miller and Smith, Inc., for Whisperwood, and Christopher Companies for Villa Ridge. Special Award for Community Concept: Reston Land Corporation for Reston. Award of Merit: Felix Construction Corporation for Solaridge Cluster Homes.

1984 The CLIOS. CLIO Awards. Award of Recognition: Reston Land Corporation for Best Regional Radio Advertisement.

1984 American Wood Council. Design for Better Living Award. *House Beautiful* Best Small House '84: Reston Land Corporation for the Classic Country Cottage.

1984 National Association of Home Builders Institute of Residential Marketing and *Builder* Magazine. MIRM (Members Institue Residential Marketing) Awards. Gold Award: Reston Land Corporation for Best Radio Commercial. Silver Awards: Reston Land Corporation for Best Overall Marketing Project and Best Special Promotion.

1984 Metropolitan Washington Sales and Marketing Council. MAME (Major Achievements in Marketing Excellence) Awards. Awards of Excellence: Reston Land Corporation for Best Color Ad, Best Radio Commercial and Best Series of Ads. Special Award of Recognition: Reston Land Corporation for the Classic Country Cottage.

1984 Fairfax County. Conservation Awards: Reston Land Corporation for Excellence in Land Conservation.

1985 Metropolitan Washington Builders Association. Finest for Family Living Awards. Award of Excellence: Fairfield Homes of Old Westbury. Energy Conservation Award: Koury Communities for Carriage Gate. Award of Merit: Regina Construction for Harbor Point.

1985 Metropolitan Washington Sales and Marketing Council. MAME (Major Achievement in Marketing Excellence) Awards. Award of Merit: Best Creative Marketing Program.

1985 American Institute of Architects. Presidential Citation: Reston Land Corporation, Robert E. Simon, the County of Fairfax, and the people of Reston for "proving conclusively that both community and the quality of life are enhanced through good design, sensitive planning, and the active involvement of caring citizens."

1985 The Advertising Club of New York. ANDY Awards. Award of Distinction: Reston Land Corporation for Best Newspaper Advertisements. Certificates of Merit: Reston Land Corporation for three Best Newspaper Advertisements.

1985 American Marketing Association/New York. EFFIE Awards. Gold Award: Reston Land Corporation for Best Real Estate Advertising Campaign.

1985 Fairfax County. Conservation Awards: Reston Land Corporation for Excellence in Land Conservation and Outstanding Commitment to Tree Preservation.

1986 National Association of Industrial and Office Parks (NAIOP). Northern Virginia NAIOP Awards. Special Award for Outstanding Achievement: Reston Land Corporation. First Place Awards: Reston Land Corporation for Reston Business Center (Best Office Park Over 100 Acres); Bay Colony Properties Company for 12200 Sunrise Valley Drive (Best Office Building Under 100,000 Square Feet); Lee Sammis Associates, Inc., for Campus Point (Best High-Tech Industrial Building over 100,000 Square Feet). Awards of Merit: Bay Colony Properties Company for Compucare Corporate Headquarters (Best Office Building Under 100,000 Square Feet); Walker and Company for Parkridge Center I (Best High-Tech Industrial Building Over 100,000 Square Feet); Lee

Sammis Associates, Inc; and Reston Land Corporation for The Branches Office Park (Best Office Park Under 100 Acres). Awards of Distinction: The Tetra Partnership for The Comsearch Building (Best Office Building Under 100,000 Square Feet).

1986 *Professional Builder* Magazine. Target Awards. Award of Excellence: Reston Land Corporation for Best Magazine Advertisement for Master Planned Community and Best Direct Mail Advertisement.

1986 Metropolitan Washington Builders Association. Finest for Family Living Awards. Award of Excellence: NVHomes for Bristol House.

1986 The Advertising Club of New York. ANDY Awards. Awards of Distinction: Reston Land Corporation for two Best Single Magazine Advertisements.

1986 Metropolitan Washington Sales and Marketing Council. MAME (Major Achievements in Marketing Excellence) Awards. Awards of Excellence: Reston Land Corporation for Best Project Brochure for a Planned Community and Best Print Media Campaign for a Planned Community. Award of Merit: Reston Land Corporation for Best Print Color Advertisement. Special Award for Best Continuing Marketing Effort for a Planned Community: Reston Land Corporation for Project of the Year.

1987 National Association of Industrial and Office Parks (NAIOP). Northern Virginia NAIOP Awards. Awards of Merit: Centennial Companies for The Summit (Best Office Building 75,000 to 150,000 Square Feet); Walker and Company for Park Ridge Center II (Best High-Tech Office Building Over 100,000 Square Feet); The Tetra Partnership for HunterLab II (Best High-Tech Office Building Under 100,000 Square Feet). Awards of Distinction: J. A. Loveless Company for Sunset Corporate Center (Best Office Building 75,000 to 150,000 Square Feet); Mulligan/Griffin and Associates for Tech Park Reston II (Best High-Tech Office Building Over 100,000 Square Feet).

1987 *Professional Builder* Magazine. Target Awards. Grand Award: Reston Land Corporation for Best Magazine Advertisement. Merit Award: Reston Land Corporatoin for Best Direct Mail Advertisement (Reston Newsletter).

1987 *Communication Arts* Magazine. Advertising Annual Awards. Award of Excellence: Reston Land Corporation for Best Consumer Magazine Advertisement Series.

1987 International Advertising Festival of New York. The New York Festival Awards. Finalist Award: Reston Land Corporation for Best Direct Mail (Reston Newsletter).

1987 Metropolitan Washington Builders Association. Finest for Family Living Awards. Awards of Excellence: Wrenn Associates, Ltd., for Fieldstone; Miller and Smith Homes for Arbor Glen; Christopher Companies for SummerRidge.

1987 Metropolitan Washington Sales and Marketing Council. MAME (Major Achievement in Marketing Excellence) Awards. Grand Awards: Reston Land Corporation for Project of the Year/Master Planned Development, Best Print Media Campaign, and Best Project Brochure. Award of Merit: Reston Land Corporation for Best Print Advertising.

1987 The CLIOS. CLIO Awards. Certificate of Excellence: Reston Land Corporation for Best Retail Services Advertisement.

1988 National Association of Industrial and Office Parks (NAIOP). Northern Virginia NAIOP Awards. First Place Awards: Lee Sammis Associates, Inc., for Audubon III, The Branches (Best Office Building Under 75,000 Square Feet) and Campus East and West Buildings, Campus Commons (Best Office Building 75,000 to 150,000 Square Feet); Walker and Company for Cascades Executive Center (Best Suburban Office Park Under twenty-five Acres). Award of Merit: Walker and Company, Parkridge Center III (Best High-Tech Office Building Over 100,000 Square Feet).

1988 National Association of Home Builders Institute of Residential Marketing and *Builder* Magazine. MIRM (Member Institute of Residential Marketing) Awards. Silver Awards: Reston Land Corporation for Best Print Media Campaign and Best Color Ad.

1988 International Advertising Festival of New York. The New York Festival Awards. Gold Medal: Reston Land Corporation for the Best Real Estate Advertising Campaign.

1988 Metropolitan Washington Sales and Marketing Council. MAME (Major Achievement in Marketing Excellence) Awards. Merit Awards: Reston Land Corporation for Best Print Advertising, Best Color Ad, and Best Special Promotion (Lake Newport Pool grand opening).

1988 Metropolitan Washington Builders Association. Finest for Family Living Awards. Awards of Excellence: cp1, Ltd., for Greenwich Point and The Meese Residence; William L. Berry and Company for Hampton Pointe. Awards of Merit: Fairfield Homes for Old Brookville; Gulick Group for Carisbrooke; and William L. Berry and Company for Hampton Pointe.

1988 Northern Virginia Board of Realtors. First Annual Northern Virginia Community Appearance Alliance Awards. Distinguished Design Award; Reston for The Branches Office Park and Lake Anne Plaza.

1988 Associated Builders and Contractors, Inc. Annual Construction Awards. Awards of Excellence: Sammis Construction Company for the Campus South Building (Best Medium Commercial $2.5-$5 million); Centennial Contractors, Inc., for the Summit at Reston, Phase II (Best Medium Commercial $5-$10 million.)

1989 *Professional Builder* Magazine. Target Awards. Award of Merit: Reston Land Corporation for Best Magazine Ad for a Master Planned Community.

1989 Metropolitan Washington Sales and Marketing Council. MAME (Major Achievement in Marketing Excellence) Awards. Award of Merit: Reston Land Corporation for Best Media Print Advertising Campaign.

APPENDIX C
Community Service Awards and Recognition

The Reston Festival

The first Dedication of Reston ceremony was held on May 21, 1966, at Lake Anne Plaza. Robert E. Simon and his wife Anne were hosts, and the principal guests were Virginia Governor Mills Godwin; United States Secretary of Housing and Urban Development Robert Weaver; and United States Secretary of the Interior Stewart Udall. An anniversary celebration was held the following year in the Lake Anne community hall with Robert Simon as host.

In 1968, under the sponsorship of the Reston Community Association, Jackie Shipp and Jackie Vergin were co- chairpersons of the Reston Spring Festival, and the initial idea was to provide a showcase for some of the extensive talent available in Reston. The Festival is an annual observance which continues to the present. The following people were chairpersons for subsequent years:

1969 - Barbara Camp and Loretta James
1970 - Victoria Westphal
1971 - Zora and Vlad Obrican
1972 - Jackie Vergin
1973 - Ann Page and Walter Ludwig
1974 - Joyce Bowen
1975 - Elinor Perez
1976 - Elinor Perez and David Hill
1977 - Marge Hope and Ed Williams
1978 - Carolyn Battle
1979 - Jeanne Lemieux
1980 - Jim Harris
1981 - Jackie Shipp
1982 and 1983 - Jackie Levy
1984 - Katherine Danish
1985, 1986, 1987, and 1988 - Melissa Kirkpatrick
1989 - Lewis and Thea Johnson

Reston Association Presidents

Elected
04/20/70—Robert Perce
01/20/71—Frederick Naef
10/03/71—John von Morse

04/12/72—Adrian Gilbert
04/12/73—Carl Stenberg
10/09/75—Fran Steinbauer
04/11/79—Frederick Diercks
12/12/79—Judi Ushio
09/01/83—Susan Jones
04/15/87—Carolyn Lindberg
04/13/88—Monroe E. "Mike"
Freeman, Jr.
04/11/89—W. M. "Mac" Murray

Restonian of the Year
Awarded annually at the Reston Spring Festival by the Reston Community Association.

1977—Lee and Max Libman
1978—Joanne Brownsword
1979—James Allred
1980—Tommy Rosamund
1981—Michelle DeCou
1982—Vernon Walker
1983—Joseph and Marcia Stowers
1984—Patrick Kane
1985—Priscilla Ames
1986—Ridge Loux
1987—Linda Singer
1988—Carolyn Lindberg
1989—Janet Howell

Community Service Award
Awarded annually at the Reston Spring Festival by the Reston Community Association.

1983—Reston Interfaith Housing
Corporation
1984—Reston-Herndon F.I.S.H. & Reston Child Development Council
1985—Reston/Nyeri Sister City Committee
1986—GRACE (Greater Reston Arts Center)
1987—Reston-Herndon Youth Club
1988—Laurel Learning Center
1989—Reston Players

The *Reston Times* selects the
Citizen of the Year:

"In recognition each year of that man or woman whose accomplishments for the public interest have left an indelible mark upon the history of Reston and Fairfax County."

1968—Robert E. Simon Jr.
1969—Jeffrey O. Wellborn
1970—Embry C. Rucker
1972—Irving Wasserman
1976—William Magness
1978—Fran Grady
1979—John Scherzer
1980—James Allred
1981—Judi Ushio
1982—Reginald Kitchen
1983—Linda Cochran and Richard
Thoesen
1984—Janet Howell
1985—Pat Noboa
1986—Matthew Wagner
1987—Caren R. Schumacher
1988—Lori Williams

No awards were given in 1971, 1973, 1974, 1975, or 1977.

Reston Community Center
Board of Governors

1978-1979

Allred, James V.—Chairperson
Davis, Nancy—Vice Chairperson
Simcox, James G.—Secretary
Edwards, David—Treasurer
Cosham, Richard
De Gree, Melvin
Demoody, Hal
Freeman, Baba
Meier, Diane
Schnore, Barbara
Walker, Elfriede

1979-1980

Davis, Nancy—Chairperson
Walker, Elfriede—Vice Chairperson
Simcox, James V. C.—Treasurer
Stillson, Marion—Secretary
Allred, James V.
Conner, Cameron
De Gree, Melvin
Hope, Marge
Howard, Katie
Mook, Jonathon
Toatley, Dave

1980-1981

Davis, Nancy—Chairperson
Walker, Elfriede—Vice Chairperson
Simcox, James V. G.—Treasurer
Stillson, Marion—Secretary
Allred, James
Conner, Cameron
De Gree, Melvin
Hope, Marge
Howard, Katie
Mook, Jonathon
Toatley, Dave

1981-1982

Walker, Elfriede—Chairperson
Stillson, Marion—Vice Chairperson
Toatley, Dave—Treasurer
Flynn, Madeline—Secretary
Bradley, Carol Ann
Conner, Cameron
Davis, Nancy
Hope, Marge
Jansons, Peggy
Simcox, Jim
Van Orsdel, Bill

1982-1983

Flynn, Madeline—Chairperson
Davis, Nancy—Vice Chairperson
Toatley, Dave—Treasurer
Bradley, Carol Ann—Secretary
Dunn, Kathleen
Fuss, Christine
Hoffman, Stuart
Jansons, Peggy
Plum, Tim
Taylor, Ron
Walker, Elfriede

1983-1984

Flynn, Madeline—Chairperson
Davis, Nancy—Vice Chairperson
Taylor, Ron—Treasurer
Jansons, Peggy—Secretary
Bradley, Carol Ann
Cole, Andrew
Hubbard, Elizabeth
McDevitt, Erin
Toatley, Dave
Trent, Gertrude
Walker, Elfriede

1984-1985

Cole, Andrew—Chairperson
Taylor, Ron—Vice Chairperson
Toatley, Dave—Treasurer
Jansons, Peggy—Secretary
Allen, Priscilla
Davis, Nancy
Elliott, Anne
Flynn, Madeline
Mustakos, Harry
O'Donnell, Lisa
Trent, Gertrude

1985-1986

Cole, Andrew—Chairperson
Flynn, Madeline—Vice Chairperson
Davis, Nancy—Treasurer
Bender, Susan—Secretary
Allen, Priscilla
Diehl, Brigid
Kaplan, Leslie
Mustakos, Harry
Rucker, Embry
Smith, Terry
Wilhelm, Jane

1986-1987

Bender, Susan—Chairperson
Cole, Andrew—Vice Chairperson
Smith, Terry—Treasurer
Flynn, Madeline—Secretary
Allen, Priscilla
Diehl, Brigid
Docktor, Gretchen
Haas, David
Hopson, Haywood
Robbins, Roberta
Rucker, Embry

1987-1988

Bender, Susan—Chairperson
Haas, David—Vice Chairperson
Smith, Terry—Treasurer
Overton, Ruth—Secretary
Cole, Andrew
Flynn, Madeline
Gordijenko, Leo
Green III, Irvin
McKelvey, Jessica
Newell, Jane
Robbins, Roberta
Roberts, Alec
Rucker, Embry

1988-1989	1989-1990
Haas, David—Chairperson	Haas, David—Chairperson
Overton, Ruth—Vice Chairperson	Overton, Ruth—Vice Chairperson
Smith, Terry—Treasurer	Smith, Terry—Treasurer
Robbins, Roberta—Secretary	Robbins, Roberta—Secretary
Bender, Susan	Bender, Susan
Cole, Andrew	Cole, Andrew
Hartnett, Tom	Hartnett, Tom
Newell, Jane	Kantrowitz, Debra Roth
Pryor, Andrea	Newell, Jane
Roth, Debra	Pryor, Andrea
Williams, Timothy	Williams, Timothy

APPENDIX D
Reston Growth

Reston's Population Growth

1970— 6,800
1971—10,200
1972—14,400
1973—20,100
1974—22,500
1975—24,700
1976—25,800
1977—28,400
1978—30,100
1979—33,200
1980—34,500
1981—36,300
1982—37,500
1983—38,300
1984—39,900
1985—43,400
1986—47,000
1987—51,500
1988—52,674
1989—53,981 *

Reston's Growth By Units

1979—11,981
1980—12,523
1981—12,848
1982—13,131
1983—13,600
1984—14,540
1985—16,069
1986—16,762
1987—17,830
1988—18,215
1989—18,628 *

* Projected
Source: Reston Land Corporation

APPENDIX E
Reston Firms
with over Five Hundred Employees

Central Intelligence Agency	Government
Emhart ATI	Professional and technical services
Fairfax County Government	Schools, public safety
Grumman Aerospace	Space station project support division
NALC Health Benefit Plan	Insurance benefits for postal workers
Piedmont Airlines Reservations Center	Airlines reservations agency
The Analytical Sciences Corp (TASC)	Strategic planning consultant for the government
Telenet	Data communications/packet switches
Unisys Corporation	Systems management
U.S. Geological Survey	Government scientific research
U.S. Sprint	Communications
Source: New Town Publications	

Reston Clusters, Apartments, and Condominiums

Name	No. Units	Year Completed	Name	No. Units	Year Completed	Name	No. Units	Year Completed
Arbor Glenn Cluster	44	1987	Hunters Green Cluster	118	1973	Walden Cluster	52	1981
Arborwood Cluster	36	1988	Hunters Square Cluster	154	1984	Walnut Ridge Cluster	42	1985
Lake Audubon Place	82	1988	Inlet Cluster	63	1972	Washington Plaza Cluster	41	1966
Barton Hill Cluster	57	1982	King Charles Common	31	1979	Waterview Cluster	90	1966
Bayfield Station Cluster	50	1984	Lake Audubon Terrace West Cluster	56	1986	Westcove Cluster	28	1982
Bennington Square Cluster	34	1983	Lakeport Cluster	83	1989	Wethersfield Cluster	65	1977
Bentana Woods East Cluster	48	1974	Lakeside Cluster	50	1970	Wheelwright Cluster	65	1976
Bentana Woods West Cluster	108	1974	Lakewinds Cluster	46	1980	Whisperhill Homeowners	146	1986
Birchfield Woods Cluster	108	1986	Lakewinds II Cluster	47	1981	Whisperwood Cluster	231	1984
Boston Ridge Cluster	99	1979	Links Pond Cluster	67	1976	Whitney Parkcenter Cluster	53	1979
Bromley Village Cluster	21	1984	Machaans Cluster	18	1977	Whitney Park East Cluster	85	1982
Brookshire Cluster	26	1967	Mallards Landing Cluster	48	1982	Winterport Cluster	79	1981
Cabots Point Cluster	40	1981	Marco Cluster	45	1977	Bantana Park Condominium	240	1975
Carriage Gate Cluster	65	1983	Mediterranean Villas Cluster	37	1971	Bristol House Condominium	152	1986
Cedar Cove Cluster	66	1984	Moorings Cluster	48	1971	Chestnut Grove Condominium	225	1972
Chadds Ford Cluster	57	1979	Newbridge Cluster	84	1975	Condominiums of Lake Anne	61	1965
Charter Oak Cluster	48	1970	Newport Cluster	32	1989	Condominiums of Lake Anne	46	1965
Chatham Colony Cluster	36	1972	North Shore Cluster	22	1972	Dockside Condominium	62	1983
Chestnut Ridge Cluster	57	1987	Northgate Square Cluster	80	1971	Glenvale Condominium	204	1974
Clubhouse Court Cluster	11	1982	Oak Spring Cluster	53	1987	Harbor Point Condominium	97	1984
Cocquina Cluster	93	1977	Old Salem Cluster	16	1985	Hunters Crossing Condominium	85	1986
Coleson Cluster	45	1967	Old Westbury Cluster	58	1984	Hunters Woods Condominium	221	1973
Colonial Green Cluster	73	1977	Orchard Green Cluster	65	1983	Island Walk Cooperative	102	1980
Colonial Oaks Homeowners	32	1980	Pinecrest Cluster	220	1974	Ivy Oak Square	96	1971
Colts Neck Cluster	60	1975	Purple Sage Cluster	177	1986	Lakeview Condominium	105	1972
Concord Green Cluster	101	1987	Regency Square Cluster	90	1970	Nantucket Condominium	40	1985
Country Court Cluster	21	1974	Saddler Oaks Cluster	63	1978	Northgate Condominium	260	1971
Country Walk Cluster	124	1984	Sanibel Cluster	68	1973	Shadowood Condominium	450	1980
Dogwood Cluster	80	1974	Sawyers Cluster	148	1977	Southgate Condominium	300	1974
Fairgreen Cluster	38	1974	Soapstone Cluster	80	1974	Springwood Council	249	1984
Fairway Cluster	30	1972	Solaridge Cluster	35	1984	Summer Ridge Condominium	168	1988
Forest Edge Cluster	107	1970	South Bay Cluster	33	1986	Thoreau Place Condominium	140	1988
Generation Cluster	125	1977	Southbridge Cluster	65	1984	Vantage Hill Condominium	152	1967
Glade Cluster	39	1977	Southgate Square Cluster	78	1972	Villa Ridge Condominium	216	1984
Glencourse Cluster	120	1979	Sunderbrier Cluster	33	1981	Waterford Square	144	1986
Golf Course Island Cluster	180	1970	Tanners Cluster	124	1978	Woodwinds I Condominium	142	1977
Golf Course Square Cluster	98	1974	The Courts Cluster	20	1978	Woodwinds II Condominium	56	1979
Golf Course View Cluster	105	1974	The Hamlet Cluster	122	1984			
Governours Square Cluster	29	1969	The Shores Cluster	65	1984			
Hampton Meadows Cluster	50	1977	The Wharf Cluster	55	1984			
Harborside Cluster	15	1979	Thornhill Cluster	88	1986			
Harpers Square Cluster	50	1983	Turnbridge Cluster	18	1986			
Hickory Cluster	90	1965	Villas De Espana Cluster	73	1975			
Hillcrest Cluster	173	1972	Wainwright Cluster	42	1966			
Hunt Club Cluster	38	1971						

INDEX

About the Author

Nan Netherton was born in Chicago and grew up in Tennessee. She and her husband, Ross, met while they were students at the University of Chicago.

The couple moved to Northern Virginia in 1951 and their three children, David, Richard, and Nancy, grew up in Fairfax County during the time when it was changing from a rural, agrarian county to a highly urbanized one. Nan and Ross began writing history together when they prepared a county civic-government directory and street map which was published by the Federation of Citizens Associations, in 1957. Nan served as historian for Fairfax County under the Office of Comprehensive Planning for ten years and has been author or co-author of a number of regional and local histories, including *Northern Virginia Heritage* (1966); *Fairfax County, Virginia; A History* (1978); *Montebello at Mount Eagle* (1981); *Clifton: Brigadoon in Virginia* (1982); *Fairfax County in Virginia* (1986); and *Arlington County in Virginia* (1987); these last two with Ross. She and Ruth Preston Rose wrote *Memories of Beautiful Burke, Virginia* in 1987 and she wrote *Books and Beyond: Fairfax County Public Library's First Fifty Years* in 1989.

Nan holds degrees from the University of Chicago and George Mason University, and serves on the Board of Directors of the Northern Virginia Association of Historians. She is shown here with her granddaughter, Jodi Marie Netherton, a Restonian by birth.

Reston

Historic Landmarks & Sites

1. A. Bowman Distillery
2. Warehouse (GRACE)
3. Robert Wiehle House
4. "Sunset Hills"
5. Wiehle pond
6. Brown's Chapel
7. E. DeLong Bowman House
8. 200 yr. old Charter Oak (fell in 1987)
9. Aesculapian Hotel
10. Thornton House
11. Patriarca House

Modern Landmarks

12. USGS
13. Lake Anne Library
14. Hunters Woods Library
15. Regional Library
16. Post Office
17. Town Center
18. Nature Center
19. Reston Hospital
20. ACCESS
21. Lake Anne Fellowship House
22. Hunters Woods Fellowship House
23. Tall Oaks Fellowship House
24. Lake Anne Village Center
25. Tall Oaks Village Center
26. Hunters Woods Village Center
27. South Lakes Village Center
28. North Point Village Center (1992)
29. Lake Anne Elementary School
30. Forest Edge School
31. Hunters Woods School
32. Dogwood School
33. Terraset School
34. Sunrise Valley School
35. Armstrong School
36. Aldrin School (1990's)
37. Langston Hughes Intermediate School
38. Herndon Intermediate School
39. Planned Intermediate School
40. South Lakes High School
41. Herndon High School
42. Planned High School